Pericles

Pericles was the most famous leader of the most famous ancient Greek democracy – and also extremely controversial in his own time and ever since. Was he a brutal imperialist ready to oppress other Greeks, or a clear-eyed defender of Athens' need for power to survive in a relentlessly hostile world? How did his intellectual training in ideas that many Athenians regarded as dangerous make him the most persuasive leader Athenian democracy ever knew? Why was his personal lifestyle so idiosyncratic? How should we evaluate his responsibility for the suffering and loss of the Peloponnesian War? Thomas R. Martin's unique emphasis on the effect on Pericles of his family's notorious history, his youthful experiences as a wartime refugee, and his unusual education reveals a brilliant politician whose hyperrationality could not, in the end, protect him or his community from tragedy.

With nearly forty years of experience teaching ancient history to non-specialist audiences, Thomas R. Martin is the author of books including surveys of ancient Greece, ancient Rome, Alexander the Great, and the works of Herodotus and Sima Qian, and An Overview of Classical Greek History online at the Perseus Project, which has been consulted by countless readers since its appearance as the first resource of its kind on the subject. He has also appeared in various documentaries on ancient history shown on television around the world.

Pericles

A Biography in Context

THOMAS R. MARTIN
College of the Holy Cross

CAMBRIDGE
UNIVERSITY PRESS

CAMBRIDGE
UNIVERSITY PRESS

One Liberty Plaza, 20th Floor, New York, NY 10006, USA

Cambridge University Press is part of the University of Cambridge.

It furthers the University's mission by disseminating knowledge in the pursuit of education, learning, and research at the highest international levels of excellence.

www.cambridge.org
Information on this title: www.cambridge.org/9780521133357

First published 2016

Printed in the United States of America by Sheridan Books, Inc.

A catalogue record for this publication is available from the British Library.

Library of Congress Cataloguing-in-Publication Data
Martin, Thomas R., author.
Pericles : a biography in context / Thomas R. Martin, College of the Holy Cross.
New York, NY: Cambridge University Press, 2016. |
Includes bibliographical references and index.
LCCN 2016009126| ISBN 9780521116459 (hardback) |
ISBN 9780521133357 (pbk.)
LCSH: Pericles, approximately 495 B.C.-429 B.C. |
Statesmen – Greece – Athens – Biography. | Athens (Greece) – Politics and government. | Athens (Greece) – History.
LCC DF228.P4 M37 2016 | DDC 938/.04092–dc23
LC record available at http://lccn.loc.gov/2016009126

ISBN 978-0-521-11645-9 Hardback
ISBN 978-0-521-13335-7 Paperback

This book is dedicated to the undergraduate students in the Department of Classics at Holy Cross in recognition of their thought-provoking questions during their ancient Greek class reading Plutarch's Life of Pericles, *and to my wife, the classicist Ivy Sui-yuen Sun, in whose scholarly company I first and always studied the unforgettable archaeological treasures of the Athens of Pericles.*

Every age has, or imagines it has, its own circumstances which render past experience no longer applicable to the present case.... And no wonder, if we read history for the facts instead of reading it for the sake of the general principles, which are to the facts as the root and sap of a tree to its leaves.

Samuel Taylor Coleridge, *The Statesman's Manual; Or, The Bible the Best Guide to Political Skill and Foresight: A Lay Sermon* (London, 1816), p. 14.

Contents

Illustrations

Maps

NB: Greek names with *os* or *on* can also be transliterated as *us* or *um* (for example, Thasos or Thasus, Phaleron or Phalerum), and those with *ai* or *aia* can also be transliterated as *ae* or *aea* or even as *e* and *ea* (for example, Aigina or Aegina or Egina, Plataia or Plataea or Platea).

Acknowledgments

I am grateful to Anastasia Graf, Beatrice Rehl, and Isabella Vitti of Cambridge University Press for their editorial guidance and endless patience, and to the production staff of the Press for their expert work. Jessica Bailot, Holy Cross Class of 2015, and Sarah Zatoonian, Holy Cross Class of 2017, deserve recognition for their careful and helpful reading of the text during a busy time. Carson Bay, Ph.D. candidate in Religions of Western Antiquity at Florida State University, provided many insightful corrections and improvements. Thanks also go to Jim Fuhr for expert crafting of the index, Ramesh Karunakaran for efficient management of final production, and Susan Thornton for responsive copy-editing. Finally, I want to express my special appreciation to the anonymous peer reviewers for their insightful, thorough, and no-holds-barred reflections at the beginning and the end of the editorial process. Their forthright criticisms motivated me to reconsider thoroughly my approach in this biography. Although I am under no illusion that the changes made in response to their observations will seem sufficient to them, I remain deeply impressed by their scholarly acumen.

Chronology

All dates are B.C.; *ca.* indicates the date is approximate.

632	Cylon of Athens attempts to take over the city-state; one of Pericles' maternal relatives is implicated in sacrilegious murder and that side of his family (the Alcmeonids) is exiled from Athens.
ca. 600–570	Cleisthenes of Sicyon rules his city-state as a tyrant; Pericles' relative Megacles of Athens marries Agariste, Cleisthenes' daughter.
ca. 590s	Pericles' relative Alcmeon wins an Olympic victory in chariot racing. He is a commander in the First Sacred War and reputedly visits King Croesus of Lydia.
ca. 546–527	Pisistratus of Athens rules his city-state as tyrant; the Alcmeonid family again goes into exile.
527	Hippias, son of Pisistratus, becomes tyrant at Athens; the Alcmeonids return.
514	The Alcmeonids go into exile again after the murder of Hippias' brother and rebuild Apollo's temple at Delphi.
511–510	Instructed by Apollo of Delphi, the Spartans use force to expel Hippias as tyrant at Athens.
507	Cleisthenes, maternal great-uncle of Pericles, creates a direct democracy as Athens' government, leading the Spartans to attack to overturn it; the Athenians successfully repel them and ask the Great King of Persia for a military alliance.
506	The Spartans again unsuccessfully attack Athens, allying with Athens' neighbors the Boeotians and Chalcidians, whom the Athenians defeat.

ca. 505	The Thebans and Aeginetans attack Athens.
ca. 500	Pericles' parents, Agariste and Xanthippus of Athens, marry.
ca. 499	Aristagoras of Miletus convinces the Athenians to send troops to support the Ionians' rebellion against Persian control.
494	The city-state of Miletus is captured as the Persians suppress the Ionian Revolt.
Mid-490s	Pericles is born.
490	The Athenians commanded by Miltiades defeat the Persians, who are accompanied by Hippias, on land at the Battle of Marathon.
ca. 489	Xanthippus prosecutes Miltiades for his failure in commanding an attack against the island of Paros.
484	Xanthippus is ostracized.
483	The Athenians vote to spend a large discovery of silver ore on building a navy instead of personal distributions of money.
480	The Persians invade Greece, winning the Battle of Thermopylae on land and drawing the Battle of Artemisium at sea; the Athenians evacuate; the Greek alliance wins the Battle of Salamis at sea.
479	The Persian invaders offer a tempting deal to the Athenians, who refuse and evacuate their land again; the Greek alliance wins the Battle of Plataea and the Battle of Mycale on land.
478	Xanthippus captures the city-state of Sestos; the Delian League, a naval alliance headed by Athens, is established by its members' oaths of permanent loyalty.
477	Aristides of Athens succeeds in having the Delian League allies voluntarily agree to assessments of annual payments, sworn to for eternity.
476	Cimon of Athens leads the Delian League to victory over the Persians at Eion.
475	Cimon captures the island of Scyros and takes back to Athens the bones of the legendary hero Theseus.
Mid-/late 470s	The Delian League attacks the islands of Carystos and Naxos; Themistocles is ostracized; Pericles is married; Pericles perhaps begins studying music with Damon.

472	Aeschylus of Athens produces the drama *Persians*, with Pericles as the *choregos*.
470s/460s(?)	Pericles studies natural science, philosophy, and persuasive argumentation with Anaxagoras of Clazomenae.
ca. 468	Cimon wins the Battle of the Eurymedon River against the Persians. An agreement may have been reached under which the Persians agree not to send military expeditions out of the eastern Mediterranean (The Peace of Callias).
ca. 465–462	The island of Thasos attempts to revolt from the Delian League and is severely punished.
ca. 464	After a giant earthquake, the helots (Greek slaves) revolt against the Spartans in the southern Peloponnese.
463	Pericles serves as one of the prosecutors of Cimon in the latter's trial for corruption.
ca. 462	Cimon leads an Athenian military force to help the Spartans in response to their appeal for aid against the helots; the Spartans then dismiss the Athenians.
ca. 461	To support radical democracy, Ephialtes of Athens and Pericles back reforms of the powers of the Areopagus Council; Cimon is ostracized.
Early 450s	Pericles persuades the Athenian democratic assembly to institute financial subsidies for service on juries; two of the Long Walls are built to connect the city of Athens to its western ports; Xanthippus, Pericles' son, is born.
458	Aeschylus' trilogy of dramas *Oresteia* is produced at Athens.
Mid-450s	The Delian League sends a large military expedition to Egypt to support a rebellion against the Persian Empire; Paralus, Pericles' son, is born; Pericles and his wife divorce.
ca. 457	The Spartans defeat the Athenians at the Battle of Tanagra; Cimon attempts to return from ostracism; the Athenians defeat the Spartans at the Battle of Oenophytae; Pericles supports recalling Cimon.
ca. 454	Pericles commands a Delian League naval expedition in the Corinthian Gulf; massive losses of men and ships end the Egyptian expedition; the Delian League treasury is moved from the Aegean island of Delos to the Acropolis in Athens.

451	The Athenian democratic assembly passes a Citizenship Law proposed by Pericles.
Late 450s/ early 440s	Pericles studies with Zeno.
ca. 450	Cimon dies on a military expedition to Cyprus; the Peace of Callias is perhaps renewed.
448	The Spartans send a military expedition to take control of the oracle of Apollo at Delphi; the Athenians send an expedition in response to take control.
447	Construction begins on the Parthenon temple at Athens; the Athenians suffer defeat at the Battle of Coronea in Boeotia; Pericles fortifies the Thracian Chersonese and settles Athenians there.
446	City-states on the island of Euboea rebel against the Delian League; the Spartans invade Athenian territory; Pericles bribes them to return home and takes Euboea.
446/5	Athens and Sparta swear to a peace treaty to last thirty years.
ca. 445	A third Long Wall is built connecting Athens and its main port of Piraeus; disenfranchised citizens at Athens are prosecuted and enslaved.
444	Pericles recommends sending settlers to Thurii in southern Italy and designates the sophist Protagoras to design its constitution.
Mid-440s	Pericles and Aspasia begin their love affair.
ca. 443	Thucydides of Athens, son of Melesias, is ostracized after heading political opposition to Pericles.
Late-440s	Pericles, son of Aspasia and Pericles, is born.
440–439	Pericles leads a Delian League force against the rebels on the island of Samos.
438	Athenian settlers found the city-state of Amphipolis in northern Greece/southern Thrace.
437	The sculptor Phidias is perhaps prosecuted for alleged sacrilege in the Parthenon project; construction begins on the Proplyaea entrance to the Acropolis.
Mid-430s	Pericles leads a naval expedition to the Black Sea (the Euxine); construction begins on the Odeon concert hall proposed by Pericles.
433	The Athenians send warships to support the Corcyreans against the Corinthians.

Late 430s	The Athenian assembly passes the Megarian Decree barring the inhabitants of the neighboring city of Megara from using the harbors of the members of the Delian League.
432	The Spartans send their final embassies to Athens refusing arbitration under the terms of the peace of 446/5 and demanding the revocation of the Megarian Decree; Pericles persuades the Athenian assembly to reject the Spartan demands.
431	The Peloponnesian War formally begins when the Spartans and their allies invade Athenian territory; the Athenians take refuge behind their fortification walls and send a naval expedition against the Peloponnese, displace the population of the island of Aegina, and attack Megara.
430	An epidemic disease (the "plague") kills many Athenians; Pericles commands a naval expedition against the Peloponnese; he is temporarily deposed from his official position on the board of Athenian generals; the epidemic kills his legitimate sons, his sister, and other family members.
429	Pericles is reelected to office as a "general"; Pericles asks the Athenian assembly to grant citizenship to his son by Aspasia; Pericles dies from the epidemic disease.

Pericles' Alcmeonid Family Tree

Except for Pericles' father, Xanthippus, and his paternal grandfather, Ariphron, this simplified version of Pericles' ancestors shows only members of his mother's family, the Alcmeonids, and only as far back in time as the first of those maternal ancestors about whom we have any reliable historical information. For more detailed information, see Davies, J. K. 1971. *Athenian Propertied Families 600–300 B.C.* (Oxford: Clarendon Press), pp. 368–385, 455–460.

== indicates marriage

--- indicates siblings

Megacles, archon in the late seventh century B.C. at time of Cylon's conspiracy

↓

Alcmeon, commander in the First Sacred War in the 590s B.C., visitor to Croesus

↓

Megacles, opponent of Pisistratus == Agariste, daughter of Cleisthenes of Sicyon

↓

Cleisthenes, democratic reformer---Hippocrates---daughter married to Pisistratus

↓

↓ Ariphron

↓ ↓

Agariste == Xanthippus

↓

Pericles

Introduction

A Biography of Pericles in the Context of the Ancient Sources

One night in Athens in the mid-490s B.C.[1] (the exact year is unknown), a rich and heavily pregnant woman named Agariste had a dream: she saw herself giving birth to a lion. A few days later her second son was born, and his parents named him Pericles. Ancient Greeks traditionally believed that dreams were sent from the gods, as they learned from the epic poems *The Iliad* and *The Odyssey* by Homer; his famous stories explored the sufferings caused by the Trojan War and expressed foundational beliefs of Greek culture. From listening to myths about ancient heroes and from hunting lions, which still roamed Europe in antiquity, Greeks learned that these animals were both powerful defenders of their own group and fierce destroyers of their prey. Agariste understood her dream to be a divine message indicating that her child was to become a very special person, for good or for bad – or for both.

Agariste's premonition about her child's future prominence proved accurate. Pericles at the height of his career became the most famous leader of the most famous and radical democracy of the most famous place of the most famous era of ancient Greece (Figure 1). During Pericles' lifetime in the fifth century B.C. (he died in 429), Athens became Greece's most influential incubator of far-reaching cultural developments, from scientific and philosophical ideas to innovative forms of art, architecture, and theater. This aspect of Athenian history has gained an appreciative reception in later times. Far less positive, however, has been the assessment of the actions of the Athenians toward other Greeks in this same

[1] From here on, all dates in this book should be understood as B.C. unless otherwise indicated.

FIGURE 1. Stone bust of Pericles. JFB/The Art Archive at Art Resource, NY.

period as they transformed themselves from their previous second-rate international status into their region's wealthiest and strongest military power. By the 430s, they controlled numerous other Greek allies in what Pericles memorably called a tyranny, according to the contemporary historian and military commander Thucydides (*The Peloponnesian War* 2.63); other contemporaries echoed that judgment, adding that Pericles led Athens as a de facto tyrant. Many modern scholars agree, labeling the Athenian-dominated alliance an empire and Pericles an imperialist, implying all the deeply negative connotations of those terms in their modern context of colonialism and oppression.

Understanding how these events took place and deciding how to evaluate their significance for our judgment of classical Athens are challenging questions, and they are especially relevant for a biography of Pericles because by the middle of the fifth century he had become Athens' most influential political leader. He was directly involved in the political and military decisions of the democratic government of Athens that led to the creation of the so-called Athenian Empire, which, its critics charge, mistreated Greeks who did not fall into line with the uncompromising leadership of the Athenians. A second challenging question is how to evaluate Pericles' responsibility for the infamous Peloponnesian War (431–404) between Athens and Sparta, each supported by its allies among other Greek states. (The name of the war is derived from the location of Sparta and most of its allies in the Peloponnese, the large peninsula that makes up southern mainland Greece.) In 431, the Athenians followed Pericles' adamant advice to make no concessions to the Spartans even if this hard-line position meant war. A generation-long conflict between the two competing states therefore broke out. Twenty-seven years later (and twenty-three years after Pericles' death), Athens' defeat in this long and bloody war proved catastrophic for his homeland.

These two aspects of Pericles' leadership – the nature of his influence during the time of Athens' greatest power and his successful advocacy of going to war with Sparta – make it imperative to ask whether, despite Pericles' lasting fame, his life in the end has to be judged a tragedy rather than a triumph. The answer to be offered here will emerge in the context of a concise biography intended for readers new to ancient Greek history. The ancient biographer and essayist Plutarch, whose writings provide the bulk of the surviving information about Pericles' life, stressed the different nature of biographical writing as compared to history: biography, he said, is the story of a life, focusing on evidence that reveals the subject's character, especially in making decisions under pressure and taking actions that affect other people. Of course, writing about the past (or the present, for that matter) involves selection of the evidence to consider, and, as Plutarch's words imply, writing biography adds to the innate uncertainty of this process by seeking to uncover the thoughts, motives, and feelings of human beings. In short, biography necessarily involves a large degree of speculation – we can never fully know what goes on in the heads and the hearts of other people (and perhaps not even in our own!). An abiding lack of certainty is simply inherent in trying to make sense of someone else's life, and it is to be expected that others will disagree, sometimes vehemently, with any biographer's interpretation of the person being profiled.

As a result, readers should expect to encounter repeated qualifications such as "probably," or "most likely," or "must have" in this book. At the same time, it seems to me that the author of a biography takes on the responsibility of presenting an interpretative evaluation of the subject and cannot always conclude by saying, "Well, we cannot decide." Certainly the study of ancient history is especially humbling because that kind of inconclusive and unsatisfactory response is often the best any scholar can offer in good conscience. And it may not be entirely wrong to regard biographers as closer to writers of fiction or fantasy than historians themselves aspire to be. My point is that readers should always be alert to the characteristics of the genre of writing that they choose to read, and that warning applies doubly to biography.

In his famous paired biographies comparing Greeks and Romans, the *Parallel Lives* (on which see later discussion), the ancient Greek author Plutarch states that he often does not spend time narrating the details of events of his subject's lifetime, even when they are major historical episodes. What matters to him in writing the story of a life, Plutarch explains, is trying to deduce meaning about his subjects' characters from their actions and words, even if those events and sayings might seem minor in the grand scheme of events. Plutarch's approach inspires the one that I will take, which aims above all at offering an evaluation of Pericles' character in action. This book therefore does not provide a balanced or comprehensive survey of the history of Athens during Pericles' time. Indeed, its narrative will not spend a great deal of time even on events important to Athenian history during Pericles' lifetime unless they seem relevant to understanding his decisions as a private individual and a political leader.

My selection of what to emphasize in telling the story of Pericles' life and evaluating his leadership instead will focus on the background to and the development of the three characteristics that for me are most important in evaluating Pericles' career: his unyielding opposition to Sparta, his reliance on reasoning and judgment based on knowledge as the basis for political persuasiveness, and his support for political and financial benefits for Athens' poorer citizens. Considering these issues will involve investigating his family history, his intellectual bent, his political skills, and his private life. This investigation calls for a thorough excavation of the historical background specific to these issues. For that reason, a significant portion of the narrative will describe relevant events dating from before Pericles' birth and during his youth, before he became politically active. These chapters will focus both on the highly contentious history of Pericles' ancestors and on the equally controversial actions of the Spartans during the conflict-filled decades of the late sixth and early fifth centuries. During these years, internal and external wars (and these latter conflicts waged against both neighboring Greeks as well as foreign invaders) determined not only the form of Athens' democratic government and political independence, but even its physical survival as a community.

This background material will reveal the degree to which Pericles' career became the story of a preeminent political leader whose ideas and policies were forever shaped by what he had as a child learned from his family about their deeply controversial history before his birth, about the treacherous about-face of Sparta in attempting to overthrow the Athenians' democracy founded by his uncle Cleisthenes after the Spartans had just expelled Athens' tyranny, and about the harsh realities of Athenian political life as revealed to the young Pericles by the exile imposed on his father. Those tough lessons were further driven home by Pericles' himself becoming a refugee while a teenager during the Persian Wars, a conflict waged by a Greek alliance to try to avoid conquest by the military forces of the gigantic empire ruled by the Persian Achaemenid dynasty. In the panic caused by this military crisis, Pericles, still too young to fight in Athens' army, was compelled to flee his homeland not once but twice during the chaos of mass evacuations of the city's population.

The detail of the opening chapters, which discuss Athenian history before Pericles' birth and during his early years, is necessary because it is my strongly held judgment that this deep background – especially how high the stakes were for Athens in these events and how vividly their reality was impressed on the young Pericles – is absolutely fundamental for understanding how Pericles came to form his unyielding attitude and policies about the necessity of Athens' possessing unassailable power, about the strict connection between Athens' power and its freedom, and, perhaps most poignantly of all, about the deep fear that Athenians should feel about the never-ending threats to their security posed by their enemies, above all the Spartans. Therefore, this biography includes an extended lead-in to Pericles' adult lifetime so that it can present evidence with which readers may reach their own judgments about the leader that Thucydides (2.65) judged to have been so overwhelmingly influential in his state's democracy that he rose to the status of its "first man" during what has sometimes been called Athens' Golden Age.

In short, the linchpin of my evaluation – and the motivation for narrating in some detail the crises in the half-century of Athenian history before Pericles rose to become a leader – is that Pericles' experiences and memories from his very early years taught him lessons that he never forgot, provoking him to formulate the policies that he ever after maintained in response to the brutal realities of political and military power as they played out in the Greek world in general and in the policies of Sparta in particular. As cognitive scientists would say, the influences on Pericles from his early life – what he heard from his parents about their family histories and then his own lived experiences – led him to develop a "memory of the future." That is, like all of us, what he heard about and experienced as repetitive phenomena during his youth – in his case, the terrible dangers threatening Athens and the necessity of asserting power to defend its freedom, the treacherous unreliability of the Spartans, and the unpredictable fate of prominent political and military leaders in democratic Athens – strongly predisposed him to expect that circumstances in his future life would correspond to those memories and that ongoing fear for the safety of his community was the only prudent attitude for an Athenian to adopt. That Pericles never wavered in his stance on these issues is a major factor that must be weighed in evaluating his leadership. Modern observers may well want to ponder whether he should have changed his mind later in life, but the fact is that he never did.

Following the background on Pericles' family and early life, the story of his life as told in this book will turn to the question of how he earned his lasting fame as a leader in competition with many other ambitious male citizens in the rough-and-tumble politics of Athens' democratic system of government. In this context, one challenging question concerns how he achieved the respect for his character and the skill in public speaking that empowered him to persuade the mass of citizens in Athens' democracy (Greek for "strength of the people") to adopt policies that he recommended. As we will see, in everything Pericles did as a leader who always had to operate under close public scrutiny and the very real possibility of punishment for promoting unpopular or unsuccessful policies, he privileged reasoned judgment based on knowledge as the key to predicting what was likely to happen and therefore as the best guide for deciding what policies and laws to propose. In other words, Pericles developed a relentless devotion to reason and knowledge as the best way to combat the disturbing and often sorrowful unpredictability of human life.

His reasoning was deeply influenced by his education and personal friendships with the most controversial thinkers of fifth-century Greece. It is remarkable that Pericles was able to rely on an intellectually grounded approach to make himself into one of the most persuasive and most celebrated political leaders in history. An aloof scholarly tone in political speeches is rarely effective in today's world, and recent psychological studies demonstrate that even scientifically grounded knowledge exercises a minimal persuasive power on people when it conflicts with their personal values and interests. It is therefore especially impressive that Pericles leveraged his notoriously intense interest in intellectual and scholarly questions into a tool for persuasive public speaking in a democracy where oratory carried great influence in political decision making. Somehow, his unvarying stress on employing knowledge-based reasoning and judgment motivated the majority of his fellow citizens – almost all of whom did not share his exceptional educational background or his interest in academic-sounding disputes – to reach difficult, dangerous, and even self-sacrificing decisions for their community.

The vast majority of citizens in Pericles' time not only lacked much, if any, high-level education, they also made do with a very modest or even poor standard of living, at least in comparison to the wealth and status of the elite members of Athenian society. The riches and fame of his family placed Pericles in the upper-class section of society. Some members of this social elite vehemently opposed democracy because it required them to share political power with the mass of citizens less affluent than they and to contribute financial resources to provide benefits for the masses. In sharp contrast to this attitude, Pericles supported measures to strengthen the political and financial interests of the majority of citizens as opposed to those of his own social class. In evaluating Pericles, it will be important to consider the likely reasons for his successful promotion of this contested policy, which at its most spectacular yielded the construction of the costly buildings, including the Parthenon temple (Figure 15), that made Golden Age Athens so famous in ancient and modern times.

Pericles' political opponents and rivals blamed him for the decisions that the male citizens of Athens had ratified in the democratic assembly (*ecclesia*) to maintain strict control of their allies in the Athenian Empire and to spend money on fabulously expensive public buildings. The denunciations of Pericles by his contemporaries could be savage. The authors of comedies mocked him for his highbrow proclivities and claimed he behaved immorally in his sexual life. Especially bitter criticisms attacked his never-wavering insistence that Athens reject the demands from Sparta that peaked in the late 430s and culminated in the Spartans' launching the Peloponnesian War; some even charged that he brought on the war to cover up scandals in his private life.

This bloody struggle of Greeks against Greeks was filled with countless disasters, including the deadly epidemic disease that killed Pericles in 429. The war finally ended in 404 with the unconditional surrender of Athens to its hated Spartan enemies, the devastation of its flourishing economy, the abolition of its democracy, and the installation of a murderous regime of Athenian collaborators, whose crimes against their fellow citizens plunged their community into a civil war that came to an end in 403 only after bloody battles of citizens in the streets. The bitterness from this internal conflict motivated the trial and execution in 399 of Socrates, an Athenian war hero and the most famous philosopher of the fifth century. In short, the Peloponnesian War was a catastrophe for Athens. Should we blame Pericles for this terrible outcome? Had his reasoning truly presented his fellow citizens with the best available choice by persuading them to wage war rather than to capitulate to the Spartans' demands? After his death, were the citizens shortsighted in abandoning his strategic policy of not attempting expansion during wartime, as Thucydides accuses them of having done? Did they in this way cause their own eventual doom, a fate that could have been prevented if they had kept to Pericles' recommended policy? Taken together, these questions about Pericles' policy concerning Sparta, as much as his insistence that Athens maintain its power over others in its own self-interest during the period of Athenian Empire, seem to me to pose the most difficult issues to analyze in the debate concerning Pericles' leadership and legacy, a debate that began in his own time and continues to this day.

Linked to issues from Pericles' public life as a leader are remarkable aspects of his private life. His home life was often turbulent. He infuriated his children by limiting their expenditures, refusing to indulge them when they appealed to him for money for splurges. He had such a bitter relationship with one of his two sons that it culminated in the accusation that he had committed adultery with a daughter-in-law. After Pericles and his wife divorced, he fell deeply in love with Aspasia, a foreign-born woman much talked about and admired for her intellectual acuity but also slandered as a brothel operator. Pericles openly expressed his affection for Aspasia and fathered a child with her named after him – but he could never marry her, the love of his life, and he could not make his son a citizen, because of a law that he himself had some years before convinced the Athenians to pass. As we will see, some Athenians claimed that Pericles' notorious relationship with Aspasia led him to force Athens into the Peloponnesian War.

Pericles exercised strict control over his personal emotions so that he could always behave with a calm dignity in the company of others. He scrupulously avoided potentially awkward social situations, especially the frequent drinking parties that were the social glue of the upper class, where overindulgence in wine could lead to embarrassing incidents and damaging gossip. The only time he was said to have wept in front of others who were not close to him – and in ancient Greek culture real men, like the warriors of Homer's *Iliad*, shed copious tears without shame in public – was when he defended Aspasia in court. But showing emotion in Athenian trials was expected; not a single anecdote exists portraying Pericles as showing emotions in public that were inappropriate to the occasion. What, then, do the stories about Pericles' private life say about his emotional life and his success – or failure – in integrating his personal choices as a man and a father with his public position as Athens' most personally disciplined leader? Did the troubles – and joys – of his personal life affect his policy recommendations? These questions, too, will figure in the evaluation of Pericles to be outlined in this biography.

Biographical information about Pericles is provided only by other people: he apparently never wrote anything for publication or preservation. There are no private letters of his, no personal journals, no public statements, and no political or reflective essays. We rely exclusively on other texts from antiquity for information on both his private life and his public career. The ancient sources that have survived (a tremendous amount has been lost in the intervening centuries) are limited – but also very interesting. I energetically encourage readers to take the characteristics (especially the shortcomings) of this biography as inducements to read for themselves the ancient texts on which its story depends so that they can critique its approach and judgments. That is the outcome that I most wish for, especially because reading ancient sources about Greek history has enriched my life so powerfully for so long.

My approach to these sources will be to take their evidence seriously unless there are clear reasons to reject their testimony; hence, they provide the context for my understanding of Pericles' biography. Keeping in mind my intended audience and the brevity of this book, I will not present much source criticism, the extremely important process through which experts tease out what is likely to be accurate and what seems mistaken or even deceptive in the accounts that we have. This choice against offering detailed source criticism will not please many scholars. What I report from the sources in this account of Pericles' life represents my judgment on what is reasonably plausible to believe from their evidence. I can add that I do not believe that it is methodologically sound to discount or disregard ancient sources just because their information seems implausible in terms of modern assumptions and assertions about how people "must" have behaved in the past. The sources on Pericles certainly do not present a uniform picture, and they are frequently difficult to understand because, to mention just one reason among many, they were written for people who often had very different views and experiences from many of us today. Nevertheless, these ancient sources are our primary evidence, and I will treat them as just that: primary. In short, my approach will be to try to tell the story of Pericles' life as it emerges from the evidence of the surviving ancient sources, without explicitly engaging discussions of modern scholars, even those specifically cited in my text. This characteristic of the book, which I recognize will be unsatisfying to some, means that readers who want to benefit from the enormous amount of stimulating and valuable scholarly work on Pericles and fifth-century Athenian history need to turn elsewhere, for example, to the list of Suggested Readings provided at this book's end. It seems appropriate to point out that a significant number of the books and articles listed there dispute or reject both my approach and my conclusions.

The surviving sources for Pericles' biography are fascinating in their varying approaches to his life, their colorful details, and, in many cases, their strongly argued judgments about him. Most of these ancient works are available in readable English translations, also listed in the Suggested Readings. They brim with stories of courage and cowardice, violence and kindness, wonders and mystery – all the stuff of lives lived fully and passionately. I will sometimes mention a specific ancient source in relation to a large theme or a direct quotation. To stress the importance and interest of the most informative ancient sources as the basis for everything that follows, I will now briefly introduce them.

Plutarch's *Life of Pericles* (hereafter cited as *Pericles*) in his *Parallel Lives* is the only surviving ancient source presenting information about Pericles' life from birth to death. An upper-class and extremely well-educated Greek living from about AD 50 to AD 120 in the time of the Roman Empire, Plutarch wrote five centuries later than Pericles' lifetime. By Plutarch's time, his beloved homeland of Greece had long been subject to the Romans. Plutarch became famous in later times mainly as the author of the *Parallel Lives*, which became popular for their exciting anecdotes and demanding moral lessons; they were favorites, for example, of Shakespeare and of the founders of the American republic. Plutarch also wrote the *Moralia*, an extensive set of essays exploring a large diversity of philosophical, religious, and personal topics. All Plutarch's works display his tremendous knowledge of earlier literature and histories. He frequently quotes from or refers to the many earlier authors whose texts he had carefully read and remembered. In fact, he preserves a very large number of so-called fragments (that is, quotations, paraphrases, and references) from "lost authors" relevant to this period of Athenian history whose works have not survived to the present.

In composing his biographies, Plutarch chooses his subjects, all of whom are men, to match Greeks with Romans. His pairing of these leaders is based on his judgment that they shared prominent aspects in their characters and experienced similar challenges during their public careers. In his stories of their lives, Plutarch explores how they succeeded – and not infrequently failed – to live up to high moral standards involving both personal ambition and duty to others. He presents most of them as successful and admirable men overall (though far from perfect), whose traits as leaders others should emulate. He treats with scrupulous fairness even the biographical subjects whom he judged to have lived in ways that others should not imitate, and he never overlooks good qualities that bad examples often display. He fully grasps that there is hardly a more effective way for human beings to learn how to live optimally and responsibly in their own lives than to reflect on the experiences of other people who have exerted themselves strenuously to live according to high standards of excellence. Plutarch writes his biographies so that people forever after could study these stories as a stimulus to reflection on how best to live their own lives.

Plutarch parallels the *Pericles* with his biography of the third-century B.C. Roman politician and commander Fabius Maximus. Fabius reached the pinnacle of political success in the Roman Republic by being elected to serve as a consul, a member of the board of two annually elected officials who served as the republic's chief leaders and military commanders. Fabius became famous for saving Rome from being captured and sacked in the Second Punic War (218–201) at the hands of the daring general Hannibal from Carthage in North Africa. To the astonishment of the panicked Romans, Hannibal had led his invading troops over the seemingly impassable heights of the snow-covered Alps Mountains into Italy to attack deep into Roman territory. When Hannibal proceeded to massacre the armies that Rome sent to stop him and then advanced his Carthaginian forces close to the capital, his invasion presented the worst threat to Rome in its history.

Fabius earned the title of Delayer (Cunctator) for his strategy of avoiding full-scale battle with Hannibal's army in Roman territory, aiming to wait out and wear down Rome's aggressive opponent in a war of attrition. Fabius' delaying tactics outraged the Roman tradition of bravely confronting its enemies, but they succeeded. Rome survived the years of Hannibal's depredations in Italy and then turned the tables on Carthage by invading its territory on the other side of the Mediterranean Sea to achieve a decisive victory, the Romans' first overseas conquest. Fabius, however, had no part in Rome's ultimate victory over the Carthaginians; he had advised against taking the war to North Africa because the risk of failure for this overseas expedition was, he judged, too great. He died in 203, with his career having reached a somber, indeed tragic, end.

In keeping with his fair-minded biographical approach, Plutarch identifies some weaknesses and failures in both Pericles and Fabius, but overall he presents them as striving to exercise thoughtful and cautious leadership in times of enormous danger. For one thing, Plutarch judges them both to have been valorously brave in war but also as appropriately reluctant when serving as commanders in the field to expose their fellow citizens to unnecessary dangers. Overall, Plutarch concludes that they were comparable for the excellence (expressed by the Greek term *aretē*, which is sometimes translated as "virtue") that they cultivated in their lives, especially in what he calls their "even-tempered way of dealing with other people" and their "behaving justly and fairly" (*Pericles* 2).

These phrases represent single words in Plutarch's original Greek (*praotēs* and *dikaiosynē*). Using only one English word as a translation for each of these terms, as is often done, seriously underplays the complexity of their ranges of meaning. It is therefore misleading to render the words in contemporary English as, respectively, "mildness" and "justice," the translations that a search in an ancient Greek dictionary would yield as primary definitions. One of the aims of this book is to try to show what I think Plutarch means in applying these complex terms to Pericles, above all when the biographer discusses what he sees as Pericles' psychology. Plutarch also refers to Pericles in his biographies of other famous leaders in fifth-century Greece, as well as in various essays, and I will sometimes mention these references when they supplement the information in his *Pericles*.

Not even Plutarch provides us with many details of Pericles' life in his earliest years. He does include Agariste's dream and one sentence about Pericles' father the war hero, and he mentions the primary role of Pericles' mother's family in expelling Athens' tyrants and establishing democracy in the late sixth century. Plutarch most likely got the story of the dream from reading Herodotus (Figure 2). Composing his work in the later fifth century, Herodotus changed history writing forever with his *Histories*, a giant and rich narrative exploring the background and events of the Persian Wars (490s to early 470s). Originally from the city of Halicarnassus (today in southwestern Turkey), Herodotus spent his life in exile as a result of political strife in his hometown; he traveled and interviewed people all around the Mediterranean world. Although Herodotus mentions his contemporary Pericles only once in his work (6.131, the dream story), his narrative provides far and away our most important evidence for the hostilities with Persia that filled the first fifteen

FIGURE 2. Back-to-back stone busts of the historians Herodotus and Thucydides. Universal Images Group/Art Resource, NY.

to twenty years of Pericles' life. Herodotus tells a vivid and action-packed story about that conflict between the Persian Empire and an alliance of thirty-one Greek states that included Athens. Herodotus is also our fullest surviving source for the history of Pericles' family from the time before he was born. The early chapters of this book will therefore draw heavily on Herodotus' *Histories* books 5–9 (the large internal divisions of ancient works are frequently called "books" rather than chapters).

Along with Plutarch's biography, Thucydides' *History of the Peloponnesian War* is today the source most often referred to for the history of Pericles' lifetime, and especially his involvement in the events leading to the Peloponnesian War. Thucydides (Figure 2) was a young adult during the height of Pericles' career as a leader at Athens in the 440s and 430s, and the historian lived at least until the end of the war in 404. Like Pericles a member of a wealthy family, Thucydides won election to the highest public office in democratic Athens, serving as a general early in the war whose history he composed. His work continues its narrative down to the events of 411, where the text breaks off for unknown reasons. Thucydides' *History* was the first major work of ancient Greek history writing focused on the author's own era. Thucydides' razor-edged analysis of the harsh realities of war and its horrifying effects on people physically and emotionally, expressed in a striking and sometimes demanding style that includes speeches in the voices of leading figures, has made his work a classic of world literature in history and political science. Plutarch knew it thoroughly.

Thucydides had unprecedented access to the inner workings of the politics of Athens and to the heat of its citizens' emotions in the stress of wartime because he had firsthand familiarity with fighting in combat as a commander and had experienced an extreme instance of the backlash that high-level public officials at Athens could expect to suffer if they failed to live up to the expectations of their fellow citizens. When, through no direct fault of his own, Thucydides' forces in northern Greece suffered a severe defeat at the hands of the dynamic Spartan commander Brasidas in 424, his fellow citizens at home in Athens exiled Thucydides for twenty years as punishment for this military setback. Rich enough to travel safely where he pleased even during an international conflict, Thucydides spent his time in banishment traveling around the theaters of war observing and talking to participants from both sides.

The account that Thucydides based on this first-person research presents an unflinchingly hard-edged narrative of events and motives. Its first two (of eight) books summarize the conflict-filled history of the international affairs of Athens over the half-century following the Persian Wars and then dramatically document Pericles' uncompromising stance on Athens' foreign policy during the outbreak and opening years of the Peloponnesian War. The sometimes telegraphically concise evidence of his section on history between about 480 and 430, the Period of Fifty Years as scholars call it, is fundamental to any attempt to evaluate the nature of Athenian foreign policy during Pericles' career. Unfortunately, however, this section says nothing of Pericles' role in these controversial events until Thucydides' narrative reaches the outbreak of the Peloponnesian War in the 430s.

At this point, Thucydides then intersperses his description of events with his versions of very influential orations by Pericles during the extremely tense period just before and then during the opening conflicts of the war. Thucydides surely heard Pericles speak in person. The historian's striking representations of Pericles' words provide our only extended report from a contemporary laying out Pericles' reasoning on two central issues. First, Thucydides portrays Pericles as insisting that the Athenians must not back down in the face of threats made by the Spartans, whom he insists they absolutely cannot trust, and that they of necessity must adopt his challenging strategy of "Athens as an island" if they are ultimately to prevail over this enemy. Second, Pericles as presented by Thucydides explains the material resources and social and political characteristics of Athens' democracy that he argues give it the power to be able to survive as a free and independent state by outlasting its enemy in a war of attrition. Like the Roman commander Fabius Maximus, whom Plutarch paired with Pericles in his *Parallel Lives*, Pericles is shown as a leader intent on preserving his homeland through a strategy of wearing down an enemy that he did not think could be defeated in a head-on confrontation of pitched battles.

In summing up Pericles, Thucydides explicitly concludes that he had been by far the most influential leader in democratic Athens and, moreover, that Pericles correctly understood what Athens needed to do, and not do, to prevail in the Peloponnesian War. In a famous phrase, Thucydides encapsulates what he saw as Pericles' overwhelmingly dominant role at Athens by saying, as mentioned previously, that "what was in name a democracy was in fact becoming *archē* by the first man" (2.65.9; usually translated as "rule," the Greek word *archē* has a semantic root meaning literally something like "to be at the head of"). The brilliant speeches that Thucydides presents Pericles as delivering in his own voice provide crucial evidence for the closing section of this biography and therefore will be presented in detail. How can it be, we have to ask, that one leader could become so overwhelmingly influential in a direct democracy famed – and sometimes vilified – for its reliance on government by committee and its hostility to the dominance of any single man? And what are we to conclude about the wisdom of the policies that Pericles so vehemently promoted to the citizens of Athens in his dramatic and effective speeches?

The only other surviving contemporary literary source with direct evidence about Pericles offers by far the most colorful ancient evidence on his character and career. This ancient source is a striking new genre of drama that emerged at Athens in the fifth century B.C.: the comic plays that scholars call Athenian Old Comedy. Like tragedies (the dramas that became central to the reputation of Athens for cultural brilliance), comedies were large-scale theater productions staged as part of large national festivals supported by public subsidies. The authors of comedies, like the authors of tragedies, competed in these festivals to win first prize for the best play. Old Comedy energetically satirized both Athens' political leaders and its social conventions through fantastic plots and continuous mockery both of characters on stage and of contemporary members of the audience; the insults were often expressed in imaginative obscenities. The only author from whose body of work complete comedies are still extant is Aristophanes. Only isolated quotations and paraphrases from the now-lost works of the many other comic dramatists survive, making these authors what are called "fragmentary sources." Numerous such "fragments" are preserved in Plutarch's *Pericles*.

Like other prominent politicians who are made fun of in these plays, Pericles came in for no-holds-barred criticism by Aristophanes and his fellow authors of comedies, especially for becoming a tyrant who exercised too much influence over the decisions made by the Athenians in their democratic form of government. Already in the 440s, the comic poet Teleclides was making fun of Pericles. In the 430s, Hermippus and Cratinus kept up this satirical criticism, raising its sting to what can only have been a painful level for someone as self-conscious about his public image as was Pericles. Cratinus in particular singled out Pericles for biting ridicule as a tyrant behaving like the king of the gods, verbal attacks that Cratinus continued in plays as late as the early 420s in the opening years of the Peloponnesian War, which he blamed Pericles for having started. Aristophanes began presenting comedies in that same decade, though not until after Pericles' death. He, too, caustically satirized Pericles, accusing him of having fomented the war for his own personal benefit. The comic poets Plato and Eupolis also included Pericles among those whom they mentioned in their politically tinged plays produced in the decades of the Peloponnesian War. Deciding what to make of this ridicule of Pericles on the public stage obviously is a major issue for any evaluation of his reputation and influence as a leader.

We know that there were also other contemporary authors who provided information about Pericles, especially Ion of Chios and Stesimbrotus of Thasos. Unfortunately, their works have not survived, except for some fragments. Ion and Stesimbrotus seem to have criticized and ridiculed Pericles, at least in part, but the almost-total loss of their sketches of him makes it impossible to understand the full context of their treatments.

Two other noncontemporary sources provide specialized narratives covering the period of Pericles' lifetime. The earlier of these two works, the *Constitution of the Athenians*, is attributed to Aristotle, the famous philosopher and scientist of the fourth century, who moved to Athens to run an academy for men with the resources and time for higher education. Aristotle's research students produced this work on the political history and the constitutional structure of contemporary Athens as part of a huge project that documented the political systems of more than 150 Greek states. The first part of this *Constitution* surveys the political development of Athens down to the restoration of democracy after the civil war of 404/403. A main theme is the ongoing conflict between Athenians who supported democracy and those who opposed it. Pericles is characterized as a "leader of the people" who made Athens more democratic against the opposition of other upper-class citizens (*Constitution* 27).

The second noncontemporary but specialized narrative source is Diodorus, a Greek from Sicily, who wrote his wide-ranging *Library of History* in the first century B.C., by which time Greece had been under Roman control for a century. Diodorus' long work attempts to knit together a universal history of the world in and around the Mediterranean and Southwest Asia down to Diodorus' day; much of what he wrote has not survived. Fortunately for us, Diodorus' account of most of the fifth century still exists. What we have begins at the time of the Persian invasion of mainland Greece in 480 and continues through the end of the century (*Library* books 11–14). More than once, Diodorus has information that no other surviving source gives us. Compared to Plutarch and Thucydides, however, Diodorus has little to say directly about Pericles.

Various other surviving works from Greco-Roman antiquity offer bits of evidence about Pericles, information that is embedded in literature as different as the complex dialogues of the renowned Athenian philosopher Plato (who wrote in the first half of the fourth century), the wildly entertaining collection of diverse nuggets of cultural history collected by Athenaeus (who wrote about AD 200), and the biographies of famous thinkers/philosophers by Diogenes Laertius (who wrote in the first half of the third century AD). All this testimony, however, consists only of anecdotes and comments about Pericles, not connected histories.

One other prominent category of literary evidence relevant to a biography of Pericles includes the earlier works that he and other Athenians of his time knew as central to Greek identity in general and Athenian identity in particular. Heading that list were Homer's massive poems from the eighth century, which explore complex issues of human conduct. Their stories raise issues extending from how men and women could and should strive for excellence and deal with failure, to the ways in which human beings should relate to the gods, whose effects on people's lives were seen as crucial but often harsh and hard to understand.

Homer was so well known and so popular that performers could make a living being paid to recite his epic poems for audiences in public and in private. In Pericles' time, everyone also knew the very short tales of talking animals collected as Aesop's *Fables*; the overt moral lessons encoded in these lively fables were staples in the education of children and were also frequently referred to in the comedies of Aristophanes. There is not space in this short book to discuss in detail the potential influence of Homer and Aesop on Pericles, but like his contemporaries he would have known their works well. Readers who immerse themselves in Homer and Aesop will greatly benefit in their understanding of the inherited context of thought in which Pericles grew up.

An indirect source of information on the cultural context in which Pericles operated also is derived from the tragic dramas produced at Athens during his lifetime. These plays present complex explorations of human conflict and morality. The tragedies that have survived remain classics of world literature. Many playwrights wrote tragedies that appeared on the Athenian stage, but some of the works of only three, Aeschylus, Sophocles, and Euripides, have survived intact. Scholars of literature and of politics disagree about how to interpret these dramas, whose plots and characters deal with multidimensional problems in life to which there are no obvious solutions. Issues of what is good and what is bad are usually not easily and completely separated in these tragedies, whether the questions and conflicts in the plays concern the actions and responsibilities of individuals or the needs and desires of the community. Aeschylus and Sophocles had a close connection to Pericles: as a young man Pericles was the producer of a tragedy by Aeschylus about the Battle of Salamis in the Persian Wars, while at the height of Pericles' political eminence he served as an elected general with Sophocles during a controversial attack on Athens' former ally Samos. There is not enough space in this book for the detailed discussion that these plays merit, giving readers all the more reason to study these moving texts on their own.

A different category of indirect textual evidence pertaining to Pericles concerns the extremely controversial fifth-century thinkers and teachers known to the Greeks as sophists (Greek for "wise men"); they are sometimes referred to today as early Greek philosophers. These intellectuals used thought experiments to speculate about the nature of the universe on the micro- and the macrocosmic level. Many people thought the sophists' conclusions were dangerous because their ideas appeared to deny the reality of the gods and, therefore, to threaten traditional religion, whose gods were believed to protect the communities that they favored but also stood ready to punish them if people openly disrespected their divine majesty. Moreover, the sophists were experts at argumentation, and in return for a hefty tuition they would teach students the skill of persuading others. Again, many people feared the damage to democratic society and politics that they believed rich men educated in persuasive speaking by these specialists could exert in winning any argument, regardless of considerations of right and justice.

One of the most controversial of the sophists, Anaxagoras from Clazomenae in Southwest Asia (today Turkey), had great influence on Pericles, as a teacher and a close friend. This association generated bitter ill will against Pericles, and it will be important for setting the context of Pericles' intellectualism to explore the evidence preserved in a variety of texts concerning the most debated ideas of Anaxagoras and other prominent sophists who were in Athens during the time of the career of Pericles. Readers should be aware that deep uncertainty about the chronologies of the careers of the sophists whom Pericles knew prevents us from being sure at precisely what period in his life he was in close contact with them. My view, which many scholars reject, is that Pericles had probably been influenced by these thinkers already by the time in the midcentury at which he began to be an effective speaker in the contentious debates of Athenian democratic politics. But even if my conclusion is wrong, presenting the sophists earlier rather than later in this biography helps to make clear a crucial point: the special characteristics of the techniques of persuasion that Pericles developed through study and practice.

In addition to literary texts, inscribed documents put on public display by Athens' democratic government in the fifth century provide a contemporary and especially valuable, if always challenging, source of information about Athenian history. Carved into stone and erected in heavily trafficked locations in the city center, these inscriptions recorded decisions reached by the male citizens who met in the democratic assembly of Athens, for everyone to see and discuss. Most surviving ancient Athenian inscriptions have been significantly damaged by the passage of time, and sometimes it is impossible to recover their words precisely, or even to determine the dates at which they were inscribed. When we can reconstruct and date inscriptions with confidence, they provide contemporary and unmediated evidence offering unique insights, particularly concerning the often-contentious relations between Athens and its allies (the members of the Athenian Empire). For this reason, these documents are important in the effort to investigate the growth of and changes in the administration of Athens' power regarding other Greek states. For the most part, however, these famous inscriptions do not give direct evidence on Pericles' position on the issues they concern. In fact, his name does not certainly appear in a single fifth-century Athenian inscription. (It has been suggested as a restoration on some damaged stones.) Moreover, the most controversial texts cited to support the notion that the Athenians developed an empire may well belong to the time of the Peloponnesian War after the death of Pericles. Since, as stated previously, this book is composed to be a biography of Pericles, not a history of fifth-century Athens, Athenian inscriptions will be discussed only when they are particularly relevant to vexed questions related to Pericles' leadership in the context of the Athenian Empire.

The art and archaeology of fifth-century Athens compose the final major source relevant for a biography of Pericles. The idealizing sculptures and soaring architecture of the major public buildings of Golden Age Athens evoked enthusiastic admiration in antiquity, and even in their ruined state today they retain the power to inspire awe. None is more famous than the Parthenon, the highly decorated and colossally expensive marble temple built on Athens' Acropolis (Figure 15), a precipitous mesa visible from a great distance, which served as the sacred heart of the city soaring far above the lower ground of the urban center. The Parthenon was a new and magnificent house for the goddess Athena, who, the Athenians believed, favored and protected them. The huge temple's artistic details posited an unprecedented claim by the Athenians about their superior position in the world. Pericles was directly and closely involved in this fifteen-year building project, and his role in overseeing the construction of the Parthenon made perhaps the greatest contribution to his enormous fame in antiquity and later (for which, see Figure 19).

As previously mentioned, the construction of the Parthenon fueled criticism from Pericles' political rivals, who claimed that he was misappropriating the allies' money to fund an undeniably spectacular but also offensively arrogant boondoggle. In addition, Pericles encountered trouble from his close friendship with the director of the Parthenon's design, the sculptor Phidias. Like his connections to Anaxagoras and Aspasia, this relationship enmeshed Pericles in a huge and dangerous controversy when Phidias was put on trial on allegations of stealing precious materials from the project and committing sacrilege by insulting the goddess with his artistic program. It will therefore be a topic in this biography to examine, at least briefly, the controversy over this most famous building of fifth-century Athens and related structures.

These are the main sources for the story of how Pericles grew to maturity and forged his career as Athens' "first man." Since in my interpretation of the story of Pericles' life the origins of fundamental aspects of his policies as a leader go back to events occurring well before his birth, I will now turn to uncovering those roots.

MAP 1. Greece and the Aegean

26°E
28°E
Hebrus
Euxine
(Black Sea)
THRACE
Byzantium
Abdera
Propontis
Thasos
CHERSONESE
Lampsacus
Cyzicus
Imbros
Sestos
Hellespont
Mt Athos
Abydos
40°N
Troy
Lemnos
Aegean Sea
Caicus
Mytilene
Lesbos
Scyros
AEOLIS
Sardis
Chios
IONIA
38°N
Ephesus
Maeander
Andros
Samos
Ceos
Tenos
Myconos
Miletus
CARIA
Delos
Paros
Leros
Naxos
Cos
Melos
Thera
Rhodes
0
50
100
150
200 km
36°N
0
25
50
75
100
125 miles

MAP 1 (*cont.*)

MAP 2. Peloponnese and Central Greece

I

The Notorious Family History of Pericles' Mother

When Agariste gave birth to her second son, women surrounded her and the new baby, as was usual during childbirth in ancient Greece. Mothers delivered babies at home, and no men were in the room. As in everyday life, female family members and household slaves controlled parts of the house that were regarded as off-limits to men. Ancient Greek fathers had relatively little direct interaction with newborns, but as the head of the household the husband had the legal right to reject the infant as illegitimate and refuse to raise it. If a father took this extreme (and rare) step, his decision obliterated the child's identity as a free citizen and condemned the helpless babe to being abandoned in the streets for anyone to find – and to sell or keep as a slave.

Family history and personal networks had an enormous influence on Athenians' lives because newborn children in ancient Athens entered a world in which deeply consequential decisions about their status began the moment they emerged from the womb and continued until they were adults: Were they genuinely their father's offspring? Were they going to be recognized as legitimate and so be raised as free members of the household? Would they later be accepted into the hereditary group (*phratry*) whose membership affected their social standing? Finally, in their late teenaged years would they be validated as full citizens by the members of the local subcommunity (*deme*) to which their father's family had always belonged? (There were some 130 to 140 separate demes constituting the Athenian democratic state as a whole.) The family, relatives, and neighbors of the children made these crucial judgments; the central government was not regularly involved in the life-altering decisions that decided individuals' status as free or slave, citizen or noncitizen.

About a week after his son's birth, Pericles' father, naked, as tradition required, picked up the new infant to carry him around the hearth. He then conducted a sacrifice, signaling the legitimacy of the child and its acceptance into the family. The joyous celebration moved on to a traditional meal of octopus and squid enjoyed with relatives. A few days later, the baby boy's parents followed tradition by formally proclaiming his name. By calling him Pericles, his mother and father were expressing hope for his future as a member of a rich and prominent family while also connecting him to his past: the *-cles* portion of the name "Pericles" is from the Greek word (*kleos*) meaning "the fame of a hero," a term familiar from Homer's poetry that expresses the goal of legendary warriors fighting to win an undying reputation for excellence. Compounded with *peri-*, *cles* makes up a name that can be roughly translated as "far famed" or "famous far around." Agariste's son was the first Athenian ever to receive this name, to judge from the surviving evidence. (It is recorded earlier in the lyric poetry of Archilochus, from the island of Paros.)

The fame evoked by Pericles' name mostly belonged to his mother's side of the family, whose history was studded with ancestors of great notoriety. The surviving ancient sources do not yield clear identities or chronologies for the earliest members of Agariste's family, and the reconstruction of her family tree that is presented here is disputed. Fortunately, however, the overall point is clear: Pericles' mother's family was both famously elite and infamously controversial.

The family became known as the Alcmeonids, "the descendants of Alcmeon." One tradition said that the family traced its roots back to Nestor from Pylos in the western Peloponnese, a heroic elder portrayed in the *Iliad* as the wisest counselor in the Greek army besieging Troy. The Alcmeonids were best known at Athens, however, for an enduring controversy that had its roots in the seventh century, in the violent aftermath of an attempted political conspiracy by rich citizens to take over Athens. The persistence of this episode in the memory of Greeks shows clearly from the fact that in the fifth century both Herodotus (*Histories* 5.71) and Thucydides (*History* 1.126) describe it and the bitter fallout from its violence that persisted down to the time of Pericles himself.

These historians record that Cylon of Athens had set the attempted coup d'état in motion. He had made himself into an international celebrity around 640 by winning a running championship in the Olympic Games (Figure 3). This glittering success helped Cylon convince Theagenes, the ruler of the state of Megara on Athens' western border, to let him marry Theagenes' daughter – it was a father's duty to arrange his daughter's

FIGURE 3. Greek vase painting of male athletes in a footrace. © The Metropolitan Museum of Art. Image source: Art Resource, NY.

marriage. Cylon's foreign bride was from the loftiest level of Greek society because her father held supreme power as a tyrant. In ancient Greece, a tyrant was a type of autocrat who had not achieved his position in a customary or perhaps even legal way, in contrast to a king, who secured his political legitimacy through inheritance, or the chief officials of an oligarchic or democratic government who held office after having been selected by their political peers.

Designation as a tyrant in ancient Greece did not automatically imply that the ruler was tyrannical in the modern sense, that is, employing coercion and violence to gain self-advantage. Greek tyrants could sometimes rule with a relatively light hand and as populists, making changes to improve the lot of less well-off citizens. Most Greek tyrannies, however, did over time become oppressive, especially in trying to perpetuate the family's rule from generation to generation. In all tyrannies, no matter how benign, the tyrant's equals in the social elite of the community hated his preeminence over them and frequently conspired to undermine his position. For this reason, such rulers regularly employed their riches to create strong bonds with influential leaders and families from other places. The sinews of power for the upper classes in ancient Greece regularly extended far beyond local political and ethnic boundaries, not unlike the ways in which modern megacompanies forge international relationships to increase their profits and their influence. Accordingly, Cylon's famous athletic triumph and his family's high standing at Athens (Olympic victors in this period were members of the rich social elite) made him an attractive choice for Theagenes in forming a mutually beneficial alliance through marriage to his daughter.

Cylon's new stardom and elite marriage soon went to his head: he conspired against his homeland. His father-in-law perhaps spurred him to this daring plan because Megara was often on hostile terms with its close neighbor Athens. Buttressed by a clique of youths from Megara and Athens, Cylon launched a sneak attack in about 632 to seize control of the Athenian Acropolis, aiming to set himself up as a tyrant like his father-in-law. Cylon's treachery failed when crowds of Athenians flocked to the city center to oppose the conspirators by force. So far as the sources allow us to see, these citizens bonded together spontaneously to risk their lives in battle to prevent one man from forcibly seizing rule over them as individuals and as a community; this is an important hint about the sense of solidarity that the mass of Athenians already at this early date felt about their political freedom as a foundation of their national identity.

Stymied by the Athenian response, Cylon and his fellow conspirators surrendered by huddling together beside a statue of the goddess Athena to secure her divine protection. The officials of Athenian government on the scene, annual magistrates called archons, promised the young men they would not be killed if they moved away from the sacred image with them. The conspirators complied. Not much later, however, they were executed, some of them while still clinging to altars in the sanctuary of a god to which they had fled in terror. Neither Herodotus nor Thucydides records how or why this bloody conclusion took place. It is clear, however, that at least some people judged it to have been a great offense for the officials to use force and violently drag suppliants away from divine protection in order to kill them, even if the criminals did ultimately deserve execution as traitors. Their deaths contrary to a sworn promise constituted an impiety, a serious crime against the gods.

According to traditional Greek religious belief, this sort of impious offense generated a curse on those responsible for the wrongdoing. The presence in the community of such wrongdoers was thought to create a sacred pollution that others feared as a danger threatening the entire population if the contamination were not expunged. The gods, it was believed, would inflict punishment on everyone in a community if it harbored even a single individual who was associated with this kind of outrage against the majesty of the divine. The well-known story of Oedipus, king of Thebes, later famous from the tragedies of Sophocles, proclaimed that truth loud and clear. It also showed that the destructive power of such a curse could endure indefinitely, as would turn out to be the case for Pericles.

This curse came to affect Pericles' life at a much later date because one of the officials in charge at Athens during the Cylon episode had been Megacles, a member of the Alcmeonid family. After the executions of the suppliant conspirators, the fear and hatred that other Athenians expressed against the family of Megacles were so intense that its living members were expelled from their homes and sent into exile, while the bones of their dead relatives were dug up to be flung outside the boundaries of Athenian territory. From the time of this seventh-century maternal ancestor down to Pericles' lifetime in the fifth century, the Alcmeonids would be remembered – by rivals of the family's eminence and wealth, anyway – as having been contaminated by the sacrilegious murders of the conspirators whom Cylon had led. The enemies of the Alcmeonids never ceased insisting that Megacles and all his descendants were accursed by the gods – and therefore a danger to the community.

The Alcmeonids apparently made a comeback relatively soon, revealing that not all Athenians believed them to be guilty of a religious crime. About 595, Megacles' son Alcmeon (the first family member by that name firmly attested in the historical record) won distinction as an Athenian commander in what was later called the First Sacred War, a war fought, the Athenians proclaimed, to avenge sacrileges that other Greeks had committed at Apollo's oracle at Delphi, the god's internationally famous sanctuary. This sacred location in central Greece attracted pilgrims from all around the Mediterranean world to ask questions of the god through his prophetess. Private individuals would line up to pose questions about their personal lives such as "Should I marry so-and-so?" or "Should I go on this trip?" Governments and rulers would send ambassadors to ask about pressing policy issues crucial to them and their communities such as "Should we go to war against our enemies right now?" or "What sacrifices should we make to appease the anger of the gods against us?"

Alcmeon probably gained his military command because, though in exile, he had retained enough influence among a number of his countrymen to win his recall to military duty when a fierce conflict involved the Athenians in high stakes – winning or losing the divine favor of the god Apollo – and required top-notch generals. When Alcmeon succeeded in that military mission, his service to Apollo on behalf of Athens was then seen by most Athenians as the necessary expiation of the family's alleged crime against the gods in the conspiracy of Cylon, thereby making possible the Alcmeonids' return to their homes. In perhaps 592, Alcmeon won the four-horse chariot race in the Olympic Games; this success in the premier event of the international festival made Alcmeon a celebrity at home. Nevertheless, his family's rivals never let the story of the Alcmeonids' inherited curse be forgotten. Pericles would have learned from his parents about the bitter weight of this accusation of inherited impiety. They were right to warn him about it because, as we will see, it would come to bedevil him long after, during Athens' conflict with Sparta in the late 430s that ignited the Peloponnesian War.

Another story Pericles would have heard was the astonishing tale of how his ancestor Alcmeon had made the family so rich. This fabulous story began when Alcmeon used his connections to do favors for officials from Lydia (a non-Greek region in what is today western Turkey) whom their king had dispatched to consult Apollo's oracle at Delphi. According to Herodotus, the ruler was Croesus. (Modern scholars tend to think Croesus' father, Alyattes, was in fact most likely the king at this time.) Croesus is still famous as the subject of the modern expression "as rich as Croesus," an allusion to the great wealth of the king that the story reveals.

Herodotus reports that when Croesus learned that Alcmeon had assisted his representatives at Delphi, he invited the helpful foreigner to visit his royal capital in Sardis. When he arrived at the Lydian court, the Athenian visitor was told he could take home as much gold as he could carry away by himself from the treasury of the stupendously rich king. Alcmeon came up with a plan to maximize his opportunity: he found a long billowing tunic to wear that he could fold up to hold pieces of gold, and then he pulled on the floppiest high boots he could get so that he could fill them, too. Once inside the royal storehouse stacked to the roof with precious metals, he packed his clothes with chunks of the valuable metal, sprinkled gold dust all through his hair, and finally stuffed his mouth with the precious powder until he puffed out his cheeks. When Croesus saw his guest stumbling out under the weight looking like a lumpy, gold-encrusted clown, the king burst out laughing and gave Alcmeon a second gift as lucrative as the one he was struggling to transport. In this wondrous fashion, Pericles' maternal ancestor became literally filthy rich. The yarn about Alcmeon's adventure was plausible because, as mentioned previously, in the Greek world of this era members of the social elites frequently established close connections with foreigners to their mutual advantage.

The history of the next generation of the Alcmeonid family again illustrated the possible consequences of international bonds among powerful members of the upper classes of different states. Cleisthenes of Sicyon (a city on the north-central coast of the Peloponnese) ruled as a tyrant from about 600 to 570. When Cleisthenes needed to find a suitable husband for his daughter Agariste (for whom Pericles' mother would later be named), he announced an international competition for her hand in marriage. Rich young men from prominent families across the Greek world flocked to Sicyon to contend for the prize of a rich bride from a ruling family. So that Cleisthenes could carefully observe the suitors' characters and performances in varied situations, from athletic contests to parties bounteously supplied with wine, the tyrant financed a series of group activities that lasted an entire year. As that probationary period neared its end, he decided that Hippocleides of Athens was the man who would earn the privilege of marrying his daughter. Not only was Hippocleides good-looking and talented, he was also related to a leading family of Corinth, a large city located nearby at the isthmus connecting the Peloponnese to mainland Greece. This marriage, then, could support Sicyon's foreign relations with two Greek states at once.

Cleisthenes arranged for a huge public festival at which the whole city would celebrate his announcement of Agariste's betrothal by dining on meat from the hundred cattle he had his servants roast for the banquet. Wine flowed endlessly, and Hippocleides kept pouring it down. Eventually, the alcohol inflamed the daring young Athenian to leap up on a table to show off his acrobatic dancing skills. After demonstrating two different dances, he topped off his performance with a shocking third style: a headstand while waving his legs around in the air. Since Greek men wore short tunics with no pants or underwear, this impressively athletic posture put his genitals on unrestricted display, bouncing around for all Cleisthenes' guests to see. The crowd exploded in an uproar. Horrified at this breach of decorum by his prospective son-in-law, Cleisthenes shouted, "Hippocleides, you have danced away your marriage!" The drunken flasher shot back, "That doesn't bother

Hippocleides" (Herodotus 6.129). In later times, Hippocleides' words became a proverbial expression to express contempt for other people's expectations of how you should behave, the equivalent in ancient Greek of "I couldn't care less!" or "Whatever!"

Cleisthenes retrieved the dignity of the occasion by proclaiming that his daughter would instead marry Megacles of Athens, with a wedding following the social norms of the groom's home state. By arranging the match on these terms, the tyrant of Sicyon could still hope to improve relations with Athens, and for certain he could cement an alliance with a very wealthy family there. This Megacles was the son of the Alcmeon who had enriched his family with his clownish antics in the Lydian royal treasure house; now, the Alcmeonids had a foreign political connection forged by a marriage that buttressed their elite status.

Even though it is hard to believe every word of the tall tales about Alcmeon in Lydia and Hippocleides in Sicyon because stories about celebrities, then and now, are infamously subject to fictive elaboration, it is still noteworthy that Herodotus narrates these incidents in colorful detail as lead-ins to the story of the dream that Pericles' mother had before his birth. The crucial point to emphasize is that the stories persisted throughout Pericles' lifetime so that they were still available for the historian to record in the later fifth century. Any contemporary with an ear for gossip would have known these accounts about Pericles' mother's family. Accordingly, the history of Pericles' ancestors was always going to be a potential issue in the public's perception of him during his political career.

The public significance of the family history of Pericles' mother continued into the next generation. A son of the Megacles who had married the daughter of the tyrant of Sicyon proved to be the crucial figure in establishing the system of democratic government under which Athens – and Pericles – reached the pinnacle of power in the fifth century. This son was Cleisthenes of Athens, named after his maternal grandfather, tyrant of Sicyon. This great-uncle of Pericles played the pivotal role in the series of violent events at the end of the sixth century that culminated in the establishment of the radical form of direct democracy that would later make Athens' government famous (or infamous, as judged by some, among whom were the founders of the United States' republic). In recognition of this achievement, Cleisthenes was later remembered as the founder of Athenian democracy.

Athens in the second half of the sixth century had been ruled by its own family of tyrants, called the Pisistratids from the name of the regime's founder, Pisistratus. He gained political control after a long and sometimes violent struggle in the 550s and 540s among three groups led by upper-class men eager to prevent their rivals from gaining an advantage over them; the Alcmeonid Megacles was the leader of one of these factions. This conflict among members of the social elite occurred at a time when Athens was suffering from serious unrest stirred up by a decades-long economic decline. These troubles had impoverished many citizens, making them desperate for reforms to alleviate their poverty.

Alliances kept shifting in this protracted conflict among elite rivals and their followers. At one point, in fact, Megacles even teamed up with Pisistratus against their other rivals, going so far as to give him his daughter in marriage. Subsequently, however, Megacles discovered that his new son-in-law was only having intercourse with his wife "not according to custom" (as Herodotus 1.61 delicately phrases it), so as to avoid having any children with her who could compete for status with the sons Pisistratus already had. When Megacles' daughter eventually told him about how she was being disrespected by her husband, her father flew into a rage at this revival of the old controversy attached to his Alcmeonid ancestors; Pisistratus claimed that Megacles' daughter was afflicted with that family's ancient curse and therefore not fit to bear legitimate children. Megacles immediately transformed his cooperation with the tyrant into bitter opposition fueled by a feeling of betrayal.

When Pisistratus finally succeeded in making himself tyrant of Athens about 546, the Alcmeonids put themselves into self-exile, once again bidding a melancholy farewell to their homes and fields at Athens. Pisistratus ended up ruling for nearly twenty years, forging a reputation as the kind of tyrant who preserved his state's legal and political traditions – except, of course, for maintaining his own supreme, dominating position. Most significant in winning the support of the poor majority of citizens were Pisistratus' decision to begin subsidies for them paid from a newly levied tax and his policy of promoting employment on public construction projects financed by public revenues. These populist financial measures won him loyalty from Athens' many citizens who had been struggling to feed their families.

When Pisistratus died in 527 – of natural causes – his son Hippias peaceably took over his father's position. To judge from an Athenian inscription (Fornara, *Translated Documents* no. 23) dated early in Hippias' reign as tyrant, at that time the new ruler was allowing leading men from other upper-class families to hold positions as high officials at Athens. So, Pisistratus' son evidently had started out by reaching some sort of compromise with his main rivals. Since one of those officials was Cleisthenes, the son of Megacles, who served as archon in 525/4 (a date including a backslash indicates an Athenian civic year, whose calendar ran from summer to summer), the Alcmeonid family had evidently been allowed to return home (again). Hippias' cooperation with his rivals for power fell apart, however, after his brother was stabbed to death in a public assassination in 514. In reality, it seems, the murdered Pisistratid was the casualty of the rage of a spurned would-be lover who disguised his rejection in romance as the opening act of a political vendetta. Hippias nevertheless feared that his brother's murder was part of a conspiracy against his rule. The tyrant therefore tightened the screws on those he perceived as his most dangerous opponents. To resist this pressure, the Alcmeonids sent themselves into exile outside Athens' territory yet another time.

By now keenly aware of the dangers to their family's well-being inherent in this refugee status, the Alcmeonids evidently had taken steps to keep their great wealth both safe and accessible while they were away from Athens. They soon set to work using their riches to undermine Hippias. At first, they assembled a military force and built a fort on the northern edge of Athenian territory. This extremely aggressive move led to overt civil war with Hippias and his supporters – and backfired when it ended in a crushing defeat that pushed the Alcmeonids back across the border and out of their homeland.

The exiles' efforts at subverting the Pisistratid regime then took a different direction. They began spending large sums making gifts to Apollo's sanctuary at Delphi, and when it needed a grand new temple, they took up the construction contract and then built – at no additional charge – a far more splendid building than the agreement called for. Herodotus adds (5.63, 65) that Cleisthenes bribed Apollo's priestess, whom the god was believed to inspire to deliver his oracular answers: the Alcmeonid paid her to tell all Spartans, regardless of what they asked, that it was their divinely mandated duty to free Athens from tyranny.

The Spartans at the time were Greece's greatest military power. Their citizens lived a life different from that of almost all other Greeks: they had enslaved the entire population of a neighboring Greek region to compel these helots ("the taken"), as they were called, to labor to provide Sparta's citizens with food and goods. The work of these slaves – their Greek neighbors – allowed Spartan men to devote themselves to military training and Spartan women to cultivate their physical fitness for healthy childbearing. To show their contempt for material riches, the Spartans banned the everyday use of money in their society. Their genuine wealth, they boasted, was what they called their "system of good law" (*eunomia*) regulating every aspect of behavior, from exercise to meals to sex. They governed themselves by consensus among their leaders, who expected deference to their decisions from the mass of citizens. The Spartans took extreme pride in what they saw as their community's special character. This self-glorification, it should be emphasized, was not diminished in their own eyes by their having enslaved tens of thousands of Greeks as helots and their having made an alliance agreeing (in the words of Herodotus 1.70) to "be ready to respond to the instructions" of Croesus, the king of Lydia, even after he had forcibly taken away the political freedom of the Greeks of Ionia (a region on the west coast of modern Turkey).

Eventually, the Spartans were worn down by the demand from Apollo's prophetess to take action against the tyranny at Athens. Oracles were always ambiguous and subject to competing interpretations of their meanings, but finally the Spartans deemed it too dangerous to disobey what appeared to be the god's will, at least on the basis of the large number of times Apollo's priestess had repeated to them the command to liberate Athens. Therefore, in 511 they assembled a modest number of troops to sail to Athens under a second-level commander. The plan was to disembark with a show of moderate strength that the leaders at Sparta evidently believed would be enough to frighten the tyrant Hippias into abdicating and then drive him and his family into exile. Athens at this time was an inferior military power to Sparta, and the Spartans were confident that there was no need to send a first-class army to expel the Pisistratids. They miscalculated. Hippias, like other successful rulers of the time, had made alliances beyond his borders, and he called in his allies the Thessalians to help defend Athens. From a prosperous region to the north in central Greece, the cavalrymen of Thessaly had a well-earned reputation as the best. The swift attacks of these skilled mounted warriors helped Hippias' forces slaughter many of the Spartans, including their overmatched general. The expedition retreated homeward to the Peloponnese in disgrace.

Humiliated by this defeat, in 510 the Spartans sent another, much larger army commanded by Cleomenes, one of their two "kings" (the Spartans' term for these special officials, who were not political monarchs but rather military and religious leaders who had inherited their positions for life by being the eldest male members of two families with special status arising from their performing traditional duties to the gods on behalf of the community). This time, the beefed-up Spartan expedition was prepared to repel cavalry charges and crushed the Thessalians. The Spartan liberators were then joined by Athenians (we do not know how many there were, but they must have been numerous) who, in Herodotus' memorable phrase (5.64), "wanted their freedom." This combined Spartan/Athenian force surrounded the Acropolis to besiege Hippias and his family, who had taken refuge behind the fortifications there. Unskilled at siege warfare, the Spartans were about to give up and go home when by pure accident they captured the Pisistratids' children; the adults had tried to sneak their young ones out to a safe location. To gain the return of their children, the tyrant and his family agreed to go into exile far away from Athens, near the site of ancient Troy in a region where they had contacts and property. As a result, Athens was released from the rule of the Pisistratids, ending thirty-six years of tyranny.

No one could have guessed what would happen next to fill the power vacuum caused by the stunningly unexpected expulsion of the tyrants. In the early sixth century before Pisistratus' reign, Athens' government had existed as a rudimentary and partial democracy dominated by the upper class, but this political system had been both turbulent and ineffective at solving the persistent economic problems afflicting the majority of the population. Reverting to that kind of government, which had proved dysfunctional and lacking the strength and will required to resist tyranny, would have been an ill-omened option in these new circumstances at Athens.

What happened next seemed at first a repetition of the political pathology that had plagued Athens in the past. Members of the elite once again ruthlessly competed to become dominant leaders. In 508, Isagoras and Cleisthenes, two men from elite Athenian families, emerged as the top contenders in this renewed contest. Isagoras had previously established a close mutual relationship with the Spartan king Cleomenes during the siege of the Pisistratids, when the two men became what the Greeks called "guest-friends." Guest-friendship was a mutually binding agreement between two prominent citizens from different places that obligated each party to support the other's interests in his own state; their descendants inherited the obligation. Since at this point Sparta was recognized as the most powerful military force in Greece and was (for the moment) basking in the admiration of those upper-class Athenians who had detested the Pisistratid tyranny, Isagoras evidently gained enough political traction from his special connection to Cleomenes to pull ahead of Cleisthenes in the race for political dominance in post-Pisistratid Athens.

Desperate to overcome Isagoras' advantage over him in this rivalry for primacy in the leadership of Athenian democracy, in 507 Cleisthenes devised a new strategy to win popular support as a counterweight to Isagoras: to counteract his rival's Spartan connection, Cleisthenes the Alcmeonid came up with a proposed reform of Athenian government that gave far greater political sway not to his fellow members of the social elite but rather to the mass of citizens, thereby increasing their social status and empowering them politically at the same time. Cleisthenes' surprising plan set Athens on a political course that in the long run made it the most direct democracy ever implemented and, to repeat a key point, established the foundation of the system of government under which his great-nephew Pericles would later achieve his own lasting fame as a political leader. Athens would become far from the only democracy in Greece, but the change was genuinely radical; forms of monarchy or oligarchy had always been the predominant types of government in the ancient world, and organizing a society on democratic principles based on widespread political rights (for men) was controversial and bound to encounter opposition. There was absolutely no general assumption that democracy was the most desirable kind of government, as it is often assumed to be in certain regions of today's world.

In proposing his plan, Cleisthenes announced that, in making these changes, he was admitting the people as a whole into the company of his "companions" (the term that ambitious upper-class men used to describe the groups of close friends and followers from their own socioeconomic level that they gathered around themselves). Therefore, Cleisthenes the Alcmeonid was paying less prominent and less wealthy Athenians a great compliment by saying that, even though they ranked as ordinary citizens, he still honored and welcomed them as members of his new community-wide entourage.

Cleisthenes, much as his grandfather from Sikyon from whom he inherited his name had, based his plan for political and social reorganization at Athens on reconfiguring and renaming traditional divisions in the community of citizens. The Athenian reformer, however, went further by creating an entirely new system for dividing the citizen body for political purposes and national defense. Previously, Athens' male population had been divided into four "tribes" (divisions based on residence, not kinship) for voting on public policies and laws, electing government officials in the assembly, and fulfilling military duties as soldiers and cavalrymen in the citizen militia that defended the state (there was no professional standing army). Cleisthenes reallotted the citizens into ten new tribes for political and military responsibilities. He promoted his new divisions of the populace as sources of national pride by naming them after legendary heroes who had specifically benefited Athens. The four tribes of the old system that he was replacing had been named after very distant ancestors of all the Ionians (the larger Greek ethnic group from which Athenians believed that they descended). Next, he distributed among his ten new tribes the 130 to 140 local urban and rural communities (the demes) in which citizens were registered. He designed the distribution of the demes among his ten divisions so that each tribe enrolled more or less the same number of people. He also set up the arrangement so that it lessened the chance that other members of the upper class could exercise too much influence by dominating the less powerful citizens from their local areas when elections for public office were held or laws were formulated in the democratic assembly.

It is important to stress that Cleisthenes established the base for the conditions under which Athens would become far more politically and socially democratic than ever before. By initiating the foundational structures of the kind of broad-based, direct democracy that characterized Athens during its Golden Age in the fifth century, Cleisthenes seemingly acted against the interests of the upper class to which he belonged. Scholars debate whether Cleisthenes invented his reforms primarily as a matter of individual self-interest in defeating Isagoras in their competition for political predominance, or because he believed that greater democracy would help the Athenian state to develop greater power to defend its freedom in a dangerous world, or because he believed that his changes needed to be made because they served the interests of justice. Most likely his motives were mixed and complex. What is clear in hindsight is that Athens eventually became far more powerful and prosperous after the reforms of Cleisthenes. This is the explicit judgment of Herodotus (5.66), whose opinion deserves our respect because he was obviously much closer to the situation than any modern historian. Athenian citizens themselves sang drinking songs whose words commemorated what they believed was the essential benefit they had gained by ousting the tyranny: "equality before the law" (*isonomia*; the song is quoted in Athenaeus 695A–B). From a family perspective, then, the mass-participation democracy of Athens of Pericles' time had been handed down from his ancestor and therefore was a system that, from the Greek point of view, he inherited a responsibility to protect.

The history of the years immediately following Cleisthenes' reforms also reveals the deepest origin of the reasons why Pericles came to believe that his fellow Athenians should never make any concessions to Sparta. In these few years at the end of the sixth century, the Spartans abruptly chose to transform themselves from the liberators of Athens into the adversaries of its political freedom under democracy. This shocking change in foreign policy originated when Isagoras realized that Cleisthenes had now gained the upper hand in the competition for political preeminence among the Athenians and therefore in 507 called for help from his guest-friend Cleomenes, still one of the two kings at Sparta. Once again reviving the memory of the story of Cylon, Isagoras asked Cleomenes to induce his fellow Spartans to compel the Athenians to expel the Alcmeonids and their supporters on the grounds that they were all cursed. Cleomenes agreed, sending a herald to proclaim this order at Athens, despite Sparta's possessing no legal or even moral standing to demand that the Athenians do anything. Some people gossiped that the Spartan leader had been so eager to respond because Isagoras had pretended not to notice when his guest-friend had an affair with his wife. When Cleisthenes heard the Spartan messenger's speech, he knew he had no option but to flee Athens. Soon thereafter, Cleomenes arrived at Athens leading a small band of soldiers that proved sufficient to support Isagoras' plans to expel his most hated rivals. The invaders rounded up and sent into exile 700 households that the Athenian conspirator identified as sharing the Alcmeonid pollution and therefore deserving to be banished from their homeland.

This expulsion affected a significant portion of the population. Counting all the members of the banned households, including slaves, 5,000 or more people had to flee. The situation was chaotic and pitiful. The narrow streets of Athens teemed with panicked refugees as they rushed to carry their small children to safety and to load whatever belongings and supplies they could hurriedly gather onto carts and donkeys. Becoming an exile in ancient Greece was about as far from a vacation abroad as it is possible to imagine. There were no international regulations protecting foreigners, no agencies to provide food or shelter, and no hope for a viable existence unless families had resources and personal connections beyond their borders on which they could rely. To make the situation even more maddening to the victims, Cleomenes had treacherously perpetrated this tremendous hardship on citizens of the very state that he had so recently liberated from tyranny on the instructions of the god of Delphi.

Cleomenes' next move gave the lie to any suggestion that he believed his drastic action in expelling the Alcmeonids and so many other

Athenians was necessary to prevent a restoration of tyranny and protect Athens' legitimate new government. To the contrary, he immediately commanded the abolition of the annually chosen council (*boulē*) of 500 citizens that Cleisthenes had made the driving engine of Athens' democratic administration. The Spartan's plan, and clearly that of Isagoras as well, was to install another government, a nondemocratic regime of a kind Athens had never had – an oligarchy consisting of 300 men. All were supporters of Isagoras. Astonishingly, the citizens in the current "Cleisthenic" council refused to obey even though they had been ordered to disband by a Spartan military commander with soldiers at his back; like the Athenians "who wanted their freedom," these citizens, too, spontaneously decided to resist an antidemocratic takeover. To overcome this resistance, Isagoras and Cleomenes then violently captured the Acropolis. By seizing this steep plateau, they controlled the sacred spot at the center of the city where the Athenians performed the religious ceremonies that maintained their good relations with their protective deities.

Before the conspirators could act to extend their hold over the rest of Athens, a remarkable event happened, again apparently spontaneously. The "rest of the Athenians had the same idea," according to Herodotus (5.72), meaning they promptly surrounded the conspirators. In other words, a mass of ordinary citizens banded together to lay siege to the Spartan king, his soldiers, and the Athenian traitors. They were willing to risk their lives to repel this threat to the democratic government that Cleisthenes had introduced. Probably these Athenians outnumbered their opponents, but nevertheless it took courage for this quickly organized crowd to confront a troop of Greece's most formidable soldiers commanded by the general who had recently routed Hippias and his Thessalian allies. Realizing after two days that the resolution of the "rest of the Athenians" to fight for their freedom was unshakable, Cleomenes and his men gave up and went home under a truce allowing them safe exit, taking Isagoras with them. To do so, they abandoned Isagoras' supporters. Some of these men were non-Athenians who had accompanied Cleomenes; some were Athenians. The "rest of the Athenians" executed them all, despite the anger this brutal punishment could be expected to provoke from both foreign states and the families of the local conspirators. Then, as now, treason earned the death penalty.

The victorious Athenians immediately sent messengers to their fellow citizens who had been exiled by Cleomenes and Isagoras to tell them to come home. Cleisthenes was one of the returnees. That there

FIGURE 4. Stone sculpture in relief of the Great King of Persia. Gianni Dagli Orti/ The Art Archive at Art Resource, NY.

is no further explicit mention of Pericles' great-uncle in the historical record perhaps means that he died soon thereafter. Whether relying on Cleisthenes' advice or not, the Athenians soon took a radical step: they dispatched ambassadors to ask for an alliance with the Persians. The Persian king ruled a huge, multiethnic empire stretching from the eastern Mediterranean and Egypt to the western edge of India; the vast revenues and population of his empire made him the leader of the greatest power of the time. It is therefore understandable that Greeks simply referred to him as the Great King (Figure 4). The Persian theory of kingship proclaimed that their monarch was the agent on earth of the supreme god Ahuramazda and that everyone else everywhere was the king's slave, regardless of whether they realized or acknowledged their inferior status. The Great King was in fact so mighty that he could displace entire populations from continent to continent. Once, when King Darius (ruled 522–486) had become intrigued by stories about how hardworking the women of the communities of Paeonia were, he had all the Paeonians and their neighbors moved from their homelands in Thrace, northeast of mainland Greece (roughly speaking, modern Bulgaria), and transplanted wholesale to Persian-controlled territory in southwestern Asia.

Mythology also taught, however, that Greeks and Persians shared a common ancestor in the hero Perseus, son of Zeus; the Persians took their name from Perseus' son Perses. These relatives had not been on friendly terms for a very long time, however. The Persians blamed the Greeks for outrages extending back to the era of the Trojan War. By Cleisthenes' time, the Persian Empire had expanded to take control of the Greeks living in western Anatolia (Asia Minor, as the Romans called it) and parts of Thrace. It was obvious from this expansion of imperial rule that Darius had his sights set on extending his control to mainland Greece. The Athenians in 507 were therefore making a risky bet in seeking to ally with him. Darius' resources totally eclipsed theirs, and their so-far-undistinguished record as a small-time military power in their local region was hardly much of a recommendation. There was no question which side would be the completely dominant partner.

The only reason that the Athenians could have been willing to take such a risk was that Cleomenes' plot with Isagoras had revealed that trusting the Spartans was a recipe for disaster. The Athenians had long realized that the Spartans exercised superior military might, but now they also knew that the Spartans were no longer going to be the guarantors of their political freedom. Cleisthenes' newly reconstituted democracy was quite simply desperate for protection from these fellow Greeks, so afraid of them that it seemed worthwhile to gamble on the very long shot of persuading the Great King to recognize them as his ally. Athenians were learning from experience the grievous lesson that fear for their national safety was going to be their constant companion.

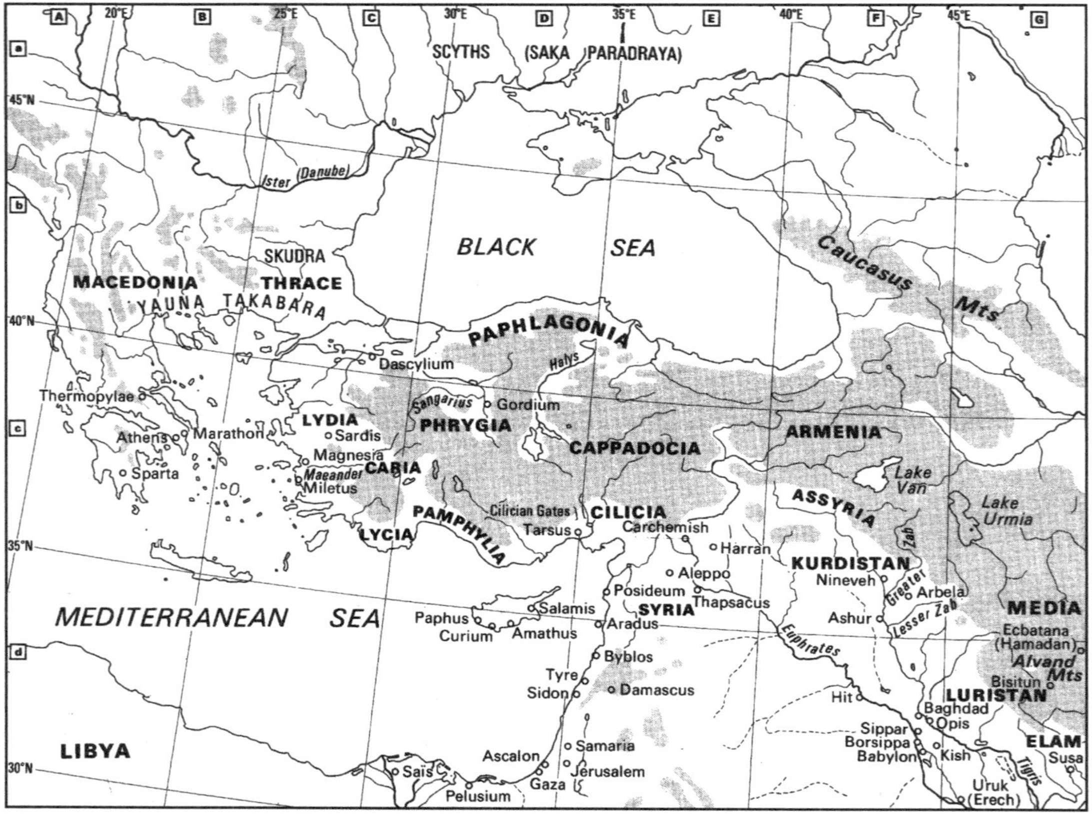

MAP 3. The Persian Empire

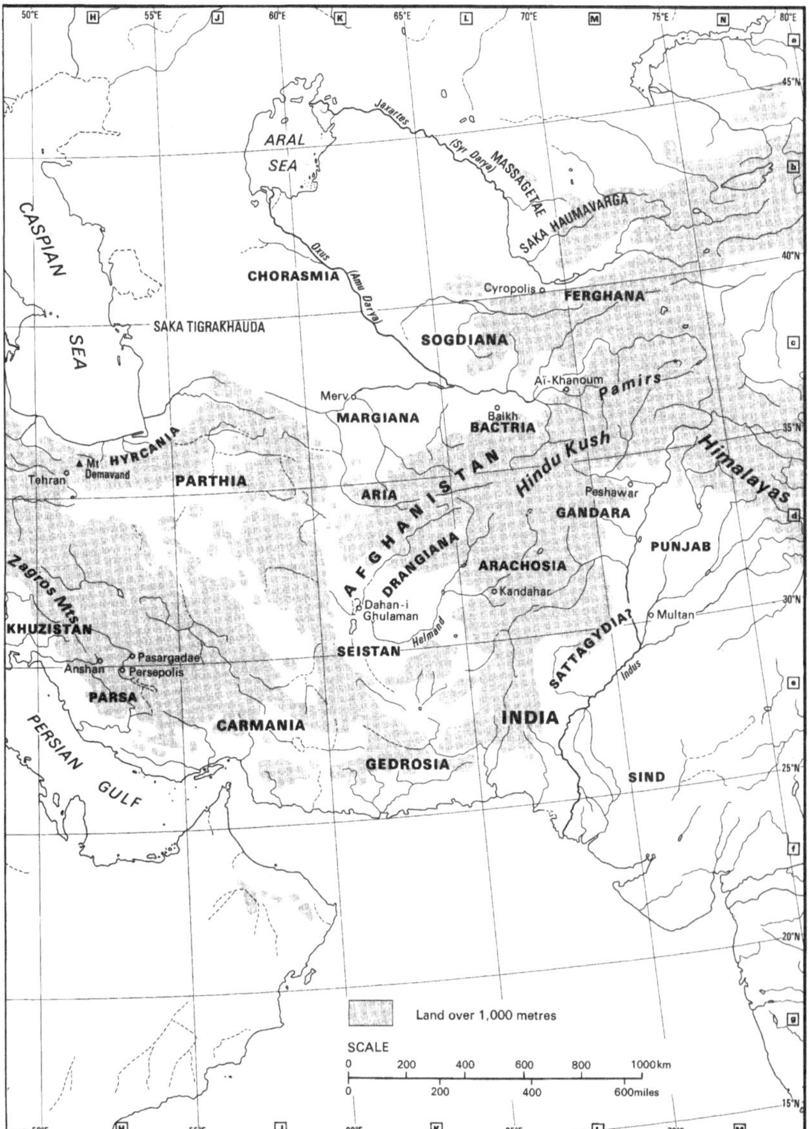

ARAL SEA
CASPIAN SEA
Jaxartes (Syr Darya)
MASSAGETAE
SAKA HAUMAVARGA
Oxus (Amu Darya)
CHORASMIA
Cyropolis
FERGHANA
SAKA TIGRAKHAUDA
SOGDIANA
Aï-Khanoum
Pamirs
Merv
MARGIANA
Balkh
BACTRIA
HYRCANIA
Mt Demavand
Tehran
PARTHIA
AFGHANISTAN
Hindu Kush
Himalayas
ARIA
Peshawar
GANDARA
PUNJAB
DRANGIANA
ARACHOSIA
Zagros Mts
Kandahar
Dahan-i Ghulaman
Multan
KHUZISTAN
Helmand
SEISTAN
SATTAGYDIA?
Pasargadae
Anshan
Persepolis
Indus
PARSA
INDIA
PERSIAN GULF
CARMANIA
GEDROSIA
SIND
Land over 1,000 metres
SCALE
0 200 400 600 800 1000 km
0 200 400 600 miles

MAP 3 (*cont.*)

2

The Harsh Lessons of the Career of Pericles' Father

The years from 511 to 507 had been tumultuous for Athenians. Cleisthenes had redirected their government in the direction of a strongly direct democracy, they had repulsed by force the attempt to seize control of their state by Cleomenes of Sparta and his Athenian collaborator Isagoras, and they had made the fateful decision to ask the Persian king for a protective alliance. As the next decades would reveal, the events of these few years deeply affected the social and political conditions of the Athens into which Pericles was to be born in the mid-490s. They also taught harsh lessons pertinent to his own career that Pericles would learn from his parents' stories about the history of Athens when they themselves were young. Those maxims were easy to summarize but disturbing to contemplate. For one, trusting the Spartans was disastrous; they might claim to support liberation, but they could do an abrupt about-face and promote tyranny when it suited them. For another, the Greeks bordering on Athenian territory (the region called Attica) were also untrustworthy; the Athenians lived in a very treacherous neighborhood with much to fear. Home was also politically hazardous; some Athenians were willing to subvert democracy and resort to tyranny or oligarchy to promote their own advantage. Finally, Pericles could always expect his opponents to try to make trouble for him by exploiting his Alcmeonid lineage and the curse attached to his mother's family. The history of the years and decades to follow would confirm and expand these warnings for Pericles as he grew up.

Pericles' mother, Agariste, married his father, Xanthippus, around 500 or a few years later. Her first child was a son, Ariphron, named after her husband's father, as was customary. She also had a daughter, but neither the baby girl's birth order nor her name is preserved in the ancient sources. Agariste was probably in her late teens at the time of the marriage, Xanthippus in his mid- to late twenties. This difference in age was customary at Athens for brides and grooms in the upper class. When Xanthippus married into the Alcmeonid family, he was stepping up the social ladder. His name, meaning something like "Blond Horse," was a kind of "horsey" name with an upper-class sound that richer Greeks liked to give their children. Nevertheless, his family's status and wealth did not approach the stratospheric socioeconomic level of his wife's clan. Likewise, her family's history was much more famous; there is no historical record of Xanthippus' ancestors before his father. Compared to the Alcmeonids, who ranked among the very wealthiest families of Athenian society, Xanthippus belonged only to a family from the "mass affluent," to use a modern oxymoron.

Pericles' father had been born early enough to grow up keenly aware of the significant political and military events at Athens in the closing years of the sixth century. During that dangerous time, Xanthippus matured from a teenager only able to watch from the sidelines to a young man expected to fight in Athens' military force, its citizen militia; in Greece at this time there was no other kind of national defense force, unless the special Spartan system should be counted as a type of full-time army. Therefore, Xanthippus could teach the lessons of this momentous period to his two sons with a special authenticity because he had first-person knowledge of the military conflicts and political dangers that so deeply affected Athens in this period. Perhaps the most pressing lesson for the boys as future politically aware Athenians was that now the adult citizens who were entitled to vote in the assembly – the legislature of Athenian democracy – were on their own in determining policy for their homeland. These men (women, though citizens, were not allowed to vote or hold a government position) would be responsible for setting policy and making laws. There would be no single ruler to leverage his wealth and personal connections with foreign powers to support Athens' economic and military needs. When Ariphron and Pericles became voting citizens at eighteen years old, they along with the rest of the free adult male population would be participating in the determination of the decisions that would guide their community's political existence and its response to military threats from both nearby Greeks and distant foreigners.

A corollary lesson to be learned was the severity of the reaction that a citizen could expect for any perceived failure to live up to the standards demanded by the Athenian population from those leading their community. The seriousness of this lesson was plain for all to see. For example, at the start of every meeting of the assembly, a herald was employed to pronounce a curse on anyone who, motivated by self-interest or treachery, turned out to give bad or misleading advice to the citizens. Equally fierce were the expectations that soldiers and generals would perform at the highest level in national defense against foreign enemies. No Athenian man of military age could forget the story that once upon a time a group of Athenian wives had surrounded the sole survivor of a military expedition that had been sent to retrieve statues of divinities from a neighboring state whose citizens had refused to return the borrowed sacred items. The enraged women had stabbed the escaped Athenian soldier to death with the long metal pins they used to fasten their clothes at the shoulder, all the while shouting at the bleeding victim to tell them where their (dead) husbands were (Herodotus 5.87).

Xanthippus knew that his sons had to absorb these sometimes-disturbing lessons because the national defense of Athens was now literally going to be self-defense: the big gamble to seek help from Persia had not paid off. On their mission in 507 to arrange an alliance with the Great King, Athens' ambassadors had advanced only as far as Sardis, the capital of Lydia, now a province on the western edge of the Persian Empire. (The Persian king ruled his wide realm by dividing the regions outside the homeland in Iran into provinces overseen by powerful governors called satraps.) When the envoys secured an audience with the satrap, Artaphrenes, he asked them who they were who were asking to become allies of the Great King, and where on earth they were from? His questions did not imply that upper-class Persians were ignorant about or uninterested in Greece. Atossa, the Persian queen, had in fact heard so much about the women of Sparta, Argos, Corinth, and Athens that she wanted her husband to launch an attack on Greece just so that she could acquire servants from those places. And Darius himself was known to be a huge fan of the internationally famous Greek wrestler Milo of Croton in the Greek-inhabited part of southern Italy. So, what Artaphrenes' questions meant was that he had never heard of Athens as being militarily or economically strong. And no wonder: Athens in this period remained still very far from having achieved the status of a power to be reckoned with in international relations.

Once the Persian governor understood what the Athenians wanted, he curtly replied that they could receive the protection of an alliance only if they submitted tokens of earth and water to the Persian king, a ceremony symbolizing that the petitioners acknowledged their utter inferiority, down to the level of these fundamental elements of human existence. If the Athenians were not willing to recognize the Great King's incomparably supreme status, Artaphrenes ordered, then they should get out of town. The representatives on their own – there was no way to communicate with the assembly back home – decided to offer the required signs of submission; they believed Athens needed the alliance that badly. When the ambassadors returned to Athens, however, their fellow citizens furiously blamed them for having agreed to such a humiliating pact. What the assembly evidently did not do, however, was send a message to the Persian king that it had rejected what their emissaries had done in Sardis. So far as King Darius knew, then, the Athenians had agreed to be his allies – on his terms, not theirs.

Athens was on its own militarily, then, when in 506 Cleomenes the Spartan king reaffirmed his true colors as a treacherous self-aggrandizer. Fuming about the affront to his self-importance from having had to listen to the insults of the Athenians who had rallied to besiege him on the Acropolis and then expelled him from their city when they thwarted his plot with the collaborator Isagoras, Cleomenes assembled a large army from all of Sparta's allies in the Peloponnese – without announcing the goal of the expedition. Secretly, he aimed to punish Athens for mocking him and to install Isagoras as its tyrant. There could be no clearer demonstration of Cleomenes' hypocrisy – and by extension of that of the majority of the leadership of Sparta, who had to approve his expedition – than this nakedly self-interested reversal of policy supporting Athens' liberation from tyranny to seeking the abolition of its democracy.

Cleomenes personally led his formidable army into the western region of Athenian territory, but he also arranged for the Boeotians and the Chalcidians, neighbors of Athens on the north and east, to attack from those other directions. The Athenians had too few citizen militiamen to face all these invasions at the same time. They decided to take the field against the instigator, Cleomenes, perhaps because he had done the unthinkable: ravaging the sanctuary of the goddess Demeter located at Eleusis in the western end of Athenian territory. This was a sacred spot whose initiation rites, the Mysteries, attracted Greeks from all over the Mediterranean world. The chances seemed slim that the Athenians could avoid defeat at the hands of a stronger opponent. At this moment, however, a dramatically unexpected turn of events occurred. To honor its alliance with Sparta, the major city-state of Corinth had sent troops to join Cleomenes' Peloponnesian army. Just before the battle against the Athenians began, however, the Corinthians balked at attacking, perhaps now for the first time learning Cleomenes' actual purpose. They concluded that they would "be doing things that are not just" (Herodotus 5.75) if they helped overthrow the democracy that Cleisthenes had established at Athens. They turned around and went home.

It appears unlikely that the Corinthians defected from the Spartan-led expedition out of fear of defeat, as the Peloponnesians' allied force was clearly superior to that of the Athenians at this point. Did they instead conclude that, by helping Sparta to gain control of Athens through a puppet tyrant, they might be adding to the strength of a superior state from their home region of the Peloponnese, a neighbor that experience showed they could not trust? Or did the Corinthians genuinely believe that it was an act contrary to justice to abolish an Athenian government with which they were not at war in order to replace it with a tyranny? The rule of a tyrant was precisely the system of government that the Corinthians themselves remembered having suffered under not so long before, until they had at last freed themselves. Or were their motives some combination of these factors? It seems to me to underestimate the strength of human motivation to rule out completely the possibility that the Corinthians were, at least in part, moved to abandon the Spartan expedition from a concern that the attack was about to perpetrate injustice, though it is also clear that it was in their own self-interest to prevent Sparta from becoming completely dominant.

In any case, the Corinthians' change of heart clearly affected others on the expedition. Cleomenes had been accompanied on this military campaign by his colleague as Spartan king, Demaratus. The latter followed the Corinthians off the battlefield to return home. His reasons are not on record. Seeing that the two Spartan kings disagreed, the rest of the Peloponnesian allies decamped, too. They presumably concluded that the dissension among their leaders meant victory was no longer likely. The Spartan army had no choice but to retreat. It is hard to call Cleomenes' and the Spartans' role in this episode anything other than dishonorable, given that he and they had switched so effortlessly from serving as Athens' liberators from the Pisistratid tyranny to acting as enemies of its reformed democracy. The episode also revealed that the Spartans depended on the support of allies to succeed in international power politics but that their leaders – in this case, the kings – did not always see eye to eye and that this disunity could swiftly change the direction of Spartan foreign policy.

The astonishing repudiation of Cleomenes' leadership by the Corinthians freed the Athenians to deal with the threat from their northern neighbors. Evidently enthused by their unforeseen escape from the Spartan-led invasion, the Athenians first crushed the Boeotians, killing many and capturing 700 more. They then ferried a force eastward across the narrow channel of sea to the adjoining island of Euboea, where the city of Chalcis was located. Winning an overwhelming victory and taking still more prisoners of war, the Athenians confiscated enough territory from upper-class landowners there to settle 4,000 Athenians to farm this conquered land – and to act as an advanced warning system of future attacks. It had become clear from this war that keeping a close eye on Euboea was going to be essential to the defense of Athens.

When the exultant Athenians returned home with their booty, they put their prisoners up for ransom at high prices. They also nailed up on the Acropolis the chains that they had used to shackle the prisoners of war, a public display of their victory and a sign of their gratitude for Athena's divine support. The proceeds from the ransoms were so large that a tenth of them was enough to pay for a statue made of bronze – and therefore expensive – of a four-horse chariot to be located on the Acropolis. It was placed there so that it was the first commemorative monument that everyone saw after entering the sacred area. The memorial sat on a base ten feet long inscribed with letters a foot high. As we know from inscriptions confirming the report of Herodotus (5.77), this text proclaimed for all to see that the "offspring of the Athenians extinguished the violent arrogance [*hubris*] of their enemies" (Fornara, *Translated Documents* no. 42). This victory was important to the democratic Athenians because it was the first demonstration that they could, if they held together, defend themselves from terrible threats and – equally significant for their future international policy, it would turn out – benefit economically by extending their power outside Athenian territory.

The turmoil of these eventful years continued unabated. Around 505, the Thebans, Athens' neighbors immediately to the north, launched a war of revenge against the Athenians. Having commanded the Boeotians during Cleomenes' failed invasion, the Thebans wanted to make up for the defeat that Athens had recently inflicted on them. Therefore, they coordinated another two-pronged attack on Athenian territory by convincing the Aeginetans to join their side in the war. Aegina was an island located close to Athens in the gulf just off its southwestern coast, so near that it was visible from the height of the Acropolis. As so often in Greek history, proximity produced conflict among neighbors: the Athenians and the Aeginetans nursed grudges against each other that reached far into the past. (For one thing, it was the Aeginetans who had not returned the divine statues mentioned in the story about the murderously furious Athenian wives whose husbands had died in war.) The chronology of the hostilities between Aegina and Athens in this period is hotly contested among scholars. The point for the biography of Pericles is that whatever the dates of these events, the conflict established a lasting enmity between these two neighbors whose consequences for Athens' foreign policy continued to loom large during Pericles' career.

The Athenians defeated the Thebans' land attack from the north. If Xanthippus was not quite old enough yet to serve in the militia, he was certainly very close to the age at which he would, like his fellow citizens, be risking his life in the battle line. He would therefore have been paying close attention to military events as the Aeginetans sent out warships for surprise attacks against Athens' western coast. These stealth missions wrecked the Athenian port of Phalerum and the adjoining coastal villages. The Aeginetans launched these raids without making a declaration of war in advance, as was expected of honorable combatants at the time, thus further confirming the danger posed by Athens' neighbors.

The damage to their western coast so outraged the Athenians that they disregarded the advice of the Delphic oracle to delay their retaliation against Aegina. They were in the midst of preparations for exacting revenge when they were stopped in their tracks by Sparta's most blatant attempt yet to suppress Athens' independence. The Spartans had learned about the Alcmeonids' having bribed the priestess of Apollo at Delphi to nag them to expel the Pisistratid tyranny from Athens, and they had also been given copies of dire oracles by Cleomenes that he reported he had found on the Acropolis, prophecies that reportedly foretold that the Athenians would do great damage to the Spartans. Apparently, the Spartans had realized that a free Athens could grow strong enough to rival their own power. So, they summoned the former Athenian tyrant Hippias from his exile to attend a meeting of all their allies at Sparta to plan for a war to restore him as ruler over Athens – and, obviously, to become the agent of the Spartans in making Athens obedient to their wishes.

When the Spartan leaders indignantly told the assembled allies how they felt insulted by the Athenians and now regretted their mistake in having removed the Pisistratid tyranny, the Corinthians once again spoke out to express what the majority of the other allies also thought but were too timid to say: "The world will be turned upside down – human beings will live in the ocean, and fish will inhabit the land – if the Spartans destroy governments built on equality in ruling and work to impose tyrannies on Greek states." There was nothing, the Corinthians continued, more unjust and more stained with bloody gore than tyranny. If the Spartans thought so highly of it, then why had they never allowed a tyrant to rule in their homeland, but only tried to impose that system of government on others? The Corinthians finished their impassioned oration with a history of the pain and suffering of their own experience of tyranny and denounced the Spartan plan to restore Hippias as "contrary to what is just" (Herodotus 5.92). The rest of the allies finally joined the Corinthians in opposing the Spartans, and Hippias had to return to exile in northwestern Anatolia, muttering frightful predictions about how the Spartans would regret this moment when the time later came for the Athenians to cause them grief.

Hippias promptly began to connive with Artaphrenes, the satrap in Sardis, to strike a deal for Persian support in restoring him as sole ruler of Athens. When the Athenians heard about Hippias' contact with this Persian governor, they sent envoys to Sardis to try to convince Artaphrenes not to support the exiled tyrant. But the satrap ordered them to take back Hippias as their tyrant if they wanted to remain safe and secure. The Athenian assembly disobeyed this command, however. This refusal moved Athens' hostile relations with the Persian Empire out into the open.

At this point (probably 499), a Greek named Aristagoras arrived in Athens from the Greek city of Miletus in western Anatolia. He had come, he claimed, to ask the Athenians to send military support to the Greeks in his region of Ionia, who with his help had just overthrown (Greek) tyrants that the Persian king had imposed on many of the states there. In truth, Aristagoras was only pretending to care about liberating the Ionians. What he really wanted was to find a way to prevent King Darius from taking revenge on him for his failure to fulfill an earlier pledge to help the Persians extend their power farther westward over the Greeks living on the islands in the Aegean Sea (the Mediterranean Sea between mainland Greece and Anatolia).

Aristagoras had traveled to Athens only because he had previously been unable to persuade the Spartans to support his scheme. Now, he skillfully played on the ancestral connection between his home state and that of the Athenians, who, legend said, had founded Miletus. Claiming that the Persians' inferior armaments (Figure 5) would make them easy to defeat, he convinced the Athenian assembly to send out a military expedition to support what modern historians call the Ionian Revolt. The Athenians outfitted twenty warships (carrying some 4,000 men). As Herodotus wryly comments on the Athenians' being persuaded by the

FIGURE 5. Greek vase painting of combat between a Greek and a Persian warrior. © The Metropolitan Museum of Art. Image source: Art Resource, NY.

deceptive Aristagoras and the dire consequences of their gullibility, "It seems to be easier to fool a crowd of 30,000 than just one person.... These ships turned out to be the beginning of evils for both Greeks and barbarians" (5.97).

The Athenian soldiers, along with a smaller number of men sent by Eretria (a city on the nearby island of Euboea) and some other allies, marched on to attack Sardis. Xanthippus was by now old enough to have been among these Athenian troops; whether he was there our sources do not say. It is noteworthy, however, that twenty years later he was assigned a military command in this area. It seems possible that he received that assignment because he had had earlier experience in this part of the Mediterranean world during the Ionian Revolt.

The Athenian expeditionary force encountered no resistance in capturing the Persian provincial capital, but the whole city swiftly went up in flames after a Greek soldier set fire to the dried reeds serving as the roof of a house, and the flames leaped from rooftop to rooftop. The conflagration burned so fast that the Greeks could not even plunder their enemies' possessions. The Ionians then rapidly retreated without a fight after the non-Greek residents of the region and their Persian overlords rallied together. Most important for later events, the inferno at Sardis incinerated a temple of the goddess called the Great Mother (Cybele), a sacrilege that the Persians would not forget.

The Persian army next crushed the Ionians at the city of Ephesus on the Anatolian coast. The Athenians were evidently not involved in the battle – they had gone home, abandoning the (in their eyes) gutless Ionians – and they refused Aristagoras' further appeals for help. When King Darius heard that the Athenians had aided the rebellious Ionians, he asked who they were, and when he heard the answer, he shot an arrow into the sky, praying, "God, please allow me to punish the Athenians." He then ordered one of his attendants to say to him three times at every dinner, "My lord, remember the Athenians" (Herodotus 5.105). No matter how many other things Darius had to deal with in his empire, he intended never to forget what he saw as the treachery of these disloyal Greeks, who, he believed, had previously accepted his terms to be his obedient allies.

Confounding the Athenians' low opinion of the Ionians' fighting spirit, the latter continued their revolt. Their intentions proved an inadequate defense, however, against the vastly superior resources of the Persian Empire. The Ionian tyrants who had been temporarily deposed at the start of the revolt accompanied the Persian army as it reconquered Ionia and the rest of western Anatolia. At the order of the Persian generals, the former tyrants sent messages to their respective states offering a deal from the Great King: he promised no retaliation and the same conditions of life as before if the Ionians would lay down their arms and resume their status as his subjects. If they refused, however, he threatened to lead their adult populations away into slavery, to castrate their sons, to ship their unmarried daughters to Afghanistan, and to give their lands away to other more compliant peoples. The Ionians defiantly persisted, fighting to retain their freedom.

The Ionians' defiance wilted, however, under the strain of the intense training in blazing summer heat needed to prepare for the combat at sea that would decide the war. Naval warfare at the time depended on sailors seated close together to operate long oars that they rowed in unison to propel their warships into battle at top speed to smash into the enemy with the rams projecting from the bows of their vessels. Relentless practice on the water exhausted the Ionians, who quit training after a week; they said they would rather become Persian slaves than keep up this grueling regimen. This less-than-heroic decision caused the Ionians' Greek allies from the island of Samos to accept – secretly – Darius' offer of a settlement so that they could save their property and shrines. When the naval battle against the Persians began, almost all the Samian warships deserted. The Persians routed this weakened Greek alliance and captured Miletus in *ca.* 494; they executed most of the men, sold the women and children into slavery, and gave the Milesians' land to their neighbors. The famous sanctuary and oracle of the god Apollo at nearby Didyma were plundered and burned. There were no longer any citizens of Miletus in Miletus.

The Persians proceeded to burn down all the rest of the Greek cities and temples in Ionia. Since the topography of the offshore islands permitted it, there Darius' soldiers "netted" the population by joining hands and then walking across the landscape to sweep up all the Greeks. Fulfilling the king's threats, Persian soldiers castrated the boys and dragged off the unmarried girls to serve in the royal harem. The king's fleet extended its conquests along the northern coast of Anatolia and the opposing European sites, taking over the cities that controlled the entrances to the Black Sea (the Euxine), which was the source of invaluable natural resources (especially grain and timber) for the Mediterranean Greeks.

Xanthippus was now mature enough to grasp the lessons of the Ionian Revolt. Above all, it was clear that any Greek alliance against the Persians could only succeed if its members remained strictly and perpetually loyal to the alliance and endured any and all hardships necessary to deter or defeat the world's strongest imperial power. Moreover, the catastrophic fate of Miletus made indisputably clear how much there was to fear from the failure of Greeks to remain united against the Persian Empire's threat to their independence from foreign rule; their literal survival was at stake. The emotional impact of this point was poignantly reinforced for Athenians when not long thereafter the playwright Phrynichus staged a drama entitled *The Capture of Miletus* in the outdoor theater at Athens used for such productions. Overcome by the pathos of the tragedy of this community of fellow Greeks, the audience of some 10,000 to 15,000 spectators broke down in pitiful weeping. Responding to the public outcry, officials fined the author 1,000 drachmas (the equivalent of around four years' wages for a workman) and banned the play from ever being performed at Athens again.

The stakes for the Greeks in a war with Persia were so sky-high, in fact, as to make it seem worthwhile to adopt an unimaginably extreme plan to escape the horrors of defeat: the entire population would abandon their homeland to move to a new settlement far away. This option was precisely what the inhabitants of the region of Caria in southwestern Anatolia debated when the Persian army approached. And a large number of Samians – those who "had something" (that is, owned property), according to Herodotus (6.22) – actually took just this step after the sack of Miletus: they all immigrated in a group to southern Italy, where they took over the city of Zancle. As difficult as it might be today to grasp the contemplation, much less the implementation, of such a momentous community migration, this is indeed what happened.

There was another thing the Athenians constantly needed to keep in mind concerning their own foreign policy: the Persian king routinely made sincere offers with attractive incentives to any state or individual willing to recognize his supremacy. The Great King was willing to "make a deal" even with bitter enemies, and he faithfully fulfilled his promises, even showing generosity to those he spared. Unlike the Spartans, he was consistent and kept his word. Events of the Ionian Revolt and its aftermath clearly documented the fact that reaching an accommodation with Persia could pay off handsomely. For example, when the Persian monarch restored the previous tyrant of Samos to his position as ruler because that Greek had helped arrange the treachery of the majority of the Samian navy, the king made good on his promise to leave property and sanctuaries on Samos undamaged as a reward for loyalty to himself. The Athenians themselves had a direct experience of this lesson when the Great King's navy captured a warship captained by Metiochus, the oldest son of the prominent Athenian Miltiades. It was Miltiades who had earlier tried to convince Darius' Ionian subjects to betray the king and therefore leave the Persian ruler to be slaughtered by the Scythians during the Persians' military campaign in Thrace before the Ionian Revolt. Darius knew about Miltiades' attempt to have him entrapped and killed – and nevertheless he treated the captured son as his own ward, presenting him money, a home, and a Persian wife; the couple's children enjoyed the status and protection of full-fledged Persians.

By far the most unforgettable demonstration of the Persian king's perpetual willingness to make mutually advantageous arrangements with Greeks who had previously been his enemies occurred when he completely reversed his former policy toward the Ionians: Darius ordered his commanders to expel from these Greek states the recently restored tyrants whom the Greeks hated and instead to install democratic governments to bestow on the Ionians the local autonomy that they had fought for in their disastrous rebellion! And not just that: Darius also compelled the Ionians to stop attacking each other and utilize arbitration in settling their interstate disputes. Finally, he established a system of taxation for them that was regarded as so reasonable that the Ionians, after they had later once again been liberated from Persian control, voluntarily maintained this arrangement without change throughout the fifth century. In short, by this time in the late 490s it was obvious that Greeks who battled the Persians so as to remain fully independent could expect the severest of punishments if they lost, but that people and states that collaborated and asked for mercy could receive extremely favorable treatment, even including forms of self-government that the king would never allow for Persians. A Greek policy maker needed to be constantly aware of how seductive it could be for allies – or even his fellow citizens – to agree to a deal with the Persian king rather than to do battle with his vastly larger military.

Unfortunately for the Athenians and the Eretrians, at this point they counted among the enemies that Darius aimed to punish rather than to reward with a deal; he was still enraged that they had joined in the attack on Sardis during the Ionian Revolt and burned down a temple. Making the situation more ominous for Athens was that in this very period, the late 490s, the Persian king had dispatched a military expedition to extend his imperial control into Macedonia (north of central mainland Greece) and had tasked ambassadors to visit many Greek states to demand that they, too, offer earth and water. Many complied, including Aegina. The Aeginetans' agreeing to the Persian demand particularly infuriated the Athenians because they believed that their close neighbors were conspiring to help the Great King gain control of Athens.

It revealed just how desperately serious was the Athenians' anxiety for their security when, in response to the looming Persian threat, they appealed to the Spartans to prevent the Aeginetans from becoming traitors to the freedom of the Greeks. In seeking the Spartans' support, the Athenians had to swallow their resentment that these fellow Greeks had not so long before launched an attack on Athens in an attempt to destroy their democracy by reinstalling Hippias, their former tyrant. The Spartans responded by sending Cleomenes, still one of their two kings, to Aegina to arrest the ringleaders of the islanders' pact with Persia. The Aeginetans summarily rejected his demands, encouraged by a letter from Cleomenes' bitter rival in the Spartan kingship, Demaratus. When the latter was deposed by a plot in which the Delphic priestess was bribed to proclaim he was a bastard and therefore an illegitimate Spartan king,

Demaratus fled to – where else would a leading Greek go to find a comfortable life in exile? – the court of the Persian king, where he became a favored adviser to Darius, who provided the fugitive Spartan former king with a lavish lifestyle. Back in Greece, Cleomenes and the new second Spartan king arrested the ten most prominent citizens of Aegina and gave them to the Athenians to keep as hostages.

When the other Aeginetans complained about this move, the Spartans yet again proved to the Athenians that they were inherently unreliable: they summarily demanded that the Athenians hand back the hostages. The Athenians refused. Hostilities with Aegina soon flared to a new intensity. When the Aeginetans captured a ship of Athenian sacred officials and confined them in chains, the Athenians put all their resources into preparing a naval attack. At this date, the Athenians' military power was still too weak to confront even the fleet of a smaller neighbor such as Aegina, so they had to ask Corinth to supply additional ships to beef up their navy. Even this strengthened force proved insufficient when, winning the first engagement but losing the next, they created a bloody stalemate. This history made yet another contribution to the Athenians' harsh realization that their close-by neighbor Aegina was dangerous, that Sparta was untrustworthy, and that overwhelming naval capacity was Athens' only hope for salvation and survival.

While the Athenians were failing to defeat the Aeginetans, Darius in 490 decided to launch a naval expedition to punish Eretria and Athens. He commanded his generals to enslave these Greeks who had defied him and take them back in chains; he intended to deport his opponents to Persia. Darius also sent Hippias on the expedition so that the exiled tyrant could be reinstalled to rule whichever Athenians would agree to live there as compliant allies of the Great King. When the Persian force reached Eretria, on the other side of the narrow channel separating the island of Euboea from Athens' territory, the Athenians dispatched the men whom they had previously settled at Chalcis to help defend the adjacent city, but they retreated when they discovered that some Eretrians were planning to make a deal with the Persians to secure personal rewards for themselves. Eretria fell when these citizens opened the gates to the attackers. The victorious Persians enslaved the Eretrians who had resisted and burned the sanctuaries there to take revenge for the incineration of the temple of the Great Mother at Sardis during the Ionian Revolt.

Hippias then led the Persians to a landing on the beach of Marathon in northeastern Attica, where the broad plain offered ideal terrain for the cavalry operations that the invaders planned. Badly outnumbered on the battlefield by the Persian troops, the Athenians sent a runner to Sparta to ask for immediate military help; he covered the 150 miles between the cities in only two days. The Spartans promised to help, but they added that they could not march out immediately because they were conducting a national religious festival whose conclusion a week later they had to await before they could launch a military campaign, for which they of course needed divine favor. The only soldiers who did arrive in time to help the Athenians were from Plataea, a tiny community immediately to the north in Boeotia. The Athenians had previously helped the Plataeans defend themselves against Thebes, their powerful and aggressive neighbor, after the Spartans had refused to support Plataea. So now, to repay their debt of honor, all the men of Plataea's citizen militia arrived to stand shoulder to shoulder with the Athenians in a fight they could hardly expect to win.

The terror felt by the Athenians at the prospect of being crushed in battle and then forcibly displaced to Persia was so intense that they freed some slaves to reward them for fighting alongside citizens in the battle. Compelling slaves to fight in battles was frequent in ancient Greek warfare, but offering them freedom was rare – a sign of how deeply apprehensive the Athenians really were. Pericles at this time would have been only a young child, four or five years old, and therefore still living with his mother and her female slaves, too young to understand why his caretakers were so upset, but he would have sensed their fear keenly. Frightening foreigners – monsters, the little boy probably imagined – were attacking, and he was sure they were going to hurt him if they won.

The majority of the Athenian commanders at Marathon were just as pessimistic. They did not want to fight, presumably thinking that they could secure a deal from the Persian king at the last minute. Miltiades, however, disagreed. He insisted to his reluctant fellow generals that their only chance to preserve Athenian freedom and property was to attack. He argued that the Greeks had a tactical advantage in the superior arms and armor of their infantry, which they should use before the Persians could fully deploy their many archers and cavalrymen. Miltiades also told his colleagues that delay favored the enemy because it gave an opening to citizens back in the city who would want to agree to a settlement with Darius to end Athens' democracy. With these arguments he shamed his colleagues by pretending not to know that their unwillingness to fight suggested that they, too, were ready to go over to the enemy side. Finally, he promised them that a victory would propel Athens to the status of "the first of the Greek states" (Herodotus 6.109). That is, he saw a successful fight for freedom from foreign domination as the way to improve the power and therefore the flourishing of Athens.

Militiades' passionate appeals persuaded the other commanders, despite the troops' fear of their enemy, whose ranks were dressed in their (to Greek eyes) intimidating foreign clothes, including pants. When sacrifices to the gods returned favorable omens, the Athenian and Plataean heavy infantry (hoplites) – apparently alone or at least ahead of any archers or cavalry – advanced toward the Persians; from their usual walking pace they broke into a run to close the final gap between the opposing lines. The Greek hoplites yelled a battle cry at the top of their lungs as they flung themselves into the shower of arrows and against the sharp points of their more numerous enemies. Scholars today still debate how great a distance the Greeks ran in clanging their way across the plain in their metal armor. It seems certain at least that their unconventional tactic surprised the Persians. Herodotus reports that they thought the Greeks had become "suicidally insane" (6.112). Incredibly, the Persian generals seem not to have been ready to deploy the cavalry that they had initially been counting on to win the day. Even so, the battle was a close contest, a fierce struggle that lasted hours. In the end, the Greeks' better armor and weapons combined with their undaunted courage prevailed in the infantry battle, and they then surged on toward the Persians' beached ships. There, the brother of the famous Athenian author Aeschylus earned eternal fame after he bled to death when a Persian chopped off his hand as he climbed up the side of an enemy warship to attack its crew. This story and more Pericles would have heard from his father, who was probably a fighter at Marathon; Xanthippus was now old enough to fight in the militia and wealthy enough to afford the bronze body armor of a heavy infantryman.

A less heroic story that Pericles certainly also later heard was the rumor that Alcmeonid family members had plotted to betray Athens at this crucial moment. After their defeat on the plain of Marathon, the story goes, the surviving Persians managed to escape on their ships, intending to land on Athens' western coast and capture the city from that direction. An Athenian became enshrined in legend for running nonstop from Marathon to the urban center to warn the citizens there to barricade the gates. (His trek of more than twenty miles from Marathon gave the name of that battle site to the running event so popular today.) Some people later accused the Alcmeonids of having signaled the Persians by flashing a shield from atop the fortification walls of Athens in a plot to restore Hippias. This was surely a slander – what possible advantage could the Alcmeonids have anticipated from restoring the tyrant they had deposed? But the story underlines that the bitterness of the rivalry between Athens' elite families never ceased and that Pericles in his career always had to be aware that his political rivals could try to use his mother's family's history to undermine his support among the people.

Unable to capture Athens, the Persian expedition went back home, delivering the captives from Eretria to Darius as instructed. Yet another demonstration of the generosity that the Great King could at any time extend occurred when, as soon as he laid eyes on the enslaved and displaced Greeks, he lost his anger at them. Instead of selling them on deeper into Asia, Darius gave them homes and land in Persia as gifts so that they could exist comfortably, living there in their own community and still speaking Greek.

In 490, then, Athens unexpectedly succeeded in defending itself against an attack by a (poorly led) contingent of the world's greatest military power. Marathon was the first time that Greeks could claim a clear victory over a Persian force. The outcome was made ambiguous, however, by the fate of the Eretrians. On the one hand, that city's capture revealed how destructive disunity among the citizens could be when some were ready to yield to the tempting possibility of collaborating with the Persian king. On the other hand, the king's ultimately forgiving treatment of the Eretrian exiles made the point that it was almost never too late for Greeks to gain the rewards of submission when dealing with this very distant relative sitting on the throne of the Persian Empire. In other words, it was never going to be a simple or straightforward choice whether to wage war against that superpower on behalf of Greek freedom, or instead make a deal with Great King.

3

Pericles Becomes a Teenager during a Family Crisis and a National Emergency

Pericles reached his teenage years in the later 480s. He was growing up in an Athens that was becoming mainland Greece's most populous city-state, the term that modern scholars have adopted to describe ancient Greek political communities consisting of a large urban center controlling a territory also populated with smaller outlying villages and farmsteads. Citizens could live anywhere in the city or the countryside. The Greek word for city-state was *polis*, the source of the modern word "politics." During the fifth century, the number of adult male citizens entitled to exercise political rights and required to serve in the citizen militia probably crested somewhere between 40,000 and 60,000. Overall, the polis of Athens grew to a population that probably totaled 250,000 or more, counting everyone: male and female citizens and their children, resident foreigners, and slaves. This was an extremely large population for an ancient Greek polis. Of the more than 1,000 ancient city-states whose existence is documented, most had far, far smaller numbers of people residing within their borders.

The territory of Athens, known as Attica, occupied a triangular peninsula of plains, hills, and small mountains in southeastern mainland Greece. Athenians, like the inhabitants of other Greek city-states, devoted the majority of their land to agriculture, but they were especially fortunate to have a coastline dotted with good ports for sea commerce. By the time Pericles was an adult, the population of Attica had grown so large that it outstripped the land's capacity to produce enough food to feed everyone. Merchants therefore began to import large amounts of essential supplies, especially raw grain, from fertile areas to the northeast in the Black Sea region and to the southeast in Egypt. These bulk imports of grain were transported aboard ships plying the Mediterranean Sea, which made for a risky business enterprise because storms could easily wreck the transport vessels.

Porridge and bread made from barley and wheat, supplemented by vegetables, olive oil, and cheese, represented the main source of nutrition for ancient Greeks. Most people could not afford meat as a regular item in their diets, and they therefore highly valued the distribution of cooked portions from large-scale animal sacrifices financed by the state. It is absolutely crucial to emphasize a fundamental truth about Athens' literal survival in the time of Pericles: if the Athenians could not guarantee the safety of their shipping by sea to import the food needed to sustain the people, they would starve to death. It is crucial to keep this brutal reality always in the forefront of any judgment about the morality of the Athenians' commitment to the central importance of maintaining and, if possible, increasing their city-state's naval power. It was a matter of life and death for them.

The Athenians helped pay for imported grain by exporting valuable goods such as wine, which was in enormous demand throughout the ancient world, and silver from the huge veins of ore that they discovered in their southern hills at the beginning of the fifth century and to which the state laid claim. This import/export trade grew so spectacularly over time that Athens' economic prosperity came largely to depend on it. So, to protect their seaborne commerce as well as to ensure their lifeline of food supplies, over time the Athenians developed fortified harbors, a proficiency at shipbuilding and sailing, and Greece's most effective navy.

Even after the Athenians' unexpected great success in winning the Battle of Marathon against the fearsome Persians in 490, few Greeks would have predicted that Pericles' home city-state was going to achieve unprecedented power, population, and prosperity. Athens had previously been overshadowed, as mentioned, by Sparta militarily and by Corinth in seagoing capability. All this was to change dramatically as Pericles grew from a child to a teenager. This period of Athenian history was nevertheless deeply marked by fear and danger. The decade of the 480s is unfortunately very poorly documented in the surviving ancient sources, but it is clear that Pericles in these years experienced emotionally wrenching and physically perilous events that burned into his mind lessons that he could never forget. The first of these disturbing episodes occurred soon after Marathon, when Pericles was still too young to grasp the full significance of what happened. But the incident's close connection to his family history meant that he would feel the weight of its consequences in time.

The incident in question involved Miltiades, who had become a national hero at Athens for his leadership in the victory at Marathon especially because no one had expected this previously second-rate Greek power to be able to repel the might of the greatest empire in existence. The Athenians' salvation through their own efforts – aided only by the small band from Plataea – made their self-confidence soar; surely, they concluded, we have the gods on our side. The voters in the democratic assembly soon acted on this confidence, letting their emotions sweep away their common sense: at Miltiades' request, they granted him a naval force to use for any purpose he determined. Astonishingly, the participants in the assembly only required him as commander of this expensive venture to promise that he would take home rich plunder, without even having to inform them where he planned to take the ships and their crews, or what he planned to do when they got there. The assembly, in other words, authorized what amounted to a pirate expedition without any knowledge or reasoning about its prospects for success. Before the battle at Marathon, Miltiades had promised that Athens would become "the first of the Greek city-states." Now, he somehow persuaded the assembly members to roll the dice in the dark so that he and they could profit from their ambition to become "number one."

Events soon revealed that Miltiades intended to attack the Greek city-state of Paros, an island in the southern Aegean Sea. His motive was personal: he blamed a Parian citizen for having ruined his chances to ingratiate himself to a high-ranking Persian who was close to King Darius. It is important, if not reassuring in the context of evaluating Athens' leaders, to be explicit about this episode. The renowned architect of the spectacular Greek victory over the Persians at Marathon had evidently been scheming to win for himself the material rewards that the enemy's monarch was known to provide so lavishly to those who favored his interests. After all, Miltiades' son was already living luxuriously off royal generosity as a favorite of the Persian ruler. It seems an inescapable conclusion that Miltiades had given in to the lure of becoming rich, regardless of the hazard that his secret plan posed to his home community.

Regrettably for Miltiades, his attack on Paros failed miserably, leaving him with a festering leg wound. When he limped home to Athens, Pericles' father, Xanthippus, prosecuted Miltiades on the legal charge of having deceived the Athenian people and squandered their resources; in the Athenian courts, private citizens, not public officials, initiated almost all prosecutions. The male citizens who made up juries, or convened in the assembly to decide certain types of major cases, had the authority and often the will to punish leaders who were charged with "having practiced deception." This charge did not necessarily have to mean that the accused had perpetrated a criminal fraud, though that could be the charge, but only that he had failed to fulfill his expected duties or fallen short in honoring his promises to benefit the city-state. In Miltiades' case, his fellow Athenians decided not to execute the former hero of Marathon but did impose a huge fine (50 talents, the equivalent of a 1,000 years' wages for a workman). Miltiades soon died of his infected wound, leaving his son, Cimon, responsible for paying off the tremendous penalty.

The sources do not document Xanthippus' motives in leading the prosecution of Miltiades. What is certain is that the prosecution reflected, or perhaps began, a bitter enmity between Pericles' family and Cimon's family, both of which ranked in the social elite. This hostility would be a legacy passed down from Xanthippus to Pericles that would have severe and enduring consequences when the son's political career later overlapped with that of Cimon and led him into a contest for prominence with this older rival. In addition, the example of how irresponsibly the assembly had authorized Miltiades' disastrous adventure would stick with Pericles as a lesson on the danger of Athens' forming its foreign policy in the absence of knowledge-based judgment.

Hostility well describes the state of domestic politics at Athens in the 480s. By late in this decade, Pericles was beginning to be old enough – his midteens – to grasp more deeply the significance of political and military events, as well as to experience the full emotional impact of the crisis that impacted his father – and by proxy his mother and siblings – during this period. That family crisis stemmed from the official procedure that Athenians called ostracism. Probably originally introduced by Cleisthenes as part of his reforms to empower his restructured democratic system of government, ostracism allowed citizens to exile a fellow citizen for a period of ten years. Once every year, the assembly voted whether to hold the procedure. If the vote was in favor of an ostracism, then two months later the balloting took place, with voters submitting *ostraca*, the term for fragments of broken terra-cotta pots or plates (Figure 6). Each participant scratched on his pottery ballot the name of the man whom he wanted banished. If 6,000 ballots were cast, then the person who received the most votes was ostracized. Within ten days, he had to leave Attica for ten years, not to return unless officially summoned.

Ostracism was not punishment for a crime. The man ostracized incurred no financial penalty, and he retained full ownership of his property at Athens. His family members could, if they wished, remain at

FIGURE 6. Ancient Greek *ostraca* (ballots for an ostracism). Gianni Dagli Orti/ The Art Archive at Art Resource, NY.

home undisturbed by any official consequence other than his compulsory absence. At the same time, this procedure imposed a terrible hardship on the banished man and the people in his family, whom he either had to uproot from their home to take with him outside the borders of Athenian territory or leave behind on their own, forced to rely on relatives and friends if they needed any help during his long absence. For all these reasons, ostracism imposed bitter personal and emotional losses on the ostracized man (it was always a man), his wife, and his children. Xanthippus, Agariste, and their children, including Pericles, would have directly experienced these dreadfully painful effects.

Why did the Athenians accept the harshness of ostracism? Perhaps it was because they remembered the repression and violence into which the tyranny of the Pisistratids had deteriorated before it had been ousted in the late 500s. In establishing their Cleisthenic democracy, the mass of Athenians had apparently decided that, to preclude the possibility that an exceptionally prominent leader would gain enough support to make himself into a tyrant, it was necessary to remove such a man from the city-state for ten years. Their hope would have been that an extended period away from Athenian politics would deprive the ostracized leader of the prestige among his followers that had made him seem such a looming threat to Athens' democracy.

John Adams (1735–1826), one of the influential founders of the United States and its second president, famously acknowledged this political motive – fear – as a cause for the creation of the Athenian institution of ostracism, commenting that "history nowhere furnishes so frank a confession of the people themselves, of their own infirmities and unfitness for managing the executive branch of government, or an unbalanced share of the legislature, as this institution" (*The Political Writings of John Adams*, ed. George Wescott Carey [2000], p. 188). This blunt judgment was one of many reasons why Adams and the other founders rejected the direct democracy of Athens as a model for their new government and insisted on forming a republic. It is hard to disagree that ostracism seems to be a manifestation of what political commentators such as Adams call the tyranny of the majority that can emerge in a democracy lacking sufficient constitutional safeguards to protect individual liberty. At the same time, however, we have to accept that, for the Athenians, their fear of losing their freedom justified this assertion of their authority over any particular person who provoked that anxiety.

The evidence for ostracisms following the Battle of Marathon in the 480s is limited but seems to support this interpretation. So far as the record shows, no one had ever been ostracized before this period (leading some scholars to think that the institution itself was not as old as the time of Cleisthenes' original reforms two decades earlier). Now, in the years after the Battle of Marathon in 490, several leading Athenians were ostracized, one after another. In Aristotle's brief survey of Athenian political history (*Constitution of the Athenians* 22), it is reported that the first men to be ostracized were banished because they were in fact suspected of aiming at becoming tyrants ruling Athens. This accusation carried the implication that they were connected to the Pisistratid family and therefore ready to collaborate with the Persian king, to rule as his toadies. After all, the former tyrant Hippias, son of Pisistratus, had accompanied the Persians to Marathon, expecting their victory would reinstall him as sole ruler of Athens.

Of course, the 6,000 or more male citizens who cast their ballots in a valid ostracism had varying motives for choosing the person whom they wanted to exile, including reasons based on nothing more than vague suspicion, or mere personal dislike or jealousy. For example, after Pericles' Alcmeonid relative Megacles was ostracized in 486, the famous fifth-century poet Pindar flattered Megacles in a (commissioned) poem by implying that he had been ostracized as the result of "envy, as repayment for his fine deeds" (*Pythian Ode* 7.15). Even more famous was a story about the 482 ostracism of the prominent leader Aristides, who was known to be exceptionally just in the way that he lived his life and conducted politics. As Aristides was walking to the balloting place for the ostracism being conducted in that year, another citizen approached him to get his help in inscribing a name on his scrap of pottery – the other man was illiterate; that was not unusual at the time and not a disqualification for citizenship or voting. When Aristides asked what name to scratch into the surface of the ballot, the man replied, "Aristides." Surprised, Aristides then asked what this Aristides – he, of course – had done to the man to deserve being ostracized. According to Plutarch (*Aristides* 7), the man said, "Why, nothing at all; I am just sick and tired of hearing everyone call Aristides 'The Just!' "

Archaeologists excavating at Athens have so far found more than 11,000 ballots. These ancient pieces of broken pottery show that some participants in the process of ostracism added to their ballot a few words or an incised drawing (in one famous case, a picture of a man dressed in Persian clothing) to express why they wanted to banish the man whose name they inscribed. As it happens, there is evidence for this practice from the very ostracism that directly affected the young Pericles: the banishment in 484 of his father, Xanthippus. Archaeologists have found a ballot bearing Xanthippus' name that includes two lines of poetry in addition to the name (Fornara, *Translated Documents* no. 41, D8). The verses are tersely expressed and difficult to interpret precisely, but they accuse Xanthippus of committing some kind of injustice in politics or government – they also allude to him as "cursed," surely a reference to his being married to Agariste, whose family, the Alcmeonids, bore the stigma of the curse that never expired, carried forward through time from the outcome of the long-ago conspiracy of Cylon. The words of the two lines do not point to any direct indication of a fear of tyranny or of traitorous behavior, but clearly this citizen strongly rejected what he saw as Xanthippus' immoral political stance or actions. Above all, he was not reluctant to add an age-old slur to emphasize his hostility to Pericles' father.

Enough citizens agreed with him to force Xanthippus to leave Athens. No details have survived about Xanthippus' experience abroad, or about the fate of his family during his period of banishment. Xanthippus was rich and, like other members of the Athenian elite, would have had contacts outside the borders of his home city-state whom he could visit, such as his wife's relatives in Sicyon. But his wife, with young children still at home, probably stayed in Athens so as not to dislodge the youngsters from their accustomed surroundings and household routines. It does not take much historical imagination, however, to envision how devastated his young son must have felt, once he fully grasped the consequences of what had been decided on the fateful day of his father's ostracism. For the child Pericles, it could only have been a terrifying catastrophe.

If it is correct that Xanthippus' family remained in Athens, then soon after the day of the balloting for the ostracism Pericles watched in dismay while his father left their house and hometown. The boy must have dimly grasped that he was unlikely to see Xanthippus again within any time frame that a child of his age could even begin to comprehend – his father was now going to be gone for approximately as long as Pericles had been alive! Regardless of how affectionate and emotionally close Pericles' father had or had not been to him (the sources are silent on this point), his soon-to-be-adolescent son could only have experienced feelings of confusion, dismay, and profound fear at his father's departure. His mother was admittedly even more socially elite than his father, with the helpful connections that resulted from such status, and she certainly would have controlled financial resources adequate to maintain the family's standard of living. Still, in a patriarchal society like that of ancient Greece, the absence of the father could only seem a frightening setback for the family's safety.

Pericles at his age would not have understood all the implications of this family crisis, but he could hardly have failed to sense – and be seriously troubled by – the worry and tension that the other adults in his immediate family were experiencing. Uncertainty always presents a gnawing threat to a child's sense of well-being and security, and anxiety that could not be resolved is certainly what Pericles would have felt from this episode. Maybe he was given the hope that he could later visit his father abroad, but nevertheless the boy's fear can only have been deep and disturbing, never to be forgotten.

Once Pericles was older and came to know more about the procedures and norms of Athenian democratic government, he would have appreciated just how powerful the will of the majority could be in this direct democracy that lacked a written constitution. To use a modern parallel, Cleisthenic democracy could operate fundamentally as government by referendum. There were in practice no binding restrictions on what could be decided by the voting public in Athenian democracy – the adult men known collectively in this sense as "the people" (demos). Long-standing traditions and the existing laws that the demos passed in the assembly served as signposts to what previously had been judged fair and right; memory of them was meant to discourage ill-considered decisions made in the heat of the moment. Nevertheless, there was no insuperable constitutional barrier to prevent a new gathering of voters deciding at any time to override the precedents or laws from the past, whether temporarily or permanently.

Pericles in his early years therefore had heart-breaking firsthand experience of the overwhelming power of the Athenian demos over individual citizens, first from the ostracism of his maternal relative Megacles and then even more so from that of his father, Xanthippus. It seems certain that Pericles absorbed deeply and indelibly the lesson that anyone aspiring to political prominence in fifth-century Athens always ran a realistic risk of suffering destructive personal consequences if he lost the favor of the majority. This sobering truth greatly complicated and deepened the challenge of acting as a genuine leader, one who could convince "the people" to adopt policies that they initially opposed, and not one who promoted only his own self-interest by operating as a craven demagogue devising ways to succeed individually by flattering and pandering to the citizens.

Four years after his father was ostracized, Pericles learned yet another painful lesson that he would always remember: the degree of danger that his city-state faced from Persia. The defeat that King Darius' expedition suffered at Marathon in 490 had enraged him as an insult to his majesty, and he had vowed to punish the Athenians and their fellow Greeks. He therefore had sent messengers all across his vast territories, from the Mediterranean shores to the western regions of the Indian subcontinent, ordering his subjects to dispatch soldiers, horses, food, supplies, transport vessels, and warships to supply a massive invasion of mainland Greece. These commands put all of western and central Asia into an uproar. The resources of the Persian monarch's empire were immense, but so were the distances. So, even four years after the orders had been sent out, the complete force had not yet gathered in one place. Darius encountered further delay when his sons by different wives began disputing among themselves who should be their father's successor as king, at about the same time that the important province of Egypt rebelled against Persian rule. Darius finally settled on his son Xerxes to be the next Great King, but Darius died soon thereafter in 486, before he could subdue Egypt or launch his megawar of revenge against the Greeks.

In the immediate aftermath of Darius' death, there had seemed to be a glimmer of hope that the danger to Greece might dissolve. Xerxes as a new king had above all to deal with the rebellion of the Egyptians because their land was such a profitable territory, yielding abundant crops of food and valuable minerals including precious metals. In addition, the rumor was, the new monarch was uninterested in pursuing his father's vendetta against the Greeks (or at least that is the report of Herodotus, whose books 7–9 give by far the most detailed account of the events of this period). By this time, Pericles was beginning his teen years, old enough to understand the frightening news that was reaching Athens about the impending threat of a Persian attack. Could he – and other Greeks – have still hoped that the invasion might not happen?

In time it became clear that the threat still loomed. What had happened was that other Persians at court had been lobbying hard for Xerxes to change his mind about invading mainland Greece. They saw a chance to increase their prestige, wealth, and personal power by sharing in the spoils of war and then by ruling the additions to the empire's provinces that the expected victory would yield. Despite the careful advice of his uncle, Artabanus, to beware of this beguiling advice and to calculate the uncertainty of such a large-scale war effort, Xerxes began to bend. He now insisted that a military expedition was appropriate to punish the Athenians for their crimes against the Persian Empire and therefore to avenge the insult to royal authority. In addition, by conquering Greek territory to expand his empire, he would be adhering to the divine mandate for all Persian kings to exercise control over the entire world. Both the guilty and the innocent, Xerxes said, would have to bear the yoke of slavery because, he maintained, there was no middle ground in the hostility between these relatives, between the Persians and the Greeks. Moreover, the victory would certainly be his, he explained, because, after all, the Greeks were so worthless that they had been conquered by the ancient hero Pelops, who had been nothing more than a lowly slave of Xerxes' ancestors. Finally, Xerxes reasoned, the Athenians would invade his territory if he did not attack them first in a preemptive strike.

Distressingly for those who saw Greek unity as the only policy with any chance of fending off the Persian juggernaut, some Greeks also persuaded Xerxes. First, there were the descendants of Pisistratus who were living in exile in Persia; the desire to return home in triumph still burned high in the tyrant's family. Its elders could promise the Great King that they would make contact with their supporters in Athens and work to prepare the way from the inside for Persian success. They could promise Xerxes that they would engineer the surrender of their city-state without a fight in return for his offering them an attractive deal. More than just a hope of collaboration was expressed by the elite family known as the Aleuadai in Thessaly, who controlled great riches and many armed followers, especially from the region's famed cavalry. They guaranteed Xerxes that they could rally support to his cause. In return, they would expect to gain complete control over the other Thessalians.

Herodotus reports that Xerxes' reluctance to undertake the invasion was finally suppressed by a terrifying divine apparition; the king yielded when faced with what he saw as a cosmic necessity to conduct a war to conquer Greece. He put down the revolt in Egypt, but then it took him four more years to gather the empire's diverse armed forces into the huge multiethnic, multilingual, and complexly structured army and navy that would finally bring to bear against Pericles' homeland the greatest and most frightening threat in the history of the world to that point. The necessary lag time in assembling the giant Persian army gave the threatened Greeks plenty of opportunity to mull over how unlikely their chance of survival was.

They learned, for one thing, that Xerxes' preparations were as global as he could make them. He became so determined to uproot the Greeks from their homeland that he schemed to smash them with a two-pronged attack launched not just from his own lands in the east but also from those of allies in the western Mediterranean. He therefore sent envoys to propose an anti-Greek alliance to the flourishing city of Carthage in western North Africa (today Tunisia), which had been founded three centuries before by Phoenicians from the eastern Mediterranean coast as a way to profit from sea trade; the Phoenicians still living in their original territory provided the major strength of the Persian navy. The Carthaginians were commercial and political rivals of the rich Greek settlements that dotted southern Italy and Sicily. Xerxes enticed Carthage to join his alliance by promising to put the Greeks into a desperate squeeze, with coordinated attacks from east and west laying open their city-states to conquest by Persians on the mainland and Carthaginians in Italy and Sicily. It seemed likely that this pincer movement would crush the Greeks.

When Xerxes finally had his total force for the invasion of Greece assembled in 480, it was almost too large to be counted. Still, the king tried, having group after group of soldiers file in and out of a marked-out space whose capacity could be estimated, allowing a final total to be calculated by multiplying that number by the number of groups who had entered. Herodotus famously reports that the total reached several millions of ground troops, while the Persian navy was said to amount to several thousand warships and transport boats. Modern source criticism judges these totals to be impossible because there could never have been enough food and water along the route to support such a vast horde of people, to say nothing of the herds of horses, oxen, mules, and other beasts of burden needed to carry equipment and to pull wagons. Most estimates today reduce the number of invaders by an order of magnitude, placing the total in the low hundreds of thousands rather than the millions. Whatever the actual numbers of men and of materiel might have been, their enormity was unprecedented. No one on earth had ever seen such a massive gathering of people, animals, and ships. The news that reached the ears of the teenaged Pericles of the magnitude of the storm that was gathering across the Aegean Sea must have sounded like the announcement of the end of times for Greece.

The reports of Xerxes' resources just kept getting more terrifying. Since storms at sea had wrecked an earlier Persian naval expedition in the wind-tossed northern Aegean Sea, the king ordered his military engineers to cut an enormous canal wide enough for two ships through the Athos peninsula that stuck out from the coast in that area. Even the architect of the project was outsized: He was said to be the tallest Persian of all – more than seven feet in height – and to speak in the loudest voice ever heard among human beings. The Greeks later said that Xerxes had the canal dug merely to show off his might and pride because, in fact, if all he was concerned about had been safe travel, he could have had his ships dragged across the peninsula on land, a common ancient technique for crossing an isthmus. The canal was such an enormous excavation that the trench through the landscape is still visible today. Xerxes also planned for the logistical challenges of supporting such a vast crowd of people and animals on the march, having dumps of food established in northern Greece in anticipation of the arrival of his army. Water was more of a problem, it would turn out, and in some cases his gigantic force drank entire rivers dry.

While these preparations were under way, Xerxes traveled with his large royal entourage from the Persian heartland in Iran to the regional capital at Sardis. From there, he sent envoys to the city-states of Greece – except for Athens and Sparta – to demand the traditional tokens of submission and to instruct the Greeks along the king's projected route to get ready to provide feasts for the ruler and his horde. Xerxes fully expected compliance from all those Greeks who had not previously agreed to his father, Darius', command to submit. He did not, however, send messengers to the Athenians (or the Spartans) because they had thrown his earlier ambassadors into deep wells to die, screaming at them that the Persians could find down there what they had come for. Killing these heralds was sacrilege. That the Athenians and the Spartans had been willing to risk the anger of the gods to dramatize their rejection of the king's demands shows how fierce was their determination to resist – or at least the determination of some of their political leaders. The Spartans had become alarmed, however, when they subsequently received bad omens, so they had sent two volunteers to Xerxes to be sacrificed as payback for his lost messengers. The king indignantly told the Spartan envoys to go back home unharmed. He would not, he said, stoop to commit the same crime that the Spartans had, and they would just have to live with their guilt.

It can only have increased the fear of the Athenians – and therefore of the young Pericles – when under these circumstances no messenger announcing a possible deal with Xerxes arrived. Persian kings were, as described earlier, often willing to come to terms very late in the game even with their worst enemies. So it was truly ominous to have no such offer on the table. This could only mean that Xerxes was so angry he could not be deterred from focusing his matchless military strength against Pericles' home city-state (and its allies).

Any possible doubt about Xerxes' merciless ferocity was erased by the report that he had his army exit its camp in western Anatolia by marching out between the two bloody halves of a dead human body – the bifurcated corpse of the son of a very rich man who had feasted the Persian army at tremendous expense, but then in return asked the king to allow him to keep one of his male children at home instead of sending them all along with the troops. Xerxes furiously replied that if he, the Great King, was going on the march with his sons, brothers, servants, and friends, then no one else should even think of doing anything other than following him with his entire family, down to his very wife. The king then had the man's son sliced in half, to frame the road as a gory reminder to all that they walked on this earth as his slaves, no matter how socially elite they might fancy themselves to be. Pericles could only have felt an escalating sense of horror at this tale of Xerxes' ferocity, soon to descend on his homeland.

Remarkably, twenty-nine other Greek communities joined the Athenians and the Spartans in refusing to knuckle under to Xerxes' demands to cease their resistance to his dominance. This alliance of thirty-one members could marshal at best a military only a fraction of the size of the Great King's. Their dread at what their fate was likely to be could only have increased when they received the next piece of shocking news: Xerxes had ordered a bridge to be built from boats lashed together to provide a crossing of the Hellespont, the swift-flowing strait about three-quarters of a mile wide at its narrowest point that separates Asia from Europe (in what is today western Turkey). When the first attempt to finish this complex bridge was destroyed by a storm, Xerxes ordered the channel's waters to be struck with a whip and then branded with a hot iron, to punish the waves' refusal to submit to his will. He also had the failed engineers beheaded. Greeks might think that this report meant that Xerxes was risking the righteous anger of the gods with his hubris of treating the sea, a force of nature, like a slave to be beaten, but they could also have no doubt that it also revealed the depth of his wrath against them.

Since Xerxes' route to the edge of southwest Asia took him near the site of Troy, the city that Greeks had long ago plundered according to the ancient legends made famous by Homer's epic poetry, the king visited there to inspect the ruins and pay his respects to the goddess Athena, who had been the patron deity of the inhabitants of Troy. The Trojans as enemies of the Greeks had been on the right side, in Xerxes' opinion. With typical Persian royal magnificence, the king had 1,000 cattle sacrificed for a splendid and enormous feast in honor of the goddess. It is important to recall that the Persians believed that they and the Greeks were descended from a common ancestor and, therefore, shared relationships with the divinities that ruled the universe. The Persian king could, in his mind, just as much expect to win the support of a Greek goddess as could his non-Persian relatives in Greece – and the Greeks, including Pericles, could well fear that Xerxes might be successful in his request for divine favor.

When the bridge across the Hellespont was finally ready, Xerxes positioned officers holding whips to hit the men to make them keep up the pace as they crossed the swaying bridge to Europe. It was part of Persian royal doctrine that the king's "slaves" (meaning everyone, whether formally enslaved or not) only behaved with discipline when they were directly threatened with punishment. Xerxes believed (rightly) that the traditional disunity prevailing among the Greek city-states left them ill equipped to beat back a major foreign threat, but, as events would prove, he was wrong to believe that citizens who are free and not subject to a king or emperor will never have the discipline to stand up to great danger. Xerxes did not believe Demaratus, an exile from Sparta who found refuge and favor as a royal adviser in Persia, when the Greek told him that the Spartans would always fight because they feared law, not a man, as their ruler.

Demaratus was exaggerating for effect, as later events at the Battle of Plataea in 479 would reveal, but he was right insofar as he meant that, even if they were scared and doubtful, even if they faced an enemy without being compelled by the whip strokes of a king's minions, Greeks could on the right occasion and with the right leadership voluntarily summon the courage to put their lives and property on the line to defend their freedom. It is crucial to realize just how desperately difficult and even fragile such a decision must always be. History fully and truly analyzed shows that it is never as straightforward or as easy to make and maintain such a choice as it is sometimes romanticized to be in movies or novels or triumphalist versions of a nation's past.

Sticking to their commitment to resist the Persians rather than seek a deal became harder still for the Greeks as more reports flowed in about the astounding extent of Xerxes' army: It was so enormous that it required seven days and seven nights of continuous marching for all the army's troops, slaves, concubines, horses, donkeys, camels, pack animals, wagons, and chariots to cross the strait. At the same time, a stupendous swarm of warships and transport vessels, perhaps around 1,000 or so at this point, had sailed across to Europe, bristling with ranks of spear-carrying marines on their decks. Greeks composed a part of Xerxes' expedition, especially in the navy, some as willing allies and some under compulsion. The "un-Greekness" (to Greek eyes) of the Persian threat was unmistakable, however, including the incredible (to Greeks) news that a woman, Artemisia of Caria, was serving as major naval commander for Xerxes.

After crossing into Europe, Xerxes forced the fighting men of all the regions he traversed to join his army as he moved westward toward Macedonia. At the place called Nine Roads, he had nine local boys and girls buried alive, so the Greeks heard, to placate the spirits of the underworld. What level of tortures would he inflict, the members of the Greek alliance worried, when he next directed his revenge against them? The places that had to provide a meal for the king's horde found themselves exhausted by the effort and impoverished by the expense. The terror in Greece to the south only increased day by day as this news flooded in. It is hard to imagine the depth of the fear and worry that Pericles and his contemporaries were experiencing.

Finally, at this very moment of growing desperation, for Pericles at least there came some good news. The danger to Athens from Xerxes' invasion had become so overwhelming that the Athenians decided they needed all the help they could get in trying to decide what to do in this crisis and how to defend their city-state from annihilation. So, the Athenian assembly agreed to send a message to all the leading men who had been ostracized in the previous years: "Come home quickly," they were told; "you are needed." It is also important to record perhaps the most significant motive in the recall of these ostracized citizens: Many of their fellow citizens were afraid that the leaders whom they had ostracized might seek revenge on their countrymen in the most damaging way possible by collaborating with Xerxes to help him capture Athens. We should not be startled by this fear of treachery because we must never underestimate the allure for individuals and communities alike of agreeing to a deal with the Persian king. He kept his word (a level of trustworthiness that Greek states such as Sparta found impossible to maintain), and he could make very attractive offers even to Greeks who had been his most fierce enemies. It is therefore remarkable that all of the ostracized Athenian leaders responded positively to the official recall and returned home, except for Hipparchus, the Pisistratid, who stayed with the Persians, his only possible source of safety. Included in the returnees was, to the delight of Pericles, his father, Xanthippus. The danger to Athens as a whole remained of course at a level beyond imagining, but to the teenager it must have seemed that somehow the gods had decided to smile on him and his family again. Calamitous events would soon shake that adolescent confidence.

4

Pericles Becomes a Refugee during Athens' Greatest Peril

Pericles' joy at the unexpected return of his father had to compete in his emotions with ever-heightening fear about the threat approaching their homeland from Persia. As King Xerxes in 480 marched southward from Macedonia toward central Greece, scouts constantly carried news of his progress to the Greek communities on his invasion route. The Greeks who had sent him tokens of submission were confident that they would not be attacked (though they might be bankrupted by the demand to supply provisions to his army and navy). On the other hand, those who had defied Xerxes' order to submit were terrified. What if some of their compatriots now changed their minds and went over to the side of the Persian king, begging for his mercy and pointing out their fellow citizens who opposed "cooperation"? But, they asked themselves, what if they, too, gave up their fight to preserve their city-state's political liberty before any blood was shed; could they then strike a deal with Xerxes for lenient treatment? After all, everyone remembered, once the rebellious Ionian Greeks had been pacified and returned to the fold as Persian subjects, Xerxes' father, Darius, had installed democracies to govern them instead of tyrannies, thereby giving the citizens control over their domestic politics.

As they could practically hear the footfalls of the unimaginably numerous enemy army approaching their borders, the Greeks who had not given earth and water to the Great King faced a life-and-death decision. It is remarkable that in the end any members at all of this anti-Persian alliance of Greek states stood fast against such seemingly overwhelming odds; that they experienced grave doubts and dissension the whole time only underlines the amazing nature of their commitment to fight to preserve their political liberty. The Athenians, or at least the majority of them, supported the decision to oppose Xerxes, even though, as events would show, they had another tempting option if they were willing to make a deal with him.

In 480 Pericles was approaching fifteen years old – an age at which he would have been following his male relatives around during this time of ultimate peril and listening in on their heated discussions as the news grew steadily worse. The Athenians faced an agonizing dilemma: to fight Xerxes or ask him for terms. Almost all the Greeks to their north had submitted to Persian hegemony, a decision that their fellow Greeks called "Medizing." This term reflected the Greek habit of referring to Persians as "Medes" (the ethnic group that had held power before the Persians themselves established their own empire over the region previously dominated by the Medes). These Medizers were not going to join other Greeks in resisting the invader and might even join in the foreign attack on their neighbors to the south. Experiencing near-paralyzing fear for their very existence, the Athenians did what Greek tradition required in such dire circumstances: ask for divine guidance. Sent to seek Apollo's advice at Delphi, the Athenians' delegates initially received a shocking reply from the god's priestess: "Escape to the ends of the earth!" (Herodotus 7.140). The envoys were overcome with despair at the god's instructions to abandon their homeland, until a local man persuaded them to plead for another, better answer. This time, they were told that Athens' only, slim hope was a "wooden wall" associated with the nearby island of Salamis, which lay close to Attica's western coast. What could this riddle mean?, they puzzled. Some back at Athens believed it meant the citizens should barricade themselves in atop the Acropolis behind its ancient fence, though there was room there for only a tiny minority of the population. The competing interpretation was that the oracle was telling the Athenians to put all their faith in their navy of warships made from wood – despite the Persians' huge advantage in the number of vessels in their invasion fleet.

Disagreement raged over the meaning of the divine message until one citizen convinced almost all the rest that the god was telling them to make their stand at sea. This remarkable personality was Themistocles, whom the historian Thucydides would later present as the forerunner of Pericles in his ability to use his judgment based on knowledge to reason out the best course of action for his city-state – and to do whatever was necessary to make that happen. Themistocles was an unconventional leader for the time, not born to riches and lacking a polished education. He liked to thumb his nose at his snobbish rivals for public influence, who looked down on him for his humble origins. Once, for example, he ostentatiously showed his unconcern for their disapproval by driving through the center of town with a chariot conspicuously transporting four prostitutes. His fiery nature and piercing intelligence, especially his ability to foresee what was likely to happen, propelled Themistocles to prominence in the desperate debates of the 480s over the fate of Athens. Pericles could see for himself from the example of Themistocles how knowledge-based skill in predicting and persuading provided a path to leadership in Athenian democracy.

The first time that Themistocles had successfully put his powers of persuasion to work on the citizens of Athens had actually been a few years before – in what turned out to be a momentous episode. In 483, a rich vein of silver ore was discovered in Athenian territory. Since the community owned the mineral rights, the profits from the strike belonged to the citizens as a whole, each of whom stood to gain an infusion of cash roughly equal to wages for ten to twenty days of work at a reasonably well-paid "blue-collar" job. This sum would have been a considerable boon for the majority, who were not well off. Themistocles, however, reasoned that the windfall should be spent on building a fleet for national defense, especially since at the time Athens was in a state of hostilities with Aegina. The Athenians already possessed some warships, but not nearly enough technologically advanced vessels to make them a naval power. Navies had always been expensive, but recent innovations in highly specialized warship construction had boosted the costs even further. The newest design produced narrow vessels that sacrificed stability and interior space for speed by stacking 170 oarsmen in three rows one atop another; the ships were therefore called triremes, "triple-rowed ships" (Figure 7). High-intensity, coordinated rowing was required to propel these state-of-the-art warships at a speed high enough to inflict maximum damage with their rams.

It was going to take a lot of money to provide Athens with a first-rate navy. Themistocles persuaded the Athenians to spend their unexpected bonus from the silver mines to finance the construction of 200 triremes, a technologically advanced navy of a size that few if any other city-states could match. As subsequent events would reveal, this decision both helped save the city-state from the Persians and gave it the military basis to rise from comparative weakness to a leading position of international power during Pericles' lifetime. Themistocles also made another key recommendation based on his study of topography by persuading the Athenians to improve and fortify their main port at Piraeus on their west coast. His argument was that securing access to the sea would assure Athens

FIGURE 7. Stone sculpture in relief of rowers in a trireme. Gianni Dagli Orti/The Art Archive at Art Resource, NY.

of a lifeline for importing essential supplies and security for deploying its naval might. Themistocles engineered this turning point in Athenian history by employing his oratorical skill in the public assembly to make a successful argument based on knowledge and reason. This ability to persuade fellow citizens gave a man great influence in the direct democracy of his home city-state, a clear lesson for the son of Xanthippus as he reached his midteens and contemplated the career in public life that was expected of him as an adult male.

The leaders of the coalition of Greeks who united to resist Xerxes convened more than once to debate their best options. After the Thessalians had Medized, the allied city-states decided on two military expeditions: a fleet sent to confront the Persians off the eastern coast of central Greece in the strait between the mainland and Artemisium on the northern end of the island of Euboea, and an infantry force dispatched to block the narrow pass of Thermopylae that snaked through the mountains separating Thessaly from the Greeks to the south. The Athenians supplied by far the largest number of the Greek warships dispatched to Artemisium, their ships under the overall command of Themistocles and buttressed by the contributions of superrich Athenians such as Cleinias, who paid to equip a trireme at his own expense. A demonstration of the ever-present danger to the Greek coalition caused by dissension among its members is that the other allies now refused to be commanded by an Athenian and insisted on having a Spartan take charge of the Greek fleet, despite Sparta's lack of experience in combat at sea. The Athenians conceded the leadership to prevent the operation from falling apart, though clearly there was a significant risk in making this concession because the Spartans were not the most qualified to assume this position. Compromise on such a crucial matter in the face of such a frightening threat was perilous, but the risk had to be accepted to prevent disunity in the Greek alliance.

It made more sense, given the Spartans' preeminence in heavy infantry warfare, that they also took the lead in assembling an allied force to blockade Thermopylae. The several thousand Greeks in this army included a troop of Thebans, who had been compelled to join because Thebes had earlier expressed support for the Persians. When Xerxes approached the pass, he was astonished to find this comparatively tiny group of Greek allies standing in the way of his army, which was at the very least an order of magnitude larger than that of his opponents. His initial attacks at the north end of the pass failed humiliatingly because the restricted space allowed only a limited number of his soldiers to enter at a time. The Greeks, entrenched behind a wall they had thrown across the road and led by the Spartans, repeatedly repelled their less well-armored and less well-trained opponents. The Persians only figured out how to overcome this blockade when a local Greek, seeking a reward from Xerxes, revealed to the Great King that a path over the mountains would let him send a contingent to outflank the enemy by attacking them from their undefended rear at the south end of the Thermopylae passage.

When the Spartan commander, Leonidas, learned of this treachery, he ordered all the loyal allies except his 300 Spartans to retreat to safety before the Persians could surround and destroy them; the Thebans he required to stay behind as a punishment for their betrayal of Greece as Medizers. Why Leonidas did not evacuate everyone from Thermopylae remains difficult to understand; there was no chance of the Greeks' prevailing over a two-pronged Persian assault. One plausible report is that he believed an oracle saying that the death of a Spartan king would act as a sacrifice to save his homeland.

Remarkably, the men of the small Boeotian city of Thespiae also refused to leave; they stayed behind voluntarily, to die – why, our sources do not say. Their choice stands, it appears, as a striking example of how sometimes people can value their principles and their reputations over their lives. Pericles would have heard about the Thespians, another example of how free people could sometimes demonstrate ultimate courage; he also would have heard about how the Spartan infantry could be the most formidable land army anywhere, when they were led by a determined and inspiring commander. This latter point provided persuasive evidence that it could be very risky indeed for other Greeks to confront Sparta's infantry in battle.

Meanwhile, severe storms at Artemisium sank or crippled hundreds of Persian naval vessels, severely reducing Xerxes' numerical advantage in warships. Still, Themistocles had to use money given to him by the Euboeans, who hoped that the Greek fleet could protect their city-states, to pass large sums under the table to the Spartan and Corinthian commanders to induce them to stay and fight; in other words, the coalition's commitment was not based solely on courage or a desire for freedom. The battle's outcome was a draw, doing significant damage to the fleets of both sides. When the Greek fleet then received the disturbing news of the annihilation of the defenders at Thermopylae, they withdrew farther south in consternation. Again, the teenaged Pericles would have heard the report of these events, among whose lessons were the somber insights that it was always crucial to include the unexpected in calculations about military tactics, and that money – lots of it, employed secretly – played an essential role in the hidden world of international relations.

This fraught period's significance for the practical education of a budding statesman continued in the aftermath of the Battles of Thermopylae and Artemisium. Rather than regroup to face the Persians on land in the plains of Boeotia, the allies from the Peloponnese, led by the Spartans, now decided – without informing the Athenians – to withdraw a long distance southwest of Athens to a location at the southern end of the isthmus, the narrow tongue of land that was the only connection between the Peloponnesian peninsula and the Greek mainland. There, they planned to erect a fortification wall blocking the isthmus to repeat the tactics employed at Thermopylae. This tactic of course ignored the reality that the Persian fleet, which though now reduced in number was still formidable, could outflank this impediment both by staging coastal raids all around the Peloponnese and by sending messengers to city-states there offering lucrative deals if they would abandon the alliance and go over to the Persian side.

Of course, this Spartan-led plan meant that the Peloponnesians were abandoning Athens (and the rest of the unconquered territory north of the isthmus) to the full fury of the Persian invasion. After the casualties to the fleet at Artemisium, the Athenians were now supplying the clear majority of the remaining Greek fleet, but not even this military reality could change the Peloponnesians' minds. When the Athenians received a report of the wall's being constructed and therefore realized that the Spartans and other Peloponnesians were about to leave them on their own to face the Persian onslaught, they somehow managed to convince the other naval commanders to keep the fleet, for the moment, in the narrow channel of water separating the northwest coast of Athenian territory from the island of Salamis.

They made this request to give themselves a bit more time to take action on a pivotal decision: They evacuated almost all of Athens' women, children, and noncombatants southwest across the intervening sea to the city of Troezen on the northeastern Peloponnesian peninsula and to the nearby islands of Aegina and Salamis. The only people who remained in the city were the die-hards who believed that the wooden-wall oracle really did refer to the fence of the Acropolis; they barricaded themselves there and prayed their interpretation was correct.

It is impossible to exaggerate the significance of the Athenians' evacuation, which Themistocles apparently persuaded them to undertake despite the reluctance of many citizens. After all, they knew that they could still make an attempt to reach a deal with Xerxes and thereby save their lives and their property. One source of inspiration for not caving in to their fears was a young member of the social elite briefly mentioned earlier, Cimon, the son of Miltiades and Hegesipyle (the daughter of a king in Thrace). In 480 Cimon was just reaching thirty years old, the minimum age for eligibility to serve in the high offices of Athenian democratic government; whether he already held such a position is not recorded. His family, previously impoverished by the fine imposed on his father as the disgraced victor of Marathon, had by now regained its wealthy status by Cimon's marriage to a rich wife and his sister Elpinice's marriage to an even richer husband.

At this moment of crisis for the Athenians – who had to be asking themselves, "Should we become refugees in a mass emigration or seek a deal from Xerxes?" – Cimon conspicuously walked through the middle of town carrying the bridle of his cavalry horse. The richest Athenian men served in that branch of the citizen militia because they could afford to provide and feed expensive warhorses from their private funds. When Cimon reached the sanctuary of Athena atop the Acropolis, he dedicated to the goddess the piece of cavalry gear he was carrying and then took down one of the infantry shields hanging on the temple's walls. He then proceeded to the seaside, showing that he was going to serve as a marine on a warship in support of the plan to fight at sea; there was no need for cavalry in a naval battle, which by now was clearly Athens' last hope for turning back the Persians. By his public gesture, Cimon was signaling to the other citizens that he was willing to subordinate his elite social status to the needs of the community at this moment of supreme danger. Other wealthy citizens also rose to the occasion. Since the public treasury was empty, the members of the Areopagus, the council of former magistrates that in this period was still composed of members of the upper class, provided eight days' wages to each of the poorer men who rowed the triremes so that they would be able to afford to provide for their families' subsistence while serving in the great battle that seemed sure to occur soon. These episodes showed two things to Pericles: Cimon took a major first step in achieving great popularity among his fellow citizens by conspicuous military service, and the naval strength of Athens depended on providing money to make it possible for less affluent citizens to row its warships.

Now that the awful moment to evacuate their homes had arrived, tens and tens of thousands of Athenians, their household slaves, and resident foreigners had to hurry to pack the limited amount of belongings that they could carry with them onto the ships transporting them to hastily arranged refugee camps in locations with no infrastructure in place. The evacuees' emotional state is hard to imagine. Worried mothers, crying children, arthritic elders, frantic servants – crowds of them jammed the roads as they made their way to the shore at the port. They were leaving behind their homes, their temples, their city, their farms, their animals – the tangible stuff of their existence; there was no doubt what the Persians would do when they arrived: mass destruction of their property. What the refugees were preserving were their lives and their intangible community. The stress that they felt is almost inconceivable, except perhaps to people who have experienced something similar in their own lives.

Among the agitated and fearful refugees was Pericles, too young to enroll as a rower or marine in the fleet. He surely saw Xanthippus on his way to the harbor to board a trireme, a sight that perhaps simultaneously inspired the son with pride at his father's courage and dread at the prospect of his parent's dying in the battle soon to begin. Xanthippus' departure took on an even deeper, almost pathetic emotional tone when the family's dog ran all the way to the port alongside his master, barking furiously from the strain of this inexplicable uproar. When his master's ship took to sea, the animal leaped into the waves to swim alongside, unwilling to be separated. When the dog finally swam ashore on Salamis, he died of the exertion. The Athenians built the loyal pet a memorial, still known as "The Dog's Monument" 600 years later.

Since still more money was needed to subsidize the many thousands of rowers needed to man the Athenian ships, Themistocles devised another typically clever, if characteristically deceptive, scheme by claiming that a piece of sacred property was missing from the Acropolis and had to be found to forestall the anger of Athena. To locate the allegedly lost item, he had the baggage of the richer refugees searched as they piled it up on the shore waiting to be evacuated. The money that the inspectors found was then used to help pay the oarsmen on whom naval operations depended.

The Greek fleet did in fact function successfully in the end, above all because Themistocles once again used knowledge, reason, and foresight to determine what needed to be done – and stopped at nothing to make it happen. First, in a speech to the allies he emphasized the importance of directing their actions according to what was probable: He reasoned that the allied Greek navy could prevail over the more numerous Persian fleet if the battle took place in the Salamis channel because that waterway was too narrow for the enemy to send in all its ships at once and allowed relatively little room for the Persians to utilize the greater maneuverability of their craft. In this restricted space, the greater mass of the Greek ships would provide them an edge in ramming their opponents' vessels, with crippling impact. Further relying on his deep knowledge of the terrain, Themistocles predicted that the Greeks could station their ships to use the tricky winds and currents in this stretch of water to make their tactics effective.

None of this tactical brilliance would matter, however, if the Peloponnesians abandoned the Greek fleet and sailed away to implement their faulty plan to defend their peninsula. Themistocles rightly foresaw that this was their intention, even after the Spartan commander claimed that he would keep the fleet at Salamis in response to the Athenian leader's final, shocking argument: If you withdraw to the Peloponnese, we the Athenians will move as an entire community to Italy, where we will make a new home and leave you to your inevitable fate at the hands of the Persians. As hard as it might seem to accept that this drastic proposal was a real option for the Athenians, it accurately reflects both the level of ultimate severity of the conflict for them and the reality that other Greek communities had gone to this extreme in the past, emigrating as groups to escape the extermination awaiting them if they stayed at home. After all, as mentioned earlier, less than fifteen years before this date a band of wealthy Samian property owners had done just that after the Persian sack of Miletus. Themistocles had no doubt about how big the stakes were for his homeland – and how little he could trust the Spartans.

Themistocles devised yet another astonishing and dangerous plan to ensure that the battle would take place off Salamis while the Greek alliance's fleet was still intact. He secretly sent a man whom he could trust – a Persian prisoner of war who worked as his children's tutor – to deliver a message to Xerxes. The Persian king at this moment was brimming with confidence because his army had already captured Athens from its valiant but hopelessly outmanned defenders on the Acropolis and burned the city, including its major shrines, as vengeance for the fire that had destroyed the temple at Sardis during the Ionian Revolt. Themistocles' messenger relayed to the king what his master told him to say: Themistocles was secretly plotting to help the king by sending him the news that the Greek fleet was preparing to sail away from Salamis, but that the king could outfox them before they escaped if he immediately sent ships to block both ends of the channel. He would then have his enemies bottled up so that he could crush them. Xerxes fell for the ruse, ordering his fleet to take up that split position; he was a victim of his pride and of his generals' failure to reason correctly about the tactical situation – or perhaps of their reluctance to express an opinion contrary to that of their supreme leader.

Despite the success of Themistocles' secret message, there still remained time for the other Greeks to sneak away while the Persians were moving their ships to block both ends of the Salamis channel. At this critical moment in the history of Greece, a remarkable display of patriotic leadership intervened. Aristides had been a political opponent of Themistocles, and no love was lost between the two men. In fact, it had been Themistocles who had successfully campaigned for Aristides to be ostracized not long before. Like Pericles' father, however, Aristides had been recalled, and he had consented to return to fight for Athens despite having been sent into exile by his fellow citizens for no good reason other than fear of his popularity. Putting aside any rancor toward his bitter rival, Aristides now went to Themistocles, the admiral of the Athenian naval contingent, to tell him what he had just learned: The Persians were blocking the Greeks in the Salamis channel. Themistocles responded by treating Aristides respectfully: He divulged that he had told Xerxes to take this action and urged his former rival to help him convince the Peloponnesians not to try to flee. Aristides agreed and made the rounds among the allies to argue for making a stand at Salamis. His words at least delayed the others long enough to allow the battle to begin before anyone could desert.

The naval battle that then took place in the channel off Salamis was a bloody struggle distinguished by heroic actions on both sides, but in the end Themistocles' reasoned prediction based on knowledge proved accurate: the Greek ships triumphed. This victory was as surprising as the much smaller one at Marathon had been, above all because, in the aftermath of the Battle of Salamis, Xerxes decided to withdraw his fleet and return to Persia. The threat to Athens was not over, however. The Persian king left behind a formidable infantry force commanded by Mardonius that in late 480 took up winter quarters in Thessaly, which remained pro-Persian. Still, how many Greeks would have predicted that their coalition navy, fractured as it was by incompatible disagreements over tactics between the Spartans and the Athenians, would defeat the vast fleet of the world's superpower at the time? Themistocles had been one of the very few to make that prediction, and his success stemmed from his skills at gathering scientific knowledge (in this case, on the nature of the terrain, tides, and winds at Salamis), at judgment and reasoning (how to use that knowledge to win a naval battle against a superior enemy), and persuasion (how to convince others to fight when the chances of success looked impossible to them). Anyone with inside information on what had happened at Salamis and with intelligent insight into why could have concluded that these qualities were key to winning leadership status in democratic Athens and in the fractious arena of Greek international politics. Pericles possessed those advantages: his father could give him an insider's account of this momentous episode, and his own intellectual capabilities could help him discern the reasons for its outcome. It is not surprising, then, that as Pericles matured, he exerted himself to develop his reasoning and his skills of persuasion to the highest degree. To do so was of the utmost importance for his homeland because, as this war was dramatically demonstrating, the very existence of Athens was at risk in the kind of conflicts that characterized the Greek world of Pericles' lifetime.

There was another equally somber, if more personal, lesson for Pericles to learn from this period, when the truth of the matter later emerged. Themistocles, a hero of Salamis, sent a second covert message to the

Persian king following this great Greek victory. This time Themistocles had Xerxes informed that he had convinced the other Greeks not to pursue the king as he made his way home to Persia. What the message said was true. Themistocles' motive in persuading the allies not to attack the retreating Persian king was so that he could lay up credit with Xerxes, in case in the future he, Themistocles, needed to find refuge from politically motivated attacks by his competitors for leadership in Athenian democracy. One of those rivals may have been Pericles' father, whom the Athenians made the overall commander of their fleet in place of Themistocles in the aftermath of the Battle of Salamis, apparently because they had become convinced that the international acclaim showered on Themistocles following the victory had made him too prominent and too prideful and therefore a potential threat to the treasured equality of their democracy.

In fact, Themistocles did come to a bad end at Athens; he was still providing valuable service to Athens in 479, but by the late 470s, when Pericles was in his early twenties and fully aware of the political scene, dire political pressures had forced Themistocles to flee his homeland. The Persian king characteristically received his former enemy with great hospitality, bestowing on Themistocles the income from multiple cities in his empire so that the former Greek hero could live at a level of opulence no Athenian could even dream of at home. Xerxes was hoping that he could at some point employ Themistocles' demonstrated brilliance to aid him in taking vengeance on the Greeks. The legend goes that when Xerxes called on him to do just that, Themistocles committed suicide rather than betray his homeland in war. Whether that story is true we cannot say, but it seems undeniable that Themistocles, like Miltiades, schemed to benefit personally from reaching out to the Great King. His exile is also evidence, once again, that political competition in Athenian democracy could be so bitter and so dangerous that would-be leaders had always to be conscious of how seriously they could be harmed by their opponents' machinations against them, if the latter could persuade the other citizens to punish them. Pericles cannot have missed the significance of these unsettling truths about, on the one hand, the great temptation for Athenian politicians to seek individual advantage from rich monarchs and, on the other, the real dangers to political leaders at Athens from a failed public career in the fierce competition of his city-state's democracy.

Themistocles' fate still lay in the future when another crucial moment arrived for the Athenians in the winter of 480–479 following the Battle of Salamis. During that season when the weather prevented major military operations, Mardonius, the Persian commander in Greece, sent the Macedonian Alexander to extend a dramatic offer to the Athenians from the Great King of Persia Xerxes himself: make an agreement with the king and you will gain unimaginable advantages. First, Xerxes will pay to rebuild all your sanctuaries that were burned down in the invasion. Second, you can retain your own territory in Greece while also seizing any other regions that you like. And, third, you can be "autonomous," meaning live according to your own laws and policies (Herodotus 8.140a). Mardonius added to the king's message that it would be the height of foolishness to refuse, especially because the king's overwhelming might was bound to prevail in the end and because the deal would guarantee that the Athenians could live in freedom and be military allies of the Great King without any trickery or deceit. Recent history clearly demonstrated that such offers were genuine and that the Persian monarch would keep his word. This proposed deal was a potential game changer for the Athenians: with Persian support, their city-state would soon become Greece's undisputed number-one power.

When the Spartans got wind of the message from Mardonius, in a panic they sent off an embassy to Athens to implore its citizens not to accept Xerxes' terms. In their inimitably off-putting approach to persuasive diplomacy, the Spartans began their appeal by blaming the Athenians for having started the war, but they then offered to pay to support the women and other household members of the Athenian population for the duration of the conflict if the Athenian assembly rejected the Persian offer.

Herodotus describes the Athenians' reaction during this epoch-changing episode in one of the most striking and moving passages of his history (8.143–144). First, the Athenians told Alexander to inform Mardonius that they would never make a deal with Xerxes. They knew that the king's resources were enormous, but they would go to battle to defend themselves and their freedom, trusting in assistance from the gods. Then turning to reply to the Spartan ambassadors, the Athenians pointedly remarked that it was shameful for these fellow Greeks to think that the Athenians would accept any amount of money or land to Medize and therefore reduce Greece to slavery. They were, the Athenians went on to say, obliged to take vengeance for their burned sanctuaries and never to betray fellow Greeks, to whom they were linked by their shared ancestry, language, religious traditions, and way of life. So, they concluded: "Know this, if you did not before: as long there is still a single Athenian surviving, there will be no agreement with Xerxes. As for your offer of financial subsidies, we decline with thanks. What we ask you to do is send your infantry as swiftly as possible to confront the foreign troops in Boeotia before they make their way further south into our territory once again." Plutarch adds (*Aristides* 10) the dramatic detail that Aristides rose in the assembly to tell the Spartan envoys to tell their population that there was not enough gold above or below the ground for the Athenians to accept as the price of the freedom of the Greeks. Pointing up to the sun, he said, "As long as that keeps crossing the sky, the Athenians will wage war against the Persians for the sake of the land that has been plundered and the sanctuaries of the gods that have been treated sacrilegiously and burned down!" Aristides ended by calling on the priests to put a curse on anyone who Medized or deserted the Greek alliance. Having received this answer, Mardonius' representatives went back to Boeotia, and the Spartan ambassadors returned home. It is hard to imagine a more ringing declaration than the Athenians' words in support of Greek freedom and in renunciation of any desire to rule other Greeks even when it would yield an advantage to Athens. (Whether the Athenians later changed their minds about this latter point is at the heart of the debate over the nature of the Athenian Empire.)

The young Pericles would have heard what his elders had said at this moment when the future of Athens literally hung in the balance, and he would have pondered what led at least most citizens to decide to resist the world's superpower. He also would have known that the Spartans did not respond promptly; their troops did not march out of the Peloponnese even after Mardonius did exactly what the Athenians had predicted, leading his men from Thessaly into Boeotia just north of the border of Attica. Dismayed at their ally's delay in sending aid, the Athenians again took the radical step of evacuating their population – including, of course, Pericles. Twice in two years, then, he and his fellow citizens left behind their homes and property, this time taking refuge by crowding onto ships to cross the strait from the mainland to Salamis and there spill out onto the beach in temporary settlements. The Athenian leaders realized that without the Spartan infantry, they had no chance to defeat the Persians on land. It was at this point that Mardonius advanced once again into Athenian territory. He then did what Persian royal diplomacy called for: he extended the same offer to the Athenians as before!

Embroiled in these amazing circumstances, the Athenians sent a mission to the Spartans to complain about their failure to send an army northward. Serving on that mission were both Cimon, famous from his action before the Battle of Salamis, and Xanthippus, now commander of the Athenian navy and holding the office of archon in 479. They and their colleague Myronides bitterly reproached the Spartans, reminding them of the very tempting offer from the Great King that the Athenians had until now rejected so that they could fight on in defense of Greece. They explicitly added, however, that without Spartan support they would have to find some other way to survive. This was a not-very-subtle hint that a deal with the Persians was still open to the Athenians. When for ten more days the Spartans made no move to send out their troops and in fact simply kept working on building a stronger wall across the isthmus, the Athenian representatives finally announced that, since the Spartans had treated them unjustly and no other allies were stepping up to aid them, they were now going to take the deal from Xerxes on whatever terms they could. All this Pericles would have learned firsthand from his father's report of his frustrating time on the mission to Sparta with Cimon and Myronides.

Were the Athenians serious about this threat to Medize? Had fear and desperation changed their minds? It is impossible to know. What we can see is the blazing heat of the emotions underlying the Athenians' predicament: While their ambassadors were at Sparta, an Athenian citizen among the refugees on Salamis proposed that the Persian offer should be accepted. A mob of male citizens then stoned him to death; when the women heard about what had happened, they rushed to stone his wife and children. The viciousness of these extralegal punishments shows the depth of feeling that the Athenians' second evacuation had evoked, their unquenchable anger at the losses that the war for their political liberty had inflicted on them. Pericles was most likely present at Salamis when even innocent children were spontaneously executed, a reminder, if he ever needed one, of how dangerous it could be at a personal level to make unpopular political proposals to the Athenian people. In this way, his second experience as a refugee deepened his understanding of what he would risk in embarking on a career as a leader at Athens – and how truly awful the consequences could be for his city-state and for him if matters went wrong.

After their inexplicable delay, the Spartans finally did send a military contingent to march to Athens – 5,000 heavy infantry accompanied by 35,000 helots as their battle support. Smoking ruins filled the territory of the Athenians. Mardonius had again laid waste to the city-state by setting buildings and property on fire after the citizens failed to accept the second offer of a deal. Joining up with the Athenians and the other allies, the Spartans now proceeded to Boeotia, where Mardonius had taken the Persian army because that region's terrain offered the best conditions for using cavalry, in which his side was superior. The opposing sides jockeyed for advantageous positions and engaged in skirmishes for some time until the ultimate confrontation took place. Today, this famous encounter in summer 479 is called the Battle of Plataea because it took place in the vicinity of that small town, renowned because its citizens had been the only Greeks to aid the Athenians at the Battle of Marathon a decade before.

Plutarch makes (*Aristides* 13) the disquieting report that during a period of inconclusive fighting preceding the main battle, some Athenians who had lost their wealth in the depredations of the war met together secretly at Plataea to form a conspiracy: they agreed either to find a way to overthrow Athens' democracy so that they could seize control, or to secure a private deal with the Persians so that they could rule as their collaborators. Both options, in other words, aimed at restoring their former riches and elite status. When Aristides, the leading Athenian general on the scene, got word of this imminent disaster, he arrested the eight most prominent conspirators while covering up the wider extent of the plot. Two of the eight escaped, and he then released the rest, hoping thereby to head off a disastrous split in the Athenian army. Apparently, he succeeded, and Athens' force remained intact. But it was a close call, and it would be a mistake to think that the Athenians fought for their freedom without having experienced almost-catastrophic dissent among themselves over what to do.

Contrary to everyone's expectations, the Greek allies won the Battle of Plataea. The Spartans were afterward hailed as the greatest contributors to the victory, but Herodotus' detailed description of the extended battle reveals a much more complicated story (9.27–88). The Spartans at Plataea were commanded by Pausanias, who after the Greek victory was eager to promote himself as the hero of the moment and claim the lion's share of the glory of this great success for himself (Figure 8). In truth, however, Pausanias as the Spartans' top general had more than once asked the Athenian soldiers to switch places with the Spartans in the Greek battle line so that his men did not have to face the Persians' elite troops, the most fearsome contingent of the enemy's line. The Athenians complied with his surprising requests; that Pausanias' men finally had to maintain their position and fight only happened because one Spartan at last refused to obey an order to move. This delay led to unexpected

FIGURE 8. Remains of the bronze "snake column" from Delphi. © Vanni Archive/Art Resource, NY.

developments that put the Spartan infantry – unwillingly – into the heart of the struggle. Furthermore, the tide of battle turned on an equally irregular event: Mardonius fell dead when he was hit by a rock thrown by a Spartan that miraculously struck him down as he sat atop his white warhorse surrounded by a thousand special guards. Demoralized at this loss, the Persian army was defeated. After their victory, the Greeks held a meeting at which Aristides convinced them to hold an annual ceremony at Plataea to celebrate the successful defense of Greece with Freedom Games celebrated every four years. The celebrants were to drink a communal toast with a libation to the gods: "I drink to those who died for the freedom of the Greeks!" (Plutarch *Aristides* 21). Finally, the allies agreed to form a joint land and sea strike force to carry the war to the Persians;

this would soon turn out to be a momentous decision for the history of Athens and Greece, as will be discussed in the next chapter.

At the time, Pericles and the other Athenian refugees could only worry and wait for a report about the battle in Boeotia. When he finally heard all the wondrous details, he had a lot to contemplate. For one thing, the Battle of Plataea reinforced the lesson that the Spartan infantry could fight very effectively – but only if it was commanded by leaders of genuine courage and charisma. Despite their reputations, the Spartans evidently could not be unquestionably relied on to sacrifice themselves for the freedom of the Greeks. Second, the way in which Mardonius died revealed again how the unexpected could determine the outcomes of even the most important struggles. Finally, the disturbing fact of the attempted conspiracy by elite citizens of his own city-state who were consumed by their desire for wealth demonstrated a line of seismic fracture in the unity of Athenian society. Anyone proposing to become a leader in Athens' democracy, Pericles could see with painful clarity, had to remain vigilant about all these possibilities.

At this point in 479 the Persian Wars were not over, but it was now clear that the invasion of mainland Greece had failed. The coalition of Greeks who refused to Medize had, to everyone's astonishment, succeeded in defending their political liberty against the greatest power their world had ever known. How was this amazing feat to be explained? Herodotus famously states (7.139) that his judgment will outrage many people: the Athenian refusal to abandon their resolution to oppose Xerxes was what saved Greece from Persian conquest. If the Athenians had moved away from their territory forever, as Themistocles had threatened they would, or if they had yielded to the temptation of the Great King's offer to dominate Greece as his collaborators, the rest of Greece could not have held out in the long term, not even if Sparta continued to resist. All the other Greeks except the Athenians would have had to submit or die. In Herodotus' memorable phrase, the Athenians were the "saviors of Greece," who "made the choice that Greece should endure in freedom." He adds that – after the gods – the Athenians were the ones who defeated the Persian king.

The majority of Pericles' contemporaries at Athens surely agreed with this assessment, a lesson that he would need to remember if he wanted to become a persuasive political leader always conscious of the weight of public opinion, the danger from foreign threat, and the possibility of subversive conspiracy at Athens. This overall point has of course been made multiple times in this book's survey of the events of Pericles' family history and his early years. Without stressing that historical background, however, I do not think it is possible to understand the story of Pericles' life or to give an informed and fair evaluation of his commitment to Athens' power as the source of its salvation in the face of so many shockingly dangerous threats presented by the city-state's ever-present enemies.

5

Pericles Becomes an Adult as Athens Builds an Empire

When in the summer of 479 the teenaged Pericles finally learned of the allies' astonishing victory over the Persians at Plataea, he could rejoice for his city-state and Greece though worrying about his father. Xanthippus was still away from home, commanding the Athenian warships in the allied fleet that sailed east across the Aegean Sea to respond to the plea of the Greeks in Ionia to free them from the Persian Empire. Now that the allied coalition had repulsed the great invasion of central Greece, the Ionians began to hope the momentum of that victory could be leveraged to force their release from the Great King's control. This continuation of hostilities with the Persians was to have a monumental significance for the history of Athens and the career of Pericles, as alluded to before, because it led to the beginning of what scholars today call the Athenian Empire.

Since the Persian commanders on the Ionian coast in 479 decided their fleet was inadequate to confront the Greek alliance at sea, they disembarked their men onto the Mycale peninsula, opposite the island of Samos. The Greeks followed them onto the land, crushing their opponents in a fierce battle in which the Athenians won the prize as the best fighters by punching through the center of the enemy line. Xanthippus' reputation for military leadership soared as a result. Among the spoils seized by the victors were chests spilling over with valuables; the Persians always took a store of treasure along on their military expeditions. The Greeks were learning that success in battle against them could be lucrative.

The Greek allies next held a conference on the island of Samos just off the coast of Ionia to debate the fate of the Greeks who were pleading for liberation. The Peloponnesians, headed by the Spartans, made the startling proposal that the Ionians should be forced to evacuate their homes and abandon their land to the Persians. It seemed impossible to defend this region forever, went the Spartan argument, and the Ionians could be resettled in the west in territories that would be seized from Greeks who had Medized in the Persian Wars. Those traitors would be punished by being expelled to fend for themselves as homeless refugees. The Athenians erupted into vociferous opposition to this grandiose scheme to reshape the population map of Greece. Peloponnesians, they shouted, had no business deciding the fate of the Athenians' close relatives. (Athens regarded itself as the ancient "mother city" from which the Ionians had originally emigrated long ago.) As the leading Athenian commander on the spot, Xanthippus was directly involved in this repudiation of the Spartan-led plan to displace the Ionians. Stunned by the Athenians' vehemence, the Peloponnesians withdrew their scheme.

No one could have fully suspected it at the time, but what happened next would profoundly affect the future of Athens as an international power and, in the long run, of Pericles as its most prominent leader: the allies from the mainland now admitted the Greeks from the islands of the eastern Aegean Sea to their naval coalition. Again, Pericles' father would have been in the middle of this momentous development. This change now pledged the original coalition members to defend the new members against any Persian threat and to seek vengeance for damage done in the Persian Wars. So that the binding nature of the allies' commitments to each other in this mutual defense and revenge pact would be unmistakable, the new members had to swear oaths calling the gods as their witnesses, pledging that they would always be faithful and never desert their fellow allies. In ancient Greece, breaking this kind of oath was regarded as an act of sacrilege drawing down divine anger on those who failed to honor their sworn commitments. This was the ultimate type of binding contract for Greeks.

The newly expanded Greek force then sailed north to the Hellespont strait, hoping to attack the remnants of the Persian land army that were still retreating from Europe to Asia in making their way home. The Greek attackers arrived too late to intercept the fleeing enemy troops. The Spartan Leotychidas, the commander of the entire fleet, then decided that the coalition's mission was complete and ordered all the Peloponnesians' warships to sail back to their home ports. The Athenians, however, led by Xanthippus, resolved to carry the war to the Persian outposts still being manned on the Chersonese (the peninsula on the western, European side of the Hellespont). This tactical split did not formally fracture the alliance, but it revealed how the goals of the Spartans and the Athenians diverged almost from the very beginning of this new stage of the Greek response to the continuing threat from the Persian Empire. The Great King's invasion of mainland Greece had failed, but his military forces and material resources remained unrivaled, and Persian royal ideology – the Great King's divinely sponsored role in the universe to exercise dominion over everyone else everywhere – persisted unchanged.

The Athenian-led portion of the alliance proceeded to besiege the Persian garrison holding Sestos on the Chersonese. After suffering through the winter of 479–478, the defenders were reduced to starvation by this encirclement. Therefore, at night they climbed out over the fortification wall under the cover of darkness. Now freed from their Persian garrison, the Greeks of Sestos invited the allies into their city. Xanthippus' men captured some of the fleeing enemy troops, including the commander Artyactes and his son. Artyactes offered the Athenians a gigantic ransom (the equivalent of 1,200,000 days' wages) to spare the lives of him and his son. When local Greeks whose sanctuary the Persian commander had previously robbed protested the possibility of Artyactes' being released, Xanthippus had him fastened to a wooden board to die of exposure before the eyes of those whom he had sacrilegiously wronged. The Persian's son was stoned to death before his crucified father's eyes to increase the latter's pain and suffering. In this episode of torture, the ferocity of feelings that the Persian Wars had provoked were on display for all to contemplate, with the Greeks – in the person of Pericles' father – emulating the Persian king with the brutal severity of their vengeance.

Unfortunately, there is no record of what Xanthippus told his sons about this episode, but it is hard to see how he could have avoided giving them an explanation of why the outrages perpetrated by Persians against Greeks demanded such a horrifying response. Revenge, not mercy, Pericles could see, was a rule in international relations. It was also obvious, moreover, that protection from Persian attack depended on maintaining a powerful naval coalition to fend off the ever-present threat from this still-formidable enemy. The risk to the Athenians in gaining the great power that ensured safety, the affair of Artyactes implied, was that in exercising their newly acquired strength they could descend to the same level of cruel brutality as their enemies.

Once it was confirmed that Mardonius' army had marched back onto Asian soil, Pericles and the other Athenians camped out on Salamis returned home from their second stint as refugees. They found their city a charred wreck, proof of the reality that the Persian threat embodied. At this moment when his father was still away fighting with the fleet, Pericles directly experienced startling evidence of how different the interests of Sparta and Athens truly were. Once the Persians had left Greece, it was time for the mainland city-states to repair their infrastructures damaged by the war, which of course was still ongoing. Under these circumstances, the most important building project for any city-state whose fortification wall surrounding its urban center had been weakened or destroyed was to reconstruct this bulwark quickly. A strong wall provided the only protection behind which citizens could hope to find safety when an enemy – foreign or domestic – invaded. At Athens, the Persians had torn down almost the city's entire defense wall. It was urgent to restore it.

It is therefore difficult to imagine the magnitude of the shock that the Athenians felt when representatives of Sparta arrived to say that their city-state had decided that Athens' wall should not be rebuilt. Equally stupefying was the additional Spartan call to the Athenians to join them in destroying the defensive walls of all the other Greek cities outside the Peloponnese. This was necessary, the Spartans argued, so that the Persians could not capture Greek fortifications to use as their own strongholds if they invaded again. This claim was a fraudulent pretext. In fact, the Spartans and their Peloponnesian allies had been surprised and dismayed by the military initiative and strength that the Athenians had demonstrated during the Persian Wars, especially with their navy. So, from naked self-interest rather than genuine concern for Greece as a whole, the Spartans and their Peloponnesian allies wanted to hamstring Athens and any of its potential allies, to prevent this newly emergent competitor from outstripping them as the acknowledged power in the international affairs of Greece.

Themistocles, who at this point was still influential at Athens even though Xanthippus had replaced him as commander of the fleet, formulated another daringly clever scheme to thwart this Spartan plot. He advised the Athenians to send him to Sparta as their representative, supposedly tasked to work out the details of this complex proposal concerning the abolition of the fortification walls. In fact, he disclosed to the assembly, he would stall the Peloponnesians long enough for the Athenians to rebuild the wall encircling their main urban area, at least if they worked really fast. Every man, woman, and child should pitch in, every building whether public or private should be raided for construction materials, and everyone should labor nonstop until the heart of Athens was protected by a wall again. And that is what the Athenians did. While Themistocles spun out the discussions at Sparta, they labored night and day to haul stone pieces of all kinds to reconstruct the wall. When the Spartans heard that the wall was actually being reconstructed, they sent men to Athens to check; Themistocles sent a secret message to his countrymen telling them to detain these spies until the project was completed. The Athenians achieved their goal: to this day, their work can still be seen in surviving sections of the wall (for example, in the Kerameikos section of Athens), where broken pieces of architecture and sculpture were stacked alongside squared blocks to make up the durable outer screen of the city's fortifications. At the same time, the massed citizens finished the thick wall protecting the port of Piraeus that they had begun to construct some years before on the recommendation of Themistocles.

Pericles, at least fifteen years old by now, would have been fully engaged in this exhausting task of refortification. As his back ached and his hands chapped from piling up heavy, sharp-edged stone fragments, the teenager had ample time to reflect on what the pressing need to do the job in such an emergency fashion revealed about the treacherous attitude of the Spartans toward his home city-state. When the wall was finished, Themistocles then announced to the stunned Spartans that they were not going to dictate to the Athenians. The Spartans tried to conceal their presumption by dishonestly claiming that they had only been urging this policy in the common interest of the Greeks. They also said they admired the Athenians' tremendous contribution in the Persian Wars. In private, however, they fumed with rage.

At this point in 478, the Athenians and the Spartans were still allied in the Persian War coalition that had recently expanded to include new members. Since the Spartans retained their position as the head of the coalition, they chose one of their own as the admiral to lead the allied fleet on its continuing mission to push back the Persians as far as possible from Greek territory in Anatolia. This commander, the Pausanias who had been at the Battle of Plataea, led the Greeks on a successful attack on Cyprus, the large island dominating the eastern Mediterranean, a region under Persian control. He then conducted the Greek warships northward to take Byzantium, the major city controlling the strait leading into the Black Sea. These successes corrupted Pausanias, who began to behave as a despot by violently mistreating women, indulging in a spectacularly ostentatious lifestyle, and behaving with imperious condescension toward the allied commanders and imposing agonizing physical punishments on their men. Most distressing of all, he reportedly conspired with the Persians to set him up as a tyrant ruling all the Greeks. Like some other Spartan leaders who began behaving badly while on command away from home – and therefore no longer under the direct scrutiny of their fellow citizens in their strictly regulated society at home, Pausanias abused his position of supreme command when he could operate without accountability.

Enraged by Pausanius' outrageous behavior, the non-Peloponnesian allies approached Aristides, who along with the much younger Cimon was on the expedition as a leader of the Athenian contingent. These Greeks urged Aristides to take over as the coalition's leader in place of the arrogant and treacherous Spartan. One version of the story is that Aristides himself had done everything he could to induce the other Greeks to make this request, but whatever the genesis of the initiative to depose Pausanias, it was successful: the allies began to treat the Athenians as their new leaders. In the meantime, when the Spartans at home were informed of Pausanias' crimes, they recalled him for trial. He was acquitted of the most serious charge – that he had been scheming to collaborate with the Persians in the expectation of gaining spectacular rewards – but his fellow Spartans decided not to send him back as the allied commander. They then dispatched a different Spartan general, but the Greeks in the fleet refused to follow his commands. They were instead looking to the Athenians for leadership. This new arrangement was going to change fundamentally the equations of power in the Greek world and launch Athens and Sparta on a collision course that would dominate Athenian foreign policy during Pericles' career as a leader. The Athenian Empire and the abiding hostility between Sparta and Athens in the later fifth century had their roots in these events.

For the time being, however, the Spartans accepted this transition in leadership because they had no further desire to take the war to the Persians; their interests were more narrowly focused on the Peloponnese and on counterbalancing the growing power of Athens by cementing their ties with other city-states nearer them. The Athenians, by contrast, aimed at forging a strong and stable naval alliance with allies in and around the Aegean Sea so that they could protect the Greeks there from the Persian Empire, ensure the sea routes for importing food to their own city-state, and take vengeance for the widespread physical damage inflicted on Athens during the Persian Wars. They were not going to forget the terrible damage that their enemies had done to their population and to their property, private and public. Indeed, they made sure they had a daily visual reminder of their sufferings by building into the north wall of the Acropolis some pieces of unfinished columns rescued from the wreckage of the temple to Athena that they had been erecting when the

Persians sacked and burned their sanctuaries in 480 and again in 479. These orphaned and scorched pieces of sculpted stone, every day silently reinforcing the Athenians' memory, were starkly visible from the city center below, called the agora, as they still are today.

The Athenians now saw their chance to seize the opportunity that Miltiades, the father of Cimon, had predicted in persuading his fellow generals to fight at Marathon: to push back the Persians and then become the number-one power in Greece. The leadership of the Greek naval alliance would allow them to enhance their own international reach and win profits from successful attacks on treasure-filled Persian garrisons in the eastern Mediterranean. Cimon had reinforced the allure of this latter possibility when he cleverly arranged for the Athenians in the coalition to receive the money from selling into slavery the Persian prisoners taken at Sestos and Byzantium. The sale proved so profitable that it paid the wages and the food costs for the Athenian sailors for four months, with enough left over to send a large amount of gold home to Athens.

Money matters almost more than anything in war, especially in prolonged conflicts like the one that confronted the Greek coalition in defending its far-flung members against the Persian Empire. It was going to take robust and regular funding to ensure that over the long term the Athenian-led alliance would remain the strongest naval force in the Mediterranean. It needed to build, equip, and repair hundreds of triremes and to pay tens of thousands of rowers. Since the members of the alliance varied widely in the size of their populations and the extent of their wealth, the different city-states could not all provide the same number of ships or pay the same amount toward the fleet's expenses. An assessment was therefore needed of the amount of appropriations due from all the members, based on an even-handed calculation of their different resources.

Aristides performed this challenging task to the universal satisfaction of the members, an incredible achievement given the tendency for contention traditionally prevailing among Greek city-states, to say nothing of the special friction in international relations that negotiations over money regularly generate. He visited the allies individually, discussed their situations, and by 477 had reached separate agreements on how much each one would provide each year. Reportedly, the total value of the payments amounted to 460 talents per year. Our sources, none of which is as old as the 470s, refer to these annual payments as *phoros* ("what is carried in"). This term is significant, if potentially controversial. Modern scholars translate *phoros* as "tribute," a word implying coercion and subjection because it is the term used to describe the compulsory payments that subjects of the Persian Empire were required to send in to the royal treasury. As the chorus of Aeschylus expresses it in a tragic play with which Pericles was closely connected (see later discussion), the payments due to the Persian king from the subjects of his empire had been compelled by "the necessities imposed by a despot" (*Persians*, lines 584–587). But in the case of this newly reformed alliance of independent Greeks, there was at this point no coercion of the members concerning finances and no violent subjection to a master. Their annual *phoros*, if that is what it was in fact called in these early years of the new coalition, was being paid voluntarily and in amounts that everyone agreed were fair. So it is important to be careful not to assume too quickly that there was any suggestion of imperial dominance by Athens over the other allies already in this foundational period.

A crucial point to keep in mind when evaluating the later history of the alliance during Pericles' career is that the allies now swore an oath that they would remain paying members of the alliance *forever*. To symbolize the eternity of their commitment, they sank ingots of iron into the sea, which indicated that they were swearing to keep their word until those lumps should rise to the surface of the sea of their own accord (Plutarch *Aristides* 25; Aristotle *Constitution of the Athenians* 23). Therefore, this sacred contract *permanently* obliged the Greeks to make their payments as enduring members of the coalition. The history of commercial law shows that contracts that are specified never to expire and that do not include "exit clauses" for the contracting parties are practically guaranteed to cause serious problems eventually. That phenomenon counts double in the even more unstable world of international relations. Events during Pericles' career would prove the doleful truth of this observation for the Athenian-led coalition formed to continue the Greeks' war for revenge on and defense against the Persians. Nevertheless, in evaluating the Athenian Empire, it is crucial never to forget that its members originally *swore before the gods* that they would *never* leave the alliance and would always contribute to paying its expenses.

In the beginning, the payments that allies made in coin (the only currency of the time) were stored on the Aegean island of Delos, which was sacred to the god Apollo and therefore an appropriate location to safeguard the coalition's treasury with divine protection. This location gives the alliance its name in modern scholarship, the Delian League (the designation that will be used in this book from here on). Although Athens was recognized as the leader of the Delian League and provided the lion's share of the warships and crews, the alliance was meant to follow a democratic process of decision making, with the allies' delegates meeting together in an assembly to hash out objectives. For now, this was the procedure that the league followed.

Pericles most likely learned from his father the details of Athens' new status as the head of a formidable naval alliance because Xanthippus was probably still alive at this date. (When exactly he died is not recorded; the absence in the sources of information about any further actions of his suggest that his death occurred sometime in the mid-470s, a date that fits with the comment of Plutarch in *Moralia* 496F that Xanthippus died before he could hear the adult Pericles give a speech in public.) Having risen to the top of the officer ranks in the Athenian navy, Xanthippus had a deep knowledge of its affairs that he could share with his sons. He could now explain to them how this permanent alliance offered unprecedented possibilities over the long term for Athens to extend its power both for national defense and for material benefits, and how crucial to its success was the ongoing infusion of funds from its members. The statue of Xanthippus that the Athenians set up on the Acropolis to honor his achievements for the city-state served as a permanent source of pride for Pericles and a constant reminder of the importance of the lessons that he had learned from all that his father told him about his experiences.

What Pericles also learned was that Aristides returned from his expedition to forge agreements on payments for Delian League members just as personally poor as when he had set out, in the same way as when he had refused to skim off valuables for himself twelve years earlier when he had been in charge of the spoils taken from the Persians at the Battle of Marathon. Themistocles allegedly made fun of his rival Aristides for refusing to enrich himself when the opportunity arose in public life. Aristides commented, "The beautiful thing that makes a true leader is inner strength to keep his hands clean!" (Plutarch *Aristides* 24). In Aristides' famed financial incorruptibility – he died so impoverished that there was no money to pay for burial rites or to provide for his children – Pericles found a model for avoiding corruption in his own behavior as a political and military leader.

The first leader to propel Athens to capitalize on its new opportunities as head of the Delian League was Cimon. Now in his early thirties, he had overcome his youthful reputation as a riotous playboy so wild that people said he took after his grandfather nicknamed "Blockhead." He was even rumored to have engaged in incest with his equally strong-willed sister, Elpinice. Cimon was never known as a great public speaker or brilliant intellectual, but rather as a charming man of great equanimity in public, whom people from all levels of society appreciated for his compassionate sociability toward everyone. Like Aristides, he was known for his financial honesty. On one famed occasion, he refused the enormous treasure offered him by a minion of the Persian king who had deserted to Greece. Cimon was also a superb military leader, able to train soldiers to exhibit top-flight discipline and loyalty because he treated all the men with fairness and compassion.

Cimon's popularity with the majority of Athenian citizens was particularly surprising because he had such strong and well-known associations with foreign states, starting with the undeniable fact that his mother was a member of a royal family in non-Greek Thrace, far to the north. In addition, he gave his three sons conspicuously non-Athenian names: "Thessalian," "Elian" (referring to Elis, a Peloponnesian town near where the Olympics were held), and, most startling of all, "Lacedaemonian" (another way of saying "Spartan"). This last name was clear evidence of Cimon's very open and very strong attachment to Sparta, whose relations with Athens back to the time of Cleisthenes had of course been rocky and often even angry. Cimon was tied to the Spartans as a formal representative of their interests at Athens, the position that was called *proxenos* ("representative on behalf of foreigners"). This designation meant that if a Spartan ever needed help when in Athens, Cimon would provide it. His pro-Spartan tendencies were especially on display when he opposed measures being debated in the Athenian assembly. He frequently rejected ideas by saying, "The Spartans aren't like that" (Plutarch *Cimon* 16). The mother of Cimon's sons was probably Isodice, who was the granddaughter of Megacles the Alcmeonid. Therefore, Cimon's marriage with Isodice made him a relative of Pericles; that meant that as a young man the latter would have heard a lot of insider talk from family members about the famed exploits of his older in-law.

What made Cimon above all a favorite of the mass of Athenian people were the material benefits that he provided for them from his enormous personal riches. In his private life, he used his great wealth to make generous distributions to poorer citizens. He welcomed anyone into his home in Athens for a meal, and he took down the fences surrounding his farms in the countryside so that anyone could gather food from his fields. When he was walking through downtown Athens, he had an entourage of young men follow him ready to switch their good-quality cloaks with any elderly pauper who approached them in rags, and to slip some coins into the hands of needy citizens who seemed down on their luck. Cimon would also give poorer men a financial subsidy to help them start on a political career. In other words, he fully supported the tenet of Athenian democracy that the rich had an obligation to spend money – and lots of it – to support the city-state, including its poorer citizens.

In his public career, Cimon also benefitted his fellow Athenians by leading the Delian League to celebrated victories that both enhanced their national security and gained them material advantages. In 476, he commanded the fleet against the Persian outpost at Eion on the Strymon River in northeastern Greece, using his foreign connections to persuade a rich Thessalian to provide a large amount of money and a cavalry contingent to support the attack. Cimon's victory at Eion removed the enemy presence from this choke point on the east-west land route from Asia toward Macedonia and central Greece, gained access for the alliance to the area's valuable gold mines and forests of timber suitable for building warships, and provided confiscated land for Athenians to farm or lease. Cimon's fame for this successful siege arose not just as a result of these gains but also because the fortress's Persian commander refused to accept an offer of safe conduct to return home. Instead, he piled up a giant heap of wood, set it on fire, and cut the throats of his wife, children, concubines, and slaves before throwing their bodies into the flames. Finally, he hurled his gold and silver treasures into the river and jumped into the roaring fire to burn to death. This startling story only increased Cimon's public visibility at Athens. The Athenians were so proud of the success at Eion that they set up inscribed monuments praising themselves as "directors of war and manly courage" (Plutarch *Cimon* 7).

In the following year, Cimon captured the Aegean island of Scyros and expelled its inhabitants as punishment for their piracy against Greek shipping. This victory gained the Athenians still more land to exploit, reinforcing the point that power yielded prosperity as well as protection. While on Scyros, the successful general discovered the bones of Theseus, the legendary architect of Athenian unity who had given up his monarchy to open the way to democracy (an exciting story narrated in Plutarch's biography of the hero). The Athenians believed that the remains of Theseus possessed a special ability to protect the community where they were buried, so returning them to Athens was a great coup that earned Cimon widespread praise. He was fast becoming Athens' most distinguished leader because his brilliant generalship was strengthening the finances of the alliance, opening up opportunities for citizens to acquire land abroad, protecting the sea-lanes for the importation of food

FIGURE 9. Greek vase painting of hoplites (heavy-armed infantry) in combat. © RMN-Grand Palais/ Art Resource, NY.

and international commerce, and buttressing the safety of his city-state against the threat of attack from a foreign enemy.

Recalling his father's prosecution of Cimon's father, Pericles well knew the history of bad feelings between Cimon's family and his own, and so he most likely heard about Cimon's accomplishments with admiration tempered by envy. Now about eighteen years old, Pericles had reached the age to participate in the ranks of Athens' citizen militia. Our sources unfortunately tell us almost nothing about Pericles' public life in this period, or indeed in the decade to follow, except for one general point and one specific activity. First, Plutarch reports (*Pericles* 7) that as a young adult Pericles displayed great bravery in wholeheartedly devoting himself to a military career. It seems likely that Pericles was hoping to follow in his father's footsteps, on the one hand, while, on the other, striving to rise eventually to the prominence that Cimon was achieving from his successes commanding the Delian League fleet. The sources preserve no details of the military campaigns in which the young Pericles participated, probably as a foot soldier in the ranks (Figure 9). It is likely that he would have served under Cimon at some point, able to observe at firsthand how his relative handled himself and his men under circumstances of great pressure and danger.

There are two more Delian League campaigns attested that probably date to the second half of the 470s. There may well have been others, but the surviving ancient sources for this period are seriously incomplete, creating considerable uncertainty about events and their chronology. First, the Athenians apparently led the allies to war against the city-state of Carystos, which was located at the southern end of the island of Euboea close to the eastern coast of Athenian territory. The Carystians had yielded to the overwhelming power of the Persians during the invasions of 490 and 480, aiding the enemy in their attacks on the mainland Greeks. The members of the league, no doubt at the insistence of the Athenians, decided to punish (but not destroy) Carystos in return for what seemed to the allies a weak-minded treachery and to compel it to join the alliance, making yearly payments to help pay the navy's expenses.

The second expedition in these years was on a larger scale and made in response to a different problem, one that foreshadowed serious difficulties ahead in the history of the Delian League. This time the league attacked one of its own members, the city-state on the southern Aegean island of Naxos. The Naxians had announced that they were leaving the alliance and would no longer be making their annual contributions (most likely of warships). They were the first Delian League member to regret their commitment to the coalition so deeply that complete withdrawal seemed the best option, despite the risk of angering the gods who punished oath breakers. Presumably, the Naxians prayed to their protective deities to recognize that justice was on their side in this dire situation.

Since Naxos had a good-sized population in a strategic location for naval operations, its departure would certainly have weakened the alliance significantly. In addition, if the other allies in the Delian League overlooked the rebellion, this would have encouraged any other disgruntled member to follow the Naxians' example. In his characteristically telegraphic style, Thucydides reports (1.98) only that the allies defeated Naxos after a siege, adding enigmatically that "it was the first allied city-state to have been enslaved contrary to what was established." There is no evidence that the Naxians were literally made into slaves or sold away. To judge from later episodes of conflict among members of the Delian League, what apparently happened – and what Thucydides' terminology implies he regarded as an injustice – was that the Naxians were compelled to give up their own warships, so that they would not constitute a military threat to the other allies, and to make large annual payments, as a punishment as well as restitution for the loss of their ships from the league's navy. So far as we know, the decision to take action against Naxos was the result of a meeting among all the other allies, the regular procedure of the league in making policy, and not simply at the behest of the Athenians.

Pericles would have known the details of this history, either from serving as a member of the Athenian military on the scene, or from attending the assembly meetings in which the results of these expeditions would have been discussed at length. There was much to think about in all this about how the Delian League should function and where Athens' best interests lay. Should the Athenians as the dominant member of the alliance allow unhappy members to leave despite their having sworn before the gods never to do that, so as to focus on a core of dedicated members whose actions and contributions would be reliable and to avoid the tensions and even hostility that suppressing the rebels would create? Or should the allies be compelled to honor their eternal oaths and make their payments to keep the league as strong as possible? What were the tangible and intangible benefits to Athens from its leadership of the league? Were the attack on and punishment of the Naxians the beginning of the Athenians' behaving as the ruler of an empire, tyrannically dominating fellow Greeks?

Without doubt the Naxians perceived their situation as oppression, and there may well have been other allies who agreed with them, even if they did not proclaim their views publicly. From the Athenians' perspective, they were acting legally, fulfilling their role as the coalition's leaders and enforcing the sworn unity of the Delian League. A policy of sticking to the letter of the law, so to speak, was considered necessary to keep alive the best hope for protection for the allies as a whole, to preserve the power and finances that depended upon unity. Of course, in hindsight the question remains open whether in the long run it would have been better to allow disgruntled allies to leave the coalition. But it is hard to see how the Athenians could have reached this conclusion at this point in time. In any case, the bitter tension arising from allies' attempting to leave the Delian League would prove to be deep, acrimonious, and long-lasting. Pericles' later career would require him to deal with this issue in the most bitter of circumstances. Already at this age we can see that he was being exposed to controversies and conflicts anticipating challenges that would later confront him with painful directness.

At this early point in the young man's public life (the end of his teenaged years and the beginning of his twenties), Pericles was reluctant to try to build a public reputation by giving speeches during debates in the Athenian democratic assembly because his physical appearance and his voice reminded some older people of Athens' first tyrant. One old geezer reportedly shouted out, "Watch out for that citizen! His oratory is just like the oratory of [the tyrant] Pisistratus!" (Valerius Maximus *Memorable Deeds and Sayings* 8.9.ext.2). As a member of a rich and prominent family and remembering the ostracisms directed against men who were accused of having favored tyranny, Pericles was concerned that he, too, might suffer that same fate. After all, his father had been ostracized even without being tainted by the charge of favoring the Pisistratids. In addition, at least some Athenians in this very period thought his older brother, Ariphron, should be ostracized, as we can see from the three ballots carrying his name that archaeologists have discovered. It was reasonable for Pericles to worry that he would be at risk if he went too far too fast in working to make himself into an influential participant in the high-risk environment of Athenian democratic politics.

Pericles did, however, achieve substantial visibility on the public scene from a different direction. By this time, stage productions of dramas (tragedies, as they are called) had become a very popular feature of major religious festivals at Athens. The authors of these plays based most of their plots on innovative reinterpretations of myths. A few tragedies, however, dealt with recent events. The audiences' emotions could be strongly affected by these productions dealing with contemporary history, as the heated reaction to Phrynichus' play *The Capture of Miletus* had earlier revealed. The dramas were staged outside in the daytime in a large theater seating around 15,000 people. High-ranking government officials were assigned to oversee these extremely popular shows. The best playwrights competed to be chosen by government officials to stage a set of three tragedies (and a fourth play combining tragedy and comedy) in festivals attended by throngs of spectators. If the tragedians' productions were successful in winning the first prize for best dramas, the stories they had told in their scripts would be talked about endlessly afterward.

Since the casts trained for months and the costumes, scenery, and stage machinery were elaborate, it was expensive to present these spectacles. The costs were paid by a combination of subsidies from public revenues and financial contributions by wealthy citizens. The latter expenditures formed part of the expectation at Athens that the rich would finance liturgies (the Greek word "liturgy" means "work for the people"). These costly public services ranged from providing money for equipping a trireme, to paying the expenses for the chorus of singers and dancers that performed in plays. The wealthy man who fulfilled a liturgy for a set of plays was called the *choregos* ("chorus organizer"). It was not his responsibility to conduct the actual training of the chorus members over the months leading up to the performances; the author of the play did that, serving as his own theatrical director. The *choregos*, fulfilling somewhat the role of a modern producer, provided funding for the substantial costs of supporting the chorus members during their repeated rehearsals and supplying their costly costumes. If a *choregos*' vocal and dance skills were good enough and he had the time, he could become a member of that group himself. His reward for his public service as a liturgist was the grateful recognition of the public for his contribution to their entertainment and education; the plays were regarded as so influential that their authors were informally referred to as teachers of the people. Finally, if the plays the *choregos* helped finance were judged by an official panel to have been the best in that year's competition, he was allowed to erect in Athens, at his own expense, a prominent stone and metal monument to commemorate his success.

A designated public official had the duty of assigning a *choregos* to the authors chosen to compete with their plays at each festival, but it is uncertain precisely how this matching of sponsor with playwright took place. A lottery was somehow involved, but it seems likely that the official had some discretion in making the assignments. It strains probability to think that the very rich citizens who agreed to serve as play sponsors could not, if they cared to, find a way to influence or even determine their assignments. For example, Themistocles served as a *choregos* in 476 for a set of plays that included the tragedy *The Phoenician Women*, which had been written by Phrynichus. This play focused on the momentous Greek victory in the Battle of Salamis in 480. Themistocles had of course been hailed as the architect of that great success, and it is hard to believe that such a renowned "fixer" would have become the producer of a theatrical commemoration of the Salamis battle purely by chance. When Phrynichus won the first prize for that year, Themistocles had a monument set up with an inscription recording this triumph.

Given this background, it is striking that the young Pericles served as a *choregos* in 472 to sponsor a trilogy in which one tragedy focused on the aftermath of the Battle of Salamis. This drama was entitled *The Persians*. (The other plays have not survived.) As mentioned earlier, the play's author was Aeschylus, who became the most respected and beloved Athenian author of tragedies in the fifth century. Why would the young Pericles want to sponsor *The Persians*? There was a risk in being associated with a play directly concerned with contemporary history, but, on the other hand, Themistocles' success showed that there could be a considerable upside in sponsoring a historically based drama that won a favorable public reaction.

The Persians is remarkable for including no Greeks among its characters, who are all Persians (played by Greek actors, of course). The setting is Persia, at the royal palace of Xerxes. The major characters are Xerxes' mother, the ghost of Xerxes' father, and Xerxes himself. The chorus consists of senior royal advisers. The script portrays the characters discussing the (to them) distressing news of the Greek victory at Salamis soon after it happened. To the ears of an Athenian audience, the dialogue presents what seems fair to call a triumphalist version of the Battle of Salamis. The magnitude of the victory is repeatedly stressed by the characters, who bewail what they recall as the destruction of "the flower of the men" of Asia and the disgrace to a king, Xerxes, whose riches and power had made him "the equal of a god."

Sponsoring this production turned out to be a good idea for the "twenty-something" Pericles, who could hope thereby to establish a foundation of goodwill in the community as part of his preparation for a major career in politics, because the play emphasizes the role of the Athenians in defeating the Persian armada. The citizens in the audience are being praised, even flattered. The specialness of Athens is particularly underlined by the repetition at different points in the play of the overarching reason why Xerxes fled from Greece in defeat and shame: the gods saved Athens. That is, divine favor protects the Athenians. The play also emphasizes, however, that human beings bear a large share of the responsibility for their own fate. Xerxes earned his punishment as cosmic retribution for his hubris, the destructive arrogance that had put him into the state of destructive delusion that Greeks called *atē*. The dialogue repeatedly makes clear that the king had failed to research and properly evaluate what was likely to result from his actions.

It is especially noteworthy that *The Persians* directs the spotlight of praise for the victory not at the commanders of the navy but on the nonelite majority in the allied Greek navy. Not only are the rowers of the fleet, to which the Athenians had contributed the largest number of warships, discussed as the key to the defeat of the larger Persian navy, but Attica is also described as "veined with treasures." These references implicitly praise the mass of Athenian citizens, who both served as oarsmen and had agreed to forgo individual payments from the income of the silver mines so that the revenue could be spent to build warships. It is especially fitting, then, that one of the most dramatic moments in the play occurs when a Persian herald who had been present at Salamis reports that the Greek rowers advanced to battle while shouting all together, "Go children of Greece, bring freedom to your ancestral land, bring freedom to your children, your wives, the sanctuaries of your ancestral gods, and the tombs of your families! Now the contest is for everything!"

There is also dialogue emphasizing the beneficial consequences of the victory for the Greeks living in Persian territory. Throughout Asia, the chorus of Persian elders laments, people no longer obey Persian laws or make tribute payments under the pressure of necessity; nor do they endure the rule of a master. Instead, with the yoke of the king's power removed from their necks, they enjoy freedom of speech. This dramatic passage presents a forceful justification for the military mission of the Athenian-led Delian League, with an implicit rebuke for the stay-at-home Spartans. Moreover, it explicitly points out that, despite his humiliating defeat, Xerxes continues to rule, meaning that the Persian Empire was not ceasing to be a threat to the Greeks.

Of course, as the other surviving plays written by Aeschylus fully reveal, the playwright was never satisfied with expressing a simple message. In *The Persians*, he fills the drama with references underlining just how scrupulous human beings must be in respecting their limits. The nature of the divine is such that it can purposely deceive people, even lead them to disaster, if they demonstrate excessive pride or fail to compensate for their intrinsic ignorance. Xerxes lost divine favor, his mother and the ghost of his dead father explain, because he showed hubris in his actions and failed to recognize that he needed to reason more deeply about what might happen in the future.

For Pericles, it made sense to want to be recognized as a sponsor of this complex set of messages. As a member of the Athenian social elite planning a future for himself in the public eye, he would benefit from being associated with the praise of the nonelite citizens of Athens that *The Persians* emphasized. As *choregos*, he could even have performed in the chorus himself and taken a prominent role in leading its songs praising his home city-state so strongly. A connection between Pericles and a dramatic affirmation of the praiseworthy exploits of the Athenians would certainly boost his standing among the masses as he mapped out how to make a name for himself in politics. And there may well have been another personal benefit to him from his connection to the production of *The Persians*: an inspiration to reflect deeply on the lessons that it implied for someone possessing the ambition to grow into the role of respected adviser of the people. In particular, Pericles would have recognized the value of the play's message concerning the need for citizens to value both humility and knowledge-based judgment in their decisions concerning public policy, and of the necessity for them to avoid the fatal trap that *atē* inflicts on those who in their successes forget that "power tends to corrupt and absolute power corrupts absolutely" (to quote the enduring truth expressed by the nineteenth-century British politician Lord Acton). To make good decisions for Athens, the male citizens setting policies for the city-state in its democratic assembly would need to hear advice from leaders who were recognized as intelligent, well informed, and persuasive speakers with impeccable reputations for proper behavior and financial honesty. The innovative, even startling steps that Pericles took to achieve that status constituted the next stage in the story of his life.

6

Pericles' Innovative Education for Leadership in Athenian Democracy

Like other sons from elite families in fifth-century Athens, Pericles while a child was taught to read, write, do basic arithmetic, and perform, or at least study, music. Boys with wealthy backgrounds often received their early education from educated slaves owned by their families or from private tutors (Figure 10). Publicly funded schools were rare at this point in Greek history. In the next stage of his education, Pericles would have focused on developing rhetorical skill as a public speaker, as preparation for making persuasive speeches to juries in court cases, in the Council of 500 that set the agenda for the assembly and conducted other public business, and at the mass meetings of the assembly. These venues were manned by groups of male citizens numbering from the hundreds to the thousands, and they were ready to shout out criticisms of ineffective orators while they were still trying to speak to the audience. Once Pericles and his contemporaries from the upper class reached their mid- to late teens, they began accompanying their fathers and uncles to be spectators as these older relatives attended meetings and gave speeches. This informal apprenticeship allowed the youngsters to observe successful – and failed – speakers, absorbing lessons about how to conduct themselves effectively in the highly combative environment of Athenian democratic politics.

Only those speakers could succeed whose arguments demonstrated a strong knowledge of history, finance, and politics; whose use of language was intelligent and artful; whose voice was strong enough to make them clearly audible when addressing large crowds both indoors and outdoors; and whose personal toughness enabled them to withstand intense public scrutiny that often involved mockery and heckling. As Pericles in the

FIGURE 10. Greek vase painting of boys receiving primary education. Berlin/ Antikensammlung Staatliche Museen/Art Resource, NY.

460s approached thirty years of age, he knew he needed special training to overcome the daunting hurdles that awaited him on his quest to become a respected and influential leader in war and peace.

A new way for young men to prepare for public careers developed in Pericles' time, a change from tradition that he embraced with enthusiasm. By the mid-sixth century, innovative Greek thinkers had been impressing – and shocking – other Greeks with their controversial ideas about the nature of the world. This intellectual revolution gained momentum after the Persian Wars when men who had become notorious for their startling theories not only about nature but also about what constituted human excellence (*aretē*) began traveling around the Greek world to attract affluent audiences curious to hear their provocative ideas. Some of these itinerant intellectuals offered instruction to young men in developing their individual excellence, especially in politics, and they charged high tuition for their courses. These teachers came to be called sophists (Greek for "men of wisdom").

Reliable evidence for the careers, chronologies, written works, spoken words, and even many of the ideas of the sophists is almost impossible to come by from the surviving ancient sources (a scholarly lament that readers will now wearily recognize but that bears repeating on this topic so important to the story of Pericles). Therefore, it is understandable that historians today disagree about how to evaluate the reports made especially by Plutarch but also by other authors (who give fewer details) that Pericles was deeply influenced by the ideas and personal guidance of some of these renowned thinkers. The sources' most significant assertion is that Pericles not only shaped his private and public behavior according to what he took away from these sophists' teachings, but that he also used these same thoughts to turn himself into Athens' most effective public speaker. This latter point is particularly surprising because, then and now, political leaders seeking to influence public opinion by employing an intellectual approach stressing new theories and a professorial or academic tone in their speeches on public policy have almost always been much more successful at irritating their audiences than persuading them.

Major uncertainty about the dates of the careers of the sophists makes it impossible to determine precisely when they arrived in Athens and when therefore Pericles could have met them in person. The contact could have begun as early as the 470s or as late as the 450s. Since the narrative of this book has now reached the 460s, I will present at this point my interpretation of the stories about Pericles and the teachers he encountered in what we might call his "higher education" because, by the end of this decade, he had made his first documented appearance speaking for the prosecution in a controversial case. There are, to be sure, strong arguments against dating the sophists' effect on Pericles to this earlier, formative period of his adult life. It is admittedly usual, in fact, for scholars to regard the influences I will describe here as belonging to periods later in Pericles' career. As mentioned in the Introduction, however, it is my view that discussing these issues at this juncture in the story of his life will help readers better understand the context through which Pericles would eventually cultivate the characteristics that led to such a high degree of success in his public speaking. In any case, since the persuasiveness of Pericles' addresses was the source of his unprecedented influence on the policies adopted by his fellow citizens, it seems appropriate to try at least to outline the special rhetorical approach that he developed rather than simply to report that he was fifth-century Athens' finest orator and leave it at that without exploring how he achieved that supreme status. (English translations and explanations of the fragments of comic playwrights and thinkers mentioned in this section can be found in the collections by Jeffrey Rusten, *The Birth of Comedy*, and Robin Waterfield, *The First Philosophers*.)

The uncertainty of the sources for this crucial aspect of Pericles' life is clearly reflected in the varying reports on who his earliest teacher was (in what I am calling his "higher education"). The first one that Plutarch mentions is Damon, an Athenian who, the biographer says (*Pericles* 4), instructed Pericles in music at an advanced level. Some scholars, however, think that it was in fact Damon's father, Damonides, who served as Pericles' first adviser and that the son only assumed that role later in the fifth century. Plutarch also mentions Damonides (*Pericles* 9), making him the teacher who recommended to Pericles that he promote the populist political agenda that Plutarch attributes to Pericles as a device to win the support of the masses. Finally, Plutarch also includes the report that Pericles' teacher in music was in fact Pythocleides (*Pericles* 4), concerning whom nothing else is recorded except that he was a follower of the extremely famous sixth-century thinker Pythagoras, who argued that mathematics held the key to understanding the nature of the universe.

The study of music in fifth-century Athens was considered educationally crucial because different rhythms, beats, and harmonic systems were thought to be directly linked to personal moral strength or weakness; that is, it was said that the music that people studied, performed, or heard deeply affected how they behaved. Therefore, music was believed to be able either to impel people to act constructively within the community, or to influence them to engage in antisocial, even criminal activity. A music teacher could become controversial if others thought that his ideas corrupted his students. A special fear at Athens was that these musical theories would inspire young men to aspire to become oligarchs or tyrants and therefore to try to undermine the existing democracy. Just these sorts of suspicions are evidently what a significant number of Athenians came to harbor about Damon, who was later ostracized.

There is no specific evidence about what Damon taught Pericles, only that he "brought Pericles up," to quote the words preserved as a fragment in Plutarch (*Pericles* 4) from a comedy by the fifth-century playwright Plato (not the fourth-century philosopher of the same name). Comedies, like tragedies, were staged at Athenian public festivals. The performances presented savagely farcical satire often expressed in colorfully obscene language and including pointed and personal criticism of leading male citizens. When the adult Pericles became a leading public figure, the authors of comedies mocked him for everything from his looks to his policies. Therefore, it is very unlikely to have been a compliment when Plato scripted one of his characters to proclaim that Damon raised Pericles. Whatever specific lessons Pericles took away from his instruction in music, it seems fair to deduce that he was inquisitive and confident enough to seek out a teacher or teachers who offered cutting-edge thinking, even at the risk of provoking the suspicions of more traditionally minded fellow citizens.

Other thinkers who reportedly influenced Pericles were also lightning rods for controversy. Zeno from Elea in southern Italy taught Pericles how to confound his opponents by constructing arguments that would refute whatever they might say. Zeno had himself been a student of Parmenides, with whom he visited Athens to give lectures. Parmenides had famously proposed an extreme view of reality as a total unity: "What is," Parmenides argued, is "one, timeless, and unchanging." This theory of radical monism directly conflicted with the experiences that human beings receive through their senses of sight, hearing, and touch. In their everyday existence, people constantly perceive innumerable sensations of disunity, movement, and change in the natural world and their own lives. Parmenides insisted, however, that human beings cannot trust their senses to provide them with an accurate representation of the nature of reality. In other words, his ideas revealed truth to be paradoxical (Greek for "what is contrary to what we expect").

Zeno gained international fame for inventing thought experiments to disprove the arguments of people who rejected Parmenides' intellectual assault on their commonsense perceptions. It is important to grasp the full implications of Zeno's teachings because from them Pericles would have learned to look beyond the surface of things, to reflect on the hidden reality that could only be uncovered by reasoning and by judgment based on knowledge. Zeno's paradoxes, as his teachings are called, included the story of an imaginary race between Achilles, the greatest physical specimen among the legendary warriors of the Trojan War, and a tortoise, a land turtle that moves at a glacial pace compared to an athletic man. Suppose, said Zeno, Achilles gives the tortoise a head start in their race. Both competitors start at the same moment. To reach the point from which the animal starts out, however, Achilles first has to cover half that distance. But while he is doing that, the tortoise is also moving ahead from the previous point that he had reached. In fact, Zeno maintained, every time Achilles moves, logic demands that he cover half the distance between him and the tortoise before he can cover the full distance separating them. The tortoise, however, is also always moving on from the point at which he had just been. This sequence, Zeno said, necessarily repeats infinitely. So, the conclusion must logically be that the fast-running fighter can never catch up to the pokey land turtle. But, then, we know that this is not what we would perceive happening if we saw a fast human runner competing with a tortoise; the human being would of course race ahead. How can this be? How can our apparent knowledge contradict the truth of logic? This is a paradox, Zeno insisted, that necessarily leaves us baffled – unless we accept the implications of Parmenides' view of the universe as unchanging, unless we accept that true and real knowledge of the nature of reality lies frustratingly hidden from our ordinary human perceptions and can only be brought to light through reasoning, not ordinary observation.

Zeno's paradox about an arrow in flight presented a similarly perplexing argument refuting the notion that there is such a phenomenon as change produced by motion. Once an archer shoots an arrow from a bow, the projectile is in fast motion, our senses tell us. But hold on, Zeno would reply. At every instant, does not the arrow occupy a space precisely identical to its own length? "Well, yes," we must answer. But, the teacher of paradoxes would continue, an object occupying a space identical to its length and therefore exactly aligned with a space of the same length is the definition of an object at rest. This thought experiment, Zeno concludes, also demonstrates that motion is impossible. Our perception of objects being in motion is therefore merely an illusion, one that fools us about the underlying reality of our existence.

Zeno's paradoxes flummoxed many people, though Aristotle argued the two summarized here were fallacious because they misused the notion of infinite divisibility of space by failing to connect it with the notion of time as also infinitely divisible. Zeno had other paradoxes harder to unravel, however, such as the exceptionally challenging one called "The Stadium," which involves the timing of the motion around a track of two separate groups of runners who are being observed by a group of stationary spectators in the stands. This paradox is too complex to include here, but it is well worth studying as a demonstration of the extreme subtlety in reasoning of which Zeno was capable and that he communicated to Pericles.

To sum up: Zeno taught Pericles to use reason to question conventional ideas about how conditions really were. How, then, did this intellectual training help Pericles in practice become a more effective public speaker addressing crowds of fellow citizens in Athens' courts and assembly? After all, his audiences were not likely to be receptive to high-sounding discussions about abstract ideas when they were judging a legal case, or deciding how to vote on a matter of government policy. My answer is that Zeno's methods of reasoning helped Pericles construct the kind of unexpected but logically compelling arguments that would be effective in refuting opponents in the combative atmosphere of Athenian public life.

Pericles' paying attention to the controversial ideas of Zeno is another piece of evidence pointing to his choosing an innovative approach to acquire the knowledge and skills that he decided would mesh with his individual capabilities. This would empower him in making the most persuasive possible arguments as a participant in Athenian democracy.

The special, even daring, character of Pericles' choices in his personal program for higher education is underlined by the identity of the intellectual who exercised by far the most influence on the aspiring leader. This deeply controversial thinker was Anaxagoras, who moved to Athens from Clazomenae in Ionia. Anaxagoras greatly upset many people because they believed that he denied the importance of the gods, or, some said, even argued that no divine beings existed at all. For example, he had enraged believers in traditional religion after he examined a piece of a meteorite that had impacted the earth and explained its shiny appearance as evidence that the sun, like the moon and other bodies visible in the heavens above, was in reality a large accumulation of molten metal bigger than the Peloponnese. Conventional religious ideas, by contrast, interpreted celestial objects as manifestations of actual deities. According to ancient belief, for example, the sun was the god Helios driving across the sky in a fiery chariot.

Anaxagoras also taught that "Mind" (*nous*) was the prime mover of everything in the universe. Some critics said that Anaxagoras meant that Mind was the god who had created all that exists and that his new idea was therefore blasphemous in denying a role to the traditional gods. Anaxagoras' intricate argument about creation proposed that Mind, infinite and pure, was the originator of everything that exists (including human beings) by imparting rotation to a primordial and eternal mixture of all possible qualities and characteristics. Our universe had originated in this common source, whose multitude of sperm (or "seeds") somehow embodied all the same qualities mixed together in each seed, but were at the same time different each from one another because their individual mixtures varied in their proportions. This theory therefore emphasized that the nature of reality resided in plurality arising from different mixtures of identical qualities. Clearly, Anaxagoras' idea of pluralism conflicted with the monism of Parmenides. Baffling in the density of its thought, Anaxagoras' abstract concept of Mind sounded to many people like another potential offense to the majesty of the traditional gods.

In a remarkable extension of his theory, Anaxagoras seems to have argued that the original plurality of seeds had most likely dispersed into innumerable parallel universes, even though human beings cannot directly perceive the existence of these multiple worlds. Finally, he added, no matter how many parallel universes might in fact exist, given that they all have the same seeds, they are all identical except in their dimensions, meaning that some are infinitely small compared to the universe that we inhabit but still of a similar nature in their essentials. It is hard to conceive of the level of perplexity that most people must have experienced when they heard about Anaxagoras' startling theory that there are many universes in existence and not just the one that we perceive in our everyday lives. Ordinary people's natural reaction to Anaxagoras' idea, which sounds astonishingly analogous to arguments made by some scientific theorists today, can only have made him seem more mysterious – and worrying.

The almost incomprehensible complexity of Anaxagoras' theories contributed to a widespread perception that his precepts for understanding the universe and humans' place in it lay so far out of the mainstream that they might prove dangerous to any city-state offering him hospitality. What if, people fretted, everything that Anaxagoras taught really did deny the power of the divine as traditionally worshipped, even if it was hard for most citizens to tell for sure what he meant? What were they to make of incidents such as when someone took the head of a dead ram to show to Pericles as a prodigy because it had only one horn protruding from the middle of its forehead instead of two horns at its temples? A famous religious expert, Lampon, who was evidently friendly with Pericles, was present when this incident occurred, and he interpreted this unusual anatomical phenomenon as a divine sign that one man (he meant Pericles) would emerge victorious from the current political competition. Anaxagoras was also present, however, suggesting that Pericles liked to host leading intellectuals for high-level conversations about their divergent ideas. The sophist had the sheep's skull cut open to show that the single horn was the result of an abnormality in the shape of the animal's brain. This physical cause for the deformity, the sophist was showing, trumped any religious explanation.

Worst of all for Anaxagoras, this kind of story made some people uneasy that Athens was harboring an atheist. Atheism generated tremendous hostility in ancient Greece because the overwhelmingly common view was that the gods, roused to anger by this supreme human insult to their influence and majesty, would punish not only the individuals who propounded such arrogant notions but also all the members of any community that allowed atheists to remain among them. The continuing presence of these sacrilegious unbelievers was thought to create a sacred pollution, which had to be cleaned up to prevent the gods from taking vengeance on everyone. To expiate the pollution, any atheist had to be permanently removed from the community. Therefore, a person's perceived failure to respect the city-state's religious norms could land him in court on a charge of "nonworship" (*asebeia*, commonly translated "impiety"). The penalty for conviction could be execution. It is reported that at some point, perhaps even as late as the 430s, Anaxagoras was indicted on just this charge. Some people said this case formed part of a plot by political rivals of Pericles to stir up resentment against him by initiating prosecutions of his friends.

Why, then, was Pericles willing to risk his reputation by associating with such a controversial foreigner? Plutarch in an extended account of Pericles' interactions with Anaxagoras (*Pericles* 4–8) implies that Pericles made this decision because he valued what he could take from the sophist's teaching not only to improve his public speaking but also to guide his approach to relating to other people. The biographer explains that Anaxagoras' teachings imparted dignity to Pericles' personal bearing and an elevation of thought to his oratory that raised him to a higher level than other leaders. In addition, Pericles took inspiration from Anaxagoras on how to use ideas from natural science to strengthen his arguments in persuading people, especially when they found themselves under severe stress. Two examples are recorded of Pericles' successful reassuring of his troops on military expeditions by using this sort of argument when the men became frightened by celestial phenomena. To calm a sailor panicked by a solar eclipse, he held his cloak up in front of the man's eyes and asked whether the lack of light now scared him. When the man said it did not, Pericles replied, "Well, then, how is what is happening different, except that something bigger than my cloak is causing the darkness?" (*Pericles* 35). And on another occasion when lightning terrified soldiers he was commanding, Pericles called them together, picked up two rocks, and struck them against each other to make a spark. "This," he said, "is lightning; the same thing happens when the clouds collide" (Frontinus *Stratagems* 1.12.10; Suda *s. v.* Pericles).

Plutarch's view that Anaxagoras' ideas shaped Pericles into a marvelously effective orator is challenging to analyze. As mentioned before, it seems highly unlikely that a (to exaggerate a bit in emphasizing the point) "mad scientist" style in public speaking would do anything except erode an orator's appeal to audiences of nonacademic citizens. What Pericles therefore took away from his time with Anaxagoras must have been deeper insights about how to infuse his speeches with a deep level of judgment based on knowledge, without destroying the ability of his logical arguments to produce favorable reactions among the members of his audiences. Somehow, it seems, Pericles learned to make his presentations impressive without, on the one hand, seeming obscure or condescending, while, on the other hand, never resorting to the lowbrow tactics that other speakers rolled out, such as making crude jokes, or shouting for emphasis, or making exaggerated hand gestures just to attract attention from the large crowds that Athenian leaders had to address. Instead, he learned how to present evidence to people in a clear and structured, even scientific, way that was appealing. This rhetorical approach then allowed him to use the idea of calculation based on what Greeks called "the probable" as a tool for constructing powerful arguments about what was likely to happen in the future and therefore to recommend which policies and actions the Athenians should choose. This was a very difficult accomplishment, and it is a shame that, since there are no verbatim speeches of Pericles surviving, we lack detailed information about what precise rhetorical techniques he adopted to become, over time, by far the most famous orator of his day. Anaxagoras taught that human beings succeed not because of luck but "by relying on the experience, memory, wisdom, skill that belong to us as human beings" (Plutarch *Moralia* 98F). Clearly, Pericles took this advice seriously and used it successfully.

Eventually, Pericles blended the diverse components of his education to create his preeminently successful style as a public speaker. The great acclaim that he garnered in fact led to his being called "Olympian," the adjective applied to Zeus, the king of the gods said to reside on the summit of Mount Olympus in central Greece. As the most powerful deity, Zeus commanded the thunder and lightning heard and seen in the skies. Some authors of comic plays had characters say that Pericles could himself produce verbal thunder and lightning when he spoke to the people, letting loose an awesome thunderbolt with his tongue. Like Zeus with his atmospheric weapons, Pericles could leave people stunned from the fiery impact of his words. Or as Eupolis had a character say in a comedy, "Persuasion sat on his lips ... he was the only speaker who left his sting in his listeners" (Diodorus 12.40).

Maybe part of the answer to the mystery of how Pericles earned the unprecedented title of "Olympian" also lies in the related question of what to make of the report that Anaxagoras' influence led Pericles to develop a highly distinctive personal style in his behavior, one that stressed dignity and reserve over the display of emotions in public, even on the occasions when it would have been understandable, even expected, to show some feeling. The most famous example of Anaxagoras' self-control occurred one day while he was talking to his followers about his theories of nature and received the news that his son had died. After a pause, Anaxagoras remarked, "I knew that I had fathered a [child who was] mortal." Plutarch was so impressed by this anecdote that he repeated the quotation three different times (*Moralia* 118D, 463D, 474D). This level of emotional restraint set a very high bar for Pericles to emulate, but, as events would reveal throughout his career, he trained himself to meet that standard in his public interactions.

Above all, Plutarch insists, Pericles' close association with Anaxagoras convinced him to learn the self-discipline of remaining unruffled in absolutely every situation, to maintain his composure and calm appearance no matter what level the provocation might reach. To prove his point, Plutarch tells the story of the man who one day followed Pericles around all day, harassing him incessantly while he conducted his business and held important conversations in the city center (*Pericles* 5). Toward evening, Pericles finally started toward home, with his obnoxious heckler following him all the way and never shutting up. By the time they reached Pericles' residence, night had fallen. Ancient Athens' winding and bumpy streets had no lighting. Pericles, in a demonstration of his studied equanimity, told one of his household slaves to light a torch and lead the man safely to his own home.

Pericles made it his habit to remain so composed in front of other people that he rarely laughed or even smiled. Moreover, he defied social convention by avoiding the drinking parties that were an evening staple of Athenian upper-class males. This kind of gathering, called in Greek a *symposium* ("a drinking together"), would assemble a small group of men for hours of conversation over endless cups of wine. One of the attendees would be appointed "the One in Charge of the Symposium" (*symposiarch*), and it was his job to determine how much to dilute the wine with water. (Drinking wine straight was seen as a dangerous road to madness.) He also decided what topics would be discussed. The emphasis at symposia could be on serious conversations about literature, philosophy, or politics. Sometimes, however, there would also be entertainment by hired musicians and dancers, often female. The evenings could turn raucous and drunken (Figure 11). Pericles always refused invitations to drinking parties so that he would never be in danger of becoming embroiled in any scenes of riotous behavior that could harm his reputation as a scandal-free statesman. He was in fact so careful not to expose himself to malicious rumors of this kind

FIGURE 11. Greek vase painting of a scene from a symposium (drinking party). © Fitzwilliam Museum, Cambridge/Art Resource, NY.

that once when he attended a family wedding, he left the festivities before the wine drinking began.

This behavior set Pericles apart from his contemporaries. The usual route to influence and officeholding in Athenian democracy required what today might be called social networking with other members of the elite, at the same time demonstrating some level of sociability with the mass of the voting population so as to prevent the perception of being one of the snobby rich – and therefore presumed to be unsympathetic to a democracy that included a majority of poor citizens. And it went without saying that no one who aimed at political prominence could afford to be labeled an atheist. It is striking, therefore, even unexpected, that Pericles chose to associate openly with people, and foreigners at that, who aroused such deep suspicions in the minds of many of his fellow Athenian citizens. The problem of understanding his choice might be lessened were we to conclude that Pericles only had contact with these thinkers significantly later in his life, after he had already established himself as a well-respected leader at Athens. One difficulty with this solution is that at that later time Pericles had even more to lose from malicious gossip than when he was younger. Another is that we would on this assumption have to disregard the tradition in the ancient sources that Pericles' exposure to the ideas and the personalities of these prominent sophists had an important, even decisive, influence on his relatively early self-development as an effective public speaker and political leader. Whatever one decides about this vexed chronological problem, it remains clear that it is important to contemplate how Pericles in his singular fashion adopted and adapted the teachings of thinkers as diverse and as controversial as Damon, Zeno, and Anaxagoras in constructing his success in public life.

It is at least clear that Pericles decided his best option was to forge a different, perhaps even unique, approach to gaining influence in Athenian democracy. There are no reports, for example, of his making lasting political alliances with rich members of the elite for mutual support in their political aims; Ephialtes, with whom he apparently later collaborated for a time, was not of that social class. Pericles also worked to keep a lower profile politically by behaving and speaking with dignity and moderation, and he made no speeches on the spur of the moment. He also made sure that he did not speak out in every debate that occurred in the assembly. Instead, he would ask his friends and associates to speak on the issue, thereby preventing the members of the assembly from becoming irritated at listening to him constantly. To display to everyone that he was a conscientious citizen, he walked down the same street every day from his home to the city center, always using the route leading directly to the locations where Athenian civic government took place. When Pericles did make a speech himself, Plutarch reports (*Moralia* 803F), he prayed to the gods that he would always remain self-aware and never utter a single word that was not fitting to the context under discussion. He was even said to have been the first to use a written text. These carefully cultivated characteristics of Pericles became so well known that a century later the famous Athenian orator Demosthenes purposely imitated them while speaking in court and the assembly so that, like Pericles, he could "become great" (Plutarch *Demosthenes* 9).

In short, Pericles was thoughtful and even cautious in his political life, just as he was, everyone agreed, careful and risk-averse when placed in charge of any military expedition manned by citizens in Athens' militia. Similarly, he made sure to be clear about his respect for religion. Yet, he was certainly not above exploiting people's superstitious awe when the situation demanded it. Once in wartime, Pericles costumed a giant from his army to resemble the conventional idea of how a male god looked and had him emerge onto the battlefield riding in a chariot drawn by white horses from a grove of trees that was dedicated to the fearsome god of the dead. The actor then called on Pericles by name and declared that the gods were helping the Athenians. This spectacle stunned the enemy, who fled the fight in a panic (Frontinus *Stratagems* 1.11.10). On the other hand, Pericles clearly conformed to traditional expectations for reverence for the divine on public occasions. In a famous later speech, for example, he eulogized those men killed in a war by artfully explaining that they had become immortal just like the gods: "For we do not see them [the gods] in person, but from the honors that they have and from the good things that they furnish [to us], we have evidence that they are deathless" (Plutarch *Pericles* 9). In the 440s, as we will see, he also directed the program to build Athens' most famous and most expensive temple honoring the goddess Athena, the Parthenon. So, no one could accuse Pericles of openly disrespecting the gods. He used his oratorical skill to emphasize that the deities were both honored and the source of benefits to humanity, and he showed through his support of the construction of the Parthenon that they deserved exceptional commemoration.

If Pericles' customary caution in his public behavior makes it challenging to imagine why he would be willing to run the risk of associating with dangerously controversial sophists, it is more understandable that he believed his carefully calculated public behavior helped him avoid generating hostility among the majority of the people (the *hoi polloi* – the "many" – as the upper class snidely called them). He was very conscious of the need to be careful about stirring up public opinion against him on the accusation that he was hostile to democracy, much less an aspirant to the status of a tyrant. After all, as a child he had had painful personal experience of the effects of ostracism on a family. What seems harder to grasp is how Pericles' caution, which apparently manifested itself as a very reserved, even an almost frosty, manner in his public life, would have helped him achieve popularity. Most likely he thought that this way of behaving would help insulate him from accusations of corruption or favoritism.

It is evident that Pericles put great effort into molding and maintaining his public image in this direction. He was known throughout his career for his incorruptibility, and not just concerning money. He refused to swear in support of another's lie even when begged to do so by a friend, a story that Plutarch found important enough to tell twice (*Moralia* 186C, 620CD). This quality reflected the justice in Pericles' life that Plutarch identified as characteristic of the man. In this context of Pericles' public self-presentation as being uncorrupted by any social, political, or financial pressures, it is also worth pointing out that Plutarch insists that Pericles and Cimon, otherwise so different in their personalities, resembled each other in another crucial aspect of their popular appeal. That similarity resulted from what Plutarch more than once says was their both displaying the quality of *praotēs*. The complex meaning of this Greek term is impossible to convey accurately in a single English word, as indicated in the Introduction. A well-known dictionary used by beginning students of ancient Greek defines it as "mildness, meekness, gentleness," but these terms seriously fail to convey the range of meaning of *praotēs*. Translating *praotēs* accurately is especially tricky when it is used to describe the quality of interacting skillfully, appropriately, and calmly with other people that made a man a success in the often confrontational and acrimonious sphere of political leadership in ancient Athens. Plutarch uses this concept in precisely this context, for example, in his biography both of the legendary Spartan leader Lycurgus and of the controversial fourth-century Athenian political leader Phocion. Neither of these men was mild or meek, to say the least. It also seems unlikely that Plutarch uses the word to mean "friendly, convivial, charming." Those terms could be used to describe the warmly hospitable Cimon but hardly the coolly austere Pericles.

Perhaps we can begin to triangulate toward a sufficiently subtle definition of the implications of Pericles' always behaving with *praotēs* by interpreting it to mean "never appearing to others in public to be perturbed or upset or frantic no matter the circumstances, even if deeply angry, worried, and/or frightened." This is precisely how Plutarch applies this notion in his description of the imperturbability of Aristides when he was experiencing hard times (*Aristides* 3). Both Cimon and Pericles had many firsthand opportunities to observe their famous older countryman demonstrating this equanimity as Aristides won unparalleled respect from his fellow citizens during and after the Persian Wars.

In addition to signifying an extreme lack of overt disturbance whatever the circumstances, *praotēs* seems to indicate a habitual quality of behaving fairly and even compassionately toward others, regardless of how they behave toward you. Cimon had apparently won the affectionate loyalty of Delian League allies by behaving this way toward them, in marked contrast to the vicious and arrogant manner of the Spartan Pausanias. Finally, to judge from the lives of the Greek leaders to whom Plutarch applies this term, this behavioral trait has a particular meaning that is relevant to serving in high public office in a democracy: showing one's fairness by never being corrupted by opportunities for taking bribes or secretly stealing money from the public treasury to enrich oneself. What needs to be remembered in dissecting Pericles' strategy for leadership success is that his always keeping his composure, his showing fairness to others, and his being dedicated to upright public service by resisting the temptation for corruption gave him an advantage in winning political support from the people.

The final point to be made here concerning Pericles' special, self-designed preparation for becoming a successful leader at Athens is that he met social expectations by making a "good" marriage, meaning he was wedded to a woman from the same socioeconomic level in Athenian society. In fact, his wife was a member of a family related to his own. The remaining evidence for her and Pericles' marital history is confusingly uncertain. They married in the mid- to late 460s, to judge from the probable birth dates of their two children born in the years 460 to 457: a son, Xanthippus, named after his paternal grandfather (as was common for the firstborn son) and the younger son, Paralus, named for a legendary hero regarded as an inspiration for the Athenian navy. Unfortunately, neither the name of Pericles' wife nor her age is recorded; she could have been as much as twenty years younger than her husband. Plutarch also claims (*Pericles* 24) that she had previously been married to Hipponicus, the son of Cimon's sister Elpinice and Callias, a man from the wealthiest family in Athens. Modern scholars agree that Plutarch's marital chronology is mistaken, concluding that she actually married Pericles before Hipponicus.

Money and politics played a role in both her marriages, as was often the case in the pairing of a husband and a wife in the ancient Greek social elite. Pericles' marriage was not a love match. He and his wife divorced after perhaps no more than a decade because, as Plutarch reports, "their life together was not satisfying" (*Pericles* 24). That Pericles had married a relative in a loveless union suggests that the primary motive of both families had been to keep inherited property within the extended clan, an important goal of upper-class marriage in ancient Greece. As part of their divorce, Pericles' wife willingly agreed to marry Hipponicus. Her son by her new husband, whom they named Callias, became the richest man in Greece, a status provided by the spectacular profits his family earned from exploiting state-granted leases to operate silver mines in Athenian territory. His grandfather later became a political associate of Pericles, apparently after having divorced Elpinice, who is on record as having criticized Pericles, as we will see, and whose brother Cimon was a rival and opponent of Pericles in politics.

It is remarkable that Pericles did not remarry after his divorce. Remaining long unmarried was frowned upon in Athenian society. As we will also see, however, his love life was not over. In fact, it had never really begun, at least to judge from the unanimous reports about the passion-filled liaison that he formed in the 440s with a remarkable non-Athenian woman, Aspasia. The controversies that the romance of Aspasia and Pericles provoked will have a significant place later on in this narrative.

By the 460s, then, Pericles had prepared himself for a career in politics at Athens through enthusiastic military service; close association with brilliant, if controversial, sophists to forge a powerful, persuasive, and idiosyncratic style of public speaking; the creation of a mode of personal conduct and demeanor in public constructed to prevent scandal and charges of financial impropriety; and a socially appropriate marriage. Until Pericles reached the age of thirty in the middle to later years of that decade, he was still too young to hold the highest civic office, that of "general" (*strategos*); a board of ten generals was elected every year. The generals both acted as the executors of military and civil decisions taken by the Athenian democratic assembly and exercised political leadership as advisers to that body. By this point, Pericles was now engaged in following and, if he dared, participating in the fierce political debates and extremely consequential actions undertaken by his fellow citizens in what would turn out to be years filled with challenges and dangers for Athens. He was now on his way to becoming the first man of Athens. It would not be a smooth road to the top.

Events in this decade deeply affected the international standing and the internal politics of Athens. Unfortunately, our sources do not tell us whether Pericles had any direct role in these important episodes. The River Eurymedon in southwestern Anatolia was the site of a massive battle on land and sea between the Delian League allies and the Persians in perhaps 468. Cimon was in command, and he had received advance intelligence that the Persians were gathering a huge force on land and at sea on the route westward from the eastern Mediterranean toward Ionia, the Aegean islands, and the Greek mainland. The only reason for such an expedition was that the Great King, still Xerxes at this date, had a plan to attack Greek settlements to the west. Cimon then devised an innovative plan for a preemptive attack to forestall another mammoth Persian invasion. He took 200 triremes and outfitted them with new planking on their decks so that more heavy infantrymen could be stationed on top, either to attack enemy ships after they had been rammed, or to be disembarked onto the beaches more easily for fighting on land. First he directed his ships against the Greek city of Phaselis, which was allied to the Great King and initially refused to cooperate with the Delian League expedition. The contingent from Chios in the league's forces, however, used their city-state's long-standing good relations with Phaselis to convince its citizens to join them against the Persians. Cimon had them pay ten talents (60,000 days' wages) as their contribution to the war effort.

The Persians' fleet outnumbered that of the league, but when they failed to rout the Greeks at sea, their ships turned tail to seek the protection of their infantry on land. This decision had disastrous consequences for them. On this one day, the Athenian-led force crushed the Persians, wrecking and capturing 200 triremes from the Phoenician contingent, the best wing of the Great King's navy, and then deploying their hoplites to rout the Persian infantry after a bloody struggle that cost many lives on both sides. When the Greeks finally captured the Persian camp, they found it stocked with treasure to plunder.

Receiving further intelligence that another 80 Phoenician warships were now on their way, Cimon launched his ships in a lightning campaign that had them attacking these enemy ships almost before they knew what was happening. Under his direction, the league's navy destroyed most of the enemy triremes and killed their crews. In all, then, the Persians had lost nearly 300 of their top warships, with some 60,000 trained crew members dead or captured, and suffered a large number of casualties among their infantry troops. The Athenians' share of the spoils was so huge that it financed building the southern wall of the Acropolis. The Battle of the Eurymedon also gave a great boost to Cimon's reputation and prominence.

The greatest significance of the Eurymedon victory was that the scope of the Persian king's defeat probably led him to agree to a nonaggression pact with the Delian League. This poorly documented agreement, today called "The Peace of Callias," has provoked unceasing scholarly disagreement. Since Thucydides does not mention it, some believe it never happened. Others date it to 449 after the momentous military events of the 450s, which will be described soon. Finally, it has been suggested that the Peace of Callias was in fact originally made after the Battle of the Eurymedon and then renewed nearly twenty years later. The terms reported for the treaty required the Persians to confine their military to the eastern Mediterranean region, thereby protecting Greece from the threat of invasion.

If the Peace of Callias in fact took place at this point, it most likely contributed to the growing discontent of some Delian League members. These allies had been chafing at what they regarded as the Athenians' now-oppressive leadership, and they also concluded that they no longer needed to keep making payments because the Persian threat had been neutralized. This latter decision caused a crisis. Thucydides reports (1.99) that the main source of conflict between Athens and the discontented

Delian League members was the failure of the latter to keep supplying their contributions, whether in money or in ships and crews. The Athenians were unyielding in their insistence that all members fulfill their sworn obligations for payments. Since over time many allies had converted their contributions of ships and crews to the equivalent in money because it was easier for them, when they then rebelled by refusing to pay anything, Athens was in a strong position to compel them because the money that the allies had been contributing had been used to expand the Athenian-led fleet. In other words, Athens now possessed the power of an imperial ruler, even if nothing had officially changed in the constitutional arrangements of the league.

The discontent exploded about 465 when the prosperous city-state on the island of Thasos in the northern Aegean revolted against the alliance. Thucydides attributes (1.100) the defection to a dispute over the Thasians' trading posts on the mainland and their gold mine there. The heat of the conflict escalated when the Athenians sent 10,000 settlers to occupy nearby territory around the Strymon River. After defeating the Thasians' navy, the league's forces encircled their city in a siege. To the Thasians, this aggression certainly constituted oppression by the Athenian-led Delian League. They might well have asked whether the Athenians had now changed their minds from the time in 480 when they had so defiantly told the Persian Great King's messenger that they rejected his backing to gain control of other regions of Greece, alleging their love of freedom and their respect for the shared cultural identity that they had in common with other Greeks. They might have questioned in addition whether the Athenians had been corrupted by their power (as Acton's famous epigram predicts will always happen). These issues remain at the heart of any evaluation of the nature and of the consequences of the so-called Athenian Empire.

The people of Thasos, seeking to oppose what they clearly regarded as Athenian-created injustice, then sent off a secret mission to Sparta to request a Peloponnesian invasion of Athenian territory. This attack would distract the Athenians to such a degree, the Thasians hoped, that the besiegers would have to return home to combat the threat from the Peloponnese. The Spartans agreed to launch an unprovoked attack on the Athenians, despite their still being allies of one another (outside the Delian League). They were preparing to dispatch this expedition against Athens when a series of unexpected events upset their plans to betray their fellow Greeks. The equally unexpected consequences of these events would change forever not only the relationship between Athens and Sparta but also the role of Pericles as a leader in Athenian democracy.

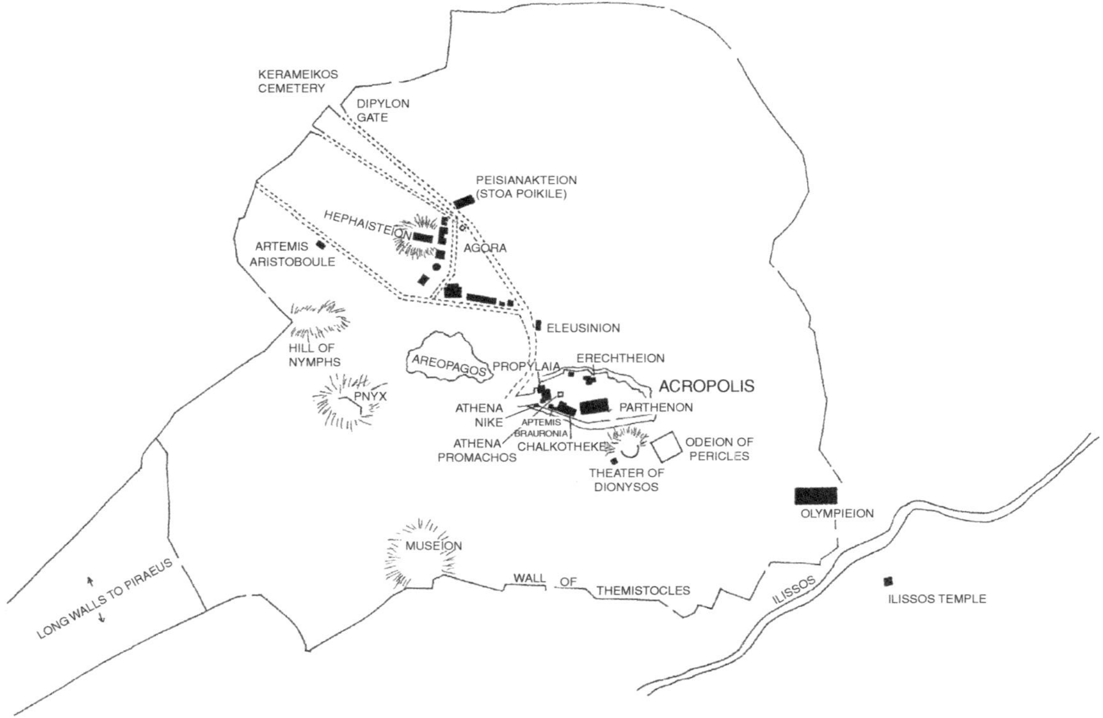

MAP 4. Athens in the late fifth century B.C.

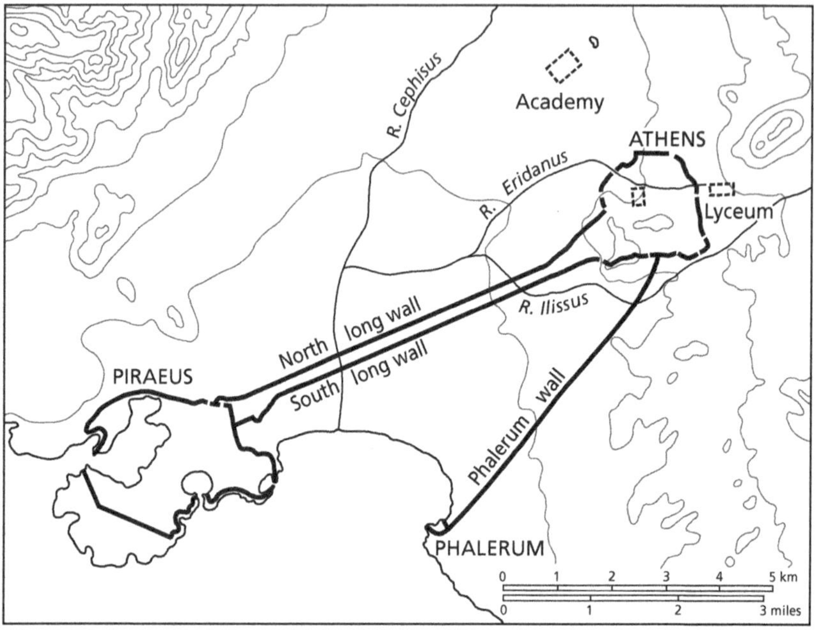

MAP 5. Athens, Piraeus, and the Long Walls

7

Pericles Becomes a Leader as Athens and Sparta Become Enemies

In about 464, not long after the Thasian envoys arrived to persuade the Spartans to attack Athens, a giant earthquake devastated Sparta. The seismic shock knocked down almost every building in town, crushing countless people. The helots, the massive slave population that the Spartans kept under oppressive control across the southern Peloponnese, seized the moment to rebel, and very violently. They were joined by some of the Greeks from Laconia (Sparta's territory) called *perioikoi* ("those who live around [us]"), who were dominated, but not enslaved, by the Spartans. The rebels slaughtered their oppressors among the ruins of Sparta and then established a fortified settlement on Mt. Ithome in Messenia to the west. Forced to fight to preserve their very existence, the Spartans could not fulfill their promise to the Thasians to invade Athenian territory.

As a result, the islanders found themselves on their own in their besieged city. By probably 462 (the chronology of all the events being narrated here for the late 460s is debatable), the citizens of Thasos had to surrender to the Athenian-led attackers. The treatment of the defeated islanders was harsh. They had to turn over their navy, their mines, and their territory on the mainland to the Delian League and demolish their fortification wall (Figure 12). Despite being deprived of the revenue from their former mineral resources and commercial outposts, they also had to pay a large fine and then resume their payments to the alliance. In evaluating the fate of Thasos, it is necessary to recognize that the Athenians had not acted alone but in company with other league members and that it was both appropriate and necessary to compel the rebel Thasians because they had originally sworn a sacred oath never to leave the alliance. For that reason, the citizens of Athens as the leaders of the Delian

FIGURE 12. Surviving portion of the fortification wall of Thasos. Gianni Dagli Orti/The Art Archive at Art Resource, NY.

League surely saw their actions as justified in enforcing the strict letter of the law, as it were.

At the same time, however, it is also likely that the rebellion of Thasos involved a dispute with Athens centering on a competition for riches and resources. Taking over Thasians' mines of precious metal and gaining control of the exploitation of and international trade in the extensive mineral resources of Thrace seem to have laid the financial base for Athens' growing prosperity during the middle decades of the fifth century. The formerly prolific coinages of the Thracians come to an end in this period, while the production of Athenian coins skyrockets. Since ancient coinages were made from valuable metal, most commonly silver, they could not be minted without supplies of real capital; they were not "fiat" currencies whose value did not depend on the contents of the pieces of money themselves but was based purely on the authority of the government to enforce acceptance of them as payments, as is the case with most modern currencies. The financial advantage that flowed to the Athenians from the punishment of the Thasians can therefore be counted as a marker of growing imperialism, when viewed through a modern lens of judgment.

Cimon had been a leading general in the league's successful mission against Thasos, but what happened on his return home reveals just how bitter the political rivalries at Athens had become. In 463, he was impeached on the accusation that, while on command duty in the north, he had accepted a bribe from the king of Macedonia to agree not to attack that mainland region, a campaign that could have seized territory for the Athenians so they could profit from its natural resources. One of the prosecutors of Cimon was Pericles. So far as we know, this was Pericles' first appearance on the main stage of Athenian politics.

There could not have been a higher-profile legal case than this one involving such social and political heavyweights. The path to its conclusion remains mysterious. At some point, Cimon's sister Elpinice made her way to Pericles' house to try to persuade him to go easy on her brother. Breaking into a smile, he said to her, a woman perhaps ten or twelve years older than he, "You are an old woman, Elpinice, an old woman, to conduct business of this kind" (Plutarch *Cimon* 14, *Pericles* 10). Was Pericles implying that this notoriously strong-willed and free-spoken woman was trying to seduce him sexually to gain his cooperation for a mutually advantageous political alliance with her brother? What, if anything, happened next between the two of them is not recorded. What is reported, however, is that at trial Cimon defended himself against the charge of having let greed cause him to fail in his public duty by arguing that he would never do such a thing because he guided his life according to the ideal of austere simplicity characteristic of the Spartans. The wealth he won from the spoils of war, he insisted, he spent to provide benefits for the entire city-state. Pericles reportedly spoke only once during the case and without vehemence, displaying *praotēs* toward the defendant. Cimon was acquitted.

The frustrating incompleteness of the sources concerning this incident makes it difficult to discern Pericles' motive. Did he simply change his mind about attacking Cimon – or should we perhaps say lose his nerve – under the intense pressure of this high-stakes prosecution during his first attempt to win a major political battle at Athens? Or did his characteristic caution lead him to back down? Or had Elpinice's mediation convinced him to ally with Cimon politically? Had he calculated that now was the moment to put aside their two families' hostility so that Athens could be stronger at a time of increasing danger in foreign affairs?

This last explanation seems plausible: Pericles intended his nonaggressive speech at the trial to help Cimon escape punishment because he had concluded that Athens at this moment needed his rival's incomparable military leadership. The 10,000 Athenian settlers who had been sent to the Strymon River region had recently been wiped out by the Thracians in a major demographic and economic setback for Athens. Cimon was the city-state's best general. If anyone could lead an expedition to repair the disaster in Thrace, Pericles would have reasoned, that man was Cimon. Plutarch attests that after his acquittal Cimon was in fact selected to command another naval expedition. Its destination is unrecorded, but it seems probable that this military mission was a response to the recent catastrophe in the north.

Any possibility that Pericles and Cimon could truly reconcile was soon foreclosed, however, by unprecedented events at Sparta. The helot revolt was still raging on in the southwestern Peloponnese. In desperation, the Spartans appealed for military support from Athens, whose army they knew had the siegecraft necessary to assault the rebel fortress on Mt. Ithome. When the ambassadors arrived to make their petition, the Athenians were unaware that the Spartans had been secretly planning, in response to the Thasians' request, to invade the land of the very same Greeks whose help Sparta was now invoking. The Spartan request generated fierce debate in the Athenian assembly. The most strident opposition to sending troops was that of Ephialtes, an established leader whose political prominence at this time exceeded that of Pericles, who was still young by Athenian standards for those speaking in the assembly and the courts. Ephialtes argued vehemently against helping this rival city-state, which he said should be left to have its arrogant sense of superiority trampled into the ground. The strongly pro-Spartan Cimon, now back home, took the opposite position with a rousing conclusion that became famous: He called on the Athenians not to allow Greece to go lame, or their own city-state to overlook its yoke mate. Cimon's dramatic argument persuaded his fellow Athenian citizens to dispatch 4,000 hoplites to Sparta under his command.

The chronology and details of this episode are muddled, but the ultimate result is not. After the Athenians arrived and the Spartans spent some time with them, the "hosts" began to worry that their "guests" were in fact dangerous. That is, the Spartans feared that the Athenians' commitment to freedom and democracy in their homeland might impel them to switch their support to the helots, who after all were enslaved Greeks still living in their home region, not foreign captives imported from abroad. The Spartans therefore decided to tell the Athenian soldiers that they were no longer needed and should return home. Stunned and infuriated by this humiliating dismissal, the Athenians marched back to Athens, probably carrying the remains of their comrades who had died while trying to storm Mt. Ithome. Cimon was disgraced, and the majority of his fellow citizens at home were outraged. The alliance between Athens and Sparta that reached back to the time of the Persian Wars was now strained just short of a formal breaking point. The consequences of this tension would affect Greek international relations from then on, spanning the rest of Pericles' political career.

The events of the helot rebellion also opened a fracture that could never be healed between Athenian leaders who favored cooperation with the Spartans and those who utterly rejected that fine-sounding idea as nothing more than disgraceful submission to an arrogant and untrustworthy rival. This disagreement simultaneously affected Athenian domestic politics. Ephialtes, supported by Pericles, convinced the assembly to redistribute the allotment of power in Athens' government by severely reducing the political and judicial competencies of the Areopagus Council, the body of former archons (men who had served a one-year term on a board of nine high officials) whose members served for life. The powers of the Areopagus, except for deciding a few special kinds of trials including homicide, were now given to the Council of 500, whose annual members were chosen by random selection from male citizens at least thirty years old; to large juries (numbering in the hundreds or thousands) also selected by lottery from the same age group to serve for a year; and to the assembly as a whole, whose attendance probably averaged around 6,000 men.

The most consequential function stripped from the Areopagus was the power to hold the mandatory annual examinations of the conduct and financial accounts of top officials who had held government posts over the past year. Moving this process of oversight to larger venues of randomly selected citizens sitting in courts of judgment meant that former officials enjoying a permanent position would not be determining the guilt or innocence of their colleagues in public office. This reform made Athenian democracy more egalitarian and less susceptible to corruption. Accountability in government thereby became solidly under the control of the majority, who were overwhelmingly not members of the social elite.

The ancient sources unanimously report that Pericles added a tremendous impetus to this radicalization of Athenian democratic government by persuading the assembly to approve a daily subsidy to be paid to jurors. This "pay for jury service," as it is sometimes called, was less than a workman could earn on a good day, but enough to buy supplies to feed his family. Since juries were convened perhaps on 150 to 200 days each year, this public funding meant a much larger number of the working population could afford to devote the time to serve in the courts and therefore to participate in deciding what the laws passed in the assembly really meant when these rules were applied in concrete instances. In legal trials at Pericles' Athens, there were no judges to make legal rulings, no permanent public prosecutors or professional lawyers, and no higher authority to tell jurors what they could and could not decide about the application of the laws. In trials that finished in a single day, the jurors listened to speakers on both sides of the case and then decided their verdict by majority vote. There was no court of appeals and no supreme court with permanent justices to review verdicts or interpret the intent of a law. There was also no written constitution to constrain the jurors in making decisions (or the assembly in establishing laws, for that matter). As Plutarch memorably phrases it (*Solon* 18), the jurors at Athens were effectively "the lords and masters of the laws."

The power to implement the laws therefore lay fully with the juries, whose members were chosen by a complex process to ensure random selection from a pool of male citizens (who, contemporary sources show, heard at home from their female relatives what the women thought about the contentious issues of the day). Since the number of jurors chosen for the pool each year – 6,000 – was large enough to provide a statistically significant sample of the population, the judicial system reflected the will of the majority, as did the legislative assembly with its attendance in the thousands. In short, the unconstrained will of the majority represented the foundational principle of the radical democracy that prevailed at Athens by the mid-fifth century.

Instituting daily subsidies for jurors paid from public funds was the first measure promoted by Pericles that led his rivals to sneer that he was spending the people's money to win their favor because he was not as wealthy as Cimon. Pericles could not afford to spend his own money to benefit the city-state the way his superrich rival did by giving clothing, food, and money to poorer citizens; paying to landscape prominent spaces in the city with plantings and shaded walks; and installing running tracks and a gymnasium for general use. Since the expenditure of public financial resources backed by Pericles recalled what Pisistratus had done in the sixth century to bolster support of his regime, it lent support to those who criticized Pericles for beginning to exercise a level of political power that amounted to a tyranny, a charge that the authors of Athenian comedies would repeat over and over in the coming years. This criticism also had a moral dimension that survives in the words of the philosopher Plato in the fourth century, who portrays Socrates as denouncing Pericles for having made the Athenians lazy, cowardly, garrulous, and greedy by initiating the subsidies (*Gorgias* 515e). Aristotle's *Constitution of the Athenians*, also written from a perspective of hindsight in the fourth century, in fact presents the conflict at fifth-century Athens over public finances as having arisen above all from the opposition of wealthy citizens to demands made by poorer citizens for the rich to elevate the well-being of the masses by subsidizing wages for public service, paying for public works projects, and supporting distributions of public money to allow ordinary citizens to attend religious festivals.

The *Constitution*, followed by Plutarch in his biography, furthermore offered the interpretation that Pericles, despite his upper-class ancestry and substantial wealth, supported the demands of the majority for the spending of public moneys in their interest. His motive, critics charged, was that, as his ancestor Cleisthenes had in the late sixth century, he was promoting this policy so that he could gain support from the mass of the people in elections for government office in Athens' democracy. With this strategy, they sneered, Pericles planned to gain political status against plutocrat rivals such as Cimon with whom he could not compete in terms of his personal riches. Others were more impressed by the revisions of the laws that the Athenians at Pericles' urging had approved by this time: The Romans, far away in Italy and plagued in their still-emerging republic by violent conflicts between the poor majority and the upper class, sent an embassy to Athens in the late 450s to study the laws there and take home ideas for improving their own legal system (Livy *From the Foundation of the City* 3.31).

The rivalry for political prominence between Pericles and Cimon came to a head when the latter vehemently opposed the reforms backed by Ephialtes and Pericles to limit the powers of the Areopagus. Cimon's political opponents attacked him for opposing the will of the majority and stressed his strongly pro-Spartan feelings, an especially contentious issue after the humiliating dismissal of the Athenian hoplites during the helot revolt. The comic poet Eupolis later satirized Cimon with verses recalling the searing tone of the debate: "From time to time he slept in Sparta, leaving his [sister] Elpinice [to sleep] alone" (Plutarch *Cimon* 15). The tide of political sentiment now turned so strongly against the hero of the victory of the Delian League over the Persians at the Eurymedon River that his fellow male citizens voted to ostracize him in 461. Sending Athens' most successful general into exile for ten years was a shocking decision. Politically, it was a win for Ephialtes and Pericles because it removed a formidable rival for influence over the people.

Cimon's ostracism was only one symptom of the now superheated level of conflict among supporters and detractors of Athens' radical democracy. Much worse was the murder of Ephialtes, one of the greatest mysteries in Athenian political history. Plutarch gives varying reports (*Pericles* 10). He believes that Ephialtes' prooligarchy political enemies arranged the plot against the fiercely prodemocracy leader, who had aroused a great deal of hostility by initiating prosecutions of several leading figures during the period when he was pushing for reform of the Areopagus' authority. Aristotle, Plutarch adds, named the assassin as a foreign hit man from Tanagra in Boeotia, which was not on good terms with Athens. Finally according to Plutarch, Idomeneus, an author writing more than a century and a half after Ephialtes' death, named Pericles as the murderer, alleging that he did the killing because he was jealous of the greater reputation of the older man.

A charge of cold-blooded murder motivated by ambition is of course tremendously serious in the evaluation of Pericles as a leader and as a person. Since Idomeneus' work has not survived, there is no way to evaluate the details of his account. All that can be said, unfortunately, is that Idomeneus was apparently the only writer to report this accusation and that Plutarch, who had read everything there was to read about Pericles, utterly rejects it. My judgment is that if the allegation against Pericles had not been a total slander made up long after the fact, then our sources, including the fifth-century comic poets, should reflect it. Since they do not, I agree with Plutarch in rejecting the notion that Pericles murdered his political ally. It is simply too difficult to see what advantage Pericles could have hoped to derive from eliminating Ephialtes. As a younger man still "on the make" politically, the always-cautious Pericles was more likely to benefit his own career by continuing to have Ephialtes as a supporter of his ambitions than by eliminating him in a way that risked prosecution for a capital crime.

In any case, there is no mistaking the strength of the venom that now poisoned Athenian politics. It was even reflected in the theater. The most highly respected author of tragedies, Aeschylus, composed a trilogy of plays set in the long-distant past at the end of the Trojan War but whose main themes spoke to the contemporary situation in Athens in the aftermath of the reforms backed by Ephialtes and Pericles. In a trilogy staged in 458 called *Oresteia* (*The Story of Orestes*), Aeschylus portrayed with unflinching explicitness the bloody violence that jealousy and rivalry could generate even among those as closely linked as wife and husband and mother and child, and how only a public judicial system could prevent an endless cycle of murderous vendettas when private motivations raged out of control. The third play put on stage a dramatization of the foundation of the Athenian judicial system, attributing this development to the will of the gods to introduce justice to a human world lost in a maze of deadly revenge. The dialogue praised respect for law and tradition without clearly taking sides in the controversy over the reforms of the Areopagus and the courts. Pericles had worked with Aeschylus in 472 when the young man served as the *choregos* for the playwright's *Persians*, and he was certainly in the audience for the *Oresteia*. He could only hope that Aeschylus' eloquent plea for political peace expressed in a tale of the past would be heard by all the combatants in the fight for political primacy in the city-state of the current day.

Athenian audiences had strong reactions to the messages of the tragedies they saw at the festival of Dionysus. They recognized that the main characters in the plots experienced catastrophe despite their status and power. These reversals of fortune happened not because the characters were evil villains but because, as fallible human beings, they could easily, if unintentionally, involve themselves in a disastrous mix of ignorance and mistakes compounded by hubris. Athenian leadership of the Delian League was becoming still more controversial during this period, and thoughtful playgoers could reflect on the possibility that Athens' current power and prosperity, managed as they were by humans, could be undermined by the same kinds of errors and excessive pride that in tragedies destroyed even heroes and heroines. In particular, the plays reminded male citizens – who governed the city-state in its assembly, council, and courts – that success created complex moral problems that self-righteous hubris could transform into communitywide disaster.

The *Oresteia* reflected contemporary events in foreign policy as well as in domestic politics by emphasizing the benefits of the alliance that, as part of the trilogy's plot, was struck between Athens and Argos, a major city-state in the northeast Peloponnese. Located between Corinth to the north and Sparta to the south, Argos occupied a highly strategic position for the balance of power in its region and could field a strong hoplite force for the frequent hand-to-hand combat of Greek warfare. After the Spartans had disgraced the Athenians by sending their hoplites home from the helot revolt and in consequence the long-standing alliance between their states had begun to dissolve, Athens had agreed to a pact with Argos, which at the time was hostile to Sparta. At the same time, the Athenians allied with the Thessalians, still famously strong in cavalry. These new alliances strengthened Athens for land warfare, which was what was needed to combat the Spartans. Pericles' role in these episodes is not recorded, but it is hard to believe that he held any position except support for agreements aimed at penning in the (in the majority view) backstabbing Spartans. When a few years later the Spartans reached a truce with the helots and *perioikoi* barricaded on Mt. Ithome to end the stalemate between their opposing armies, the Athenians resettled the surviving rebels in Naupactus, on the northern side the Corinthian Gulf and therefore out of easy reach of Spartan retribution. The Athenians had captured this territory from the locals and now used it to make clear their attitude toward the Spartans: they hated them. No one could any longer hope that the decades-old alliance between Athens and Sparta had a future. War was on everyone's mind.

The Athenians' concern with defending themselves against the now-enemy Spartans led the assembly also to make an alliance with Megara, the city-state on Athens' western border with which relations had often been rocky. The Athenians helped the Megarians build a pair of fortification walls protecting a corridor from their urban center to their eastern port, ensuring that the city-state had access to the sea and its resources even when attacked by land. They also installed a garrison of their own troops in the western port of Megara on the Corinthian Gulf. This arrangement enraged the Corinthians, to the west of Megara, who saw it as a threat to their safety. From this point on, they regarded the Athenians with "intense hatred" (Thucydides 1.103).

By the early 450s, with pure hate as the state of relations between Athens and the two major city-states in the Peloponnese, Sparta and Corinth, the Athenians had become preoccupied with war. Their assembly held mandatory discussions ten times a year over whether to be at war or peace. On average, from this time forward their military forces were fighting somewhere two out of every three years. Greece was now a battlefield for the Athenians much of the time. Poignant proof is seen in an inscription from this period (Fornara, *Translated Documents* no. 78; Figure 13) commemorating Athenians who had died in battles fought on the north coast of the Peloponnese, on Aegina (the island just west of Athens), and at Megara. Athens' (and the Delian League's) enemies in this Greek versus Greek conflict of the 450s that scholars call "the First Peloponnesian War" were a mixture of Peloponnesians: Spartans, Corinthians, Epidaurians, and Sicyonians. That hatred was the order of the day was bloodily confirmed when Athenian troops from the garrison

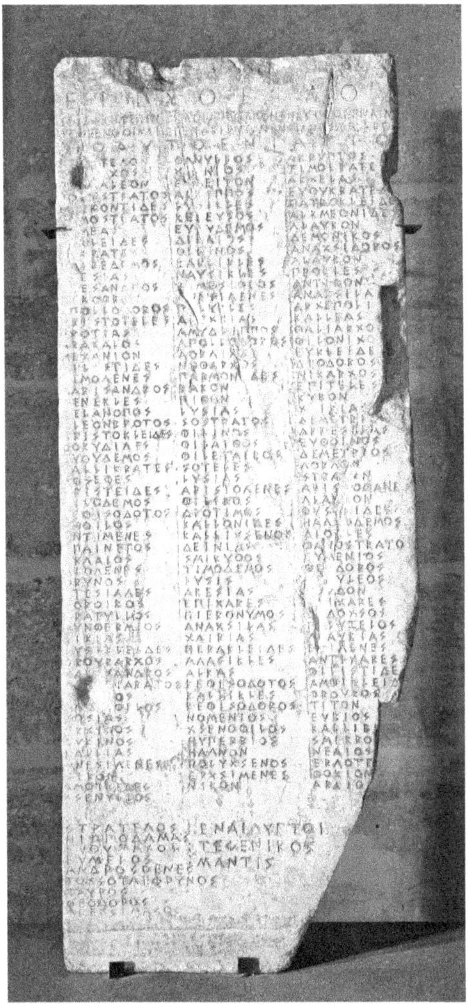

FIGURE 13. Athenian inscription listing soldiers killed in war. © RMN-Grand Palais/Art Resource, NY.

at Megara stoned to death – the method of executing traitors – a band of Corinthian soldiers that had lost their way and been trapped.

It was not just in Greece, however, that Athens and its Delian League allies expended blood and treasure in this period. The same inscription just mentioned also lists Athenian war casualties in Cyprus, Phoenicia, and Egypt. These expeditions dispatched all the way to the eastern end of the Mediterranean Sea were perhaps meant to demonstrate to the Delian League allies the vitality of Athens' continuing leadership against the Persians, despite the league's internal troubles and the volatile state of relations with Sparta and Corinth. The campaign against Cyprus was large and expensive: 200 triremes and some 40,000 men. These ships were then diverted southward across the sea from Cyprus to the Nile River delta in response to an appeal from the Libyan ruler Inarus for help in liberating Egypt from Persian control. This was an extremely ambitious risk for the league because Persia was still a superpower. In the beginning, the Greeks were successful, capturing two-thirds of the capital city of Egypt. This setback provoked the Persian king to send an envoy, Megabazus, to the Spartans to urge them to attack the Athenians and provide the Peloponnesians with money for military operations. He evidently stayed on in Sparta for a considerable time, more than enough for the Athenians to hear about his mission. Eventually, however, Megabazus returned to Persia, disgusted at the Spartans' spending the Great King's money "in other ways" (Thucydides 1.109). Still, as far as the Athenians were concerned, that the Spartans had contemplated cooperation with Persia against Athens was despicable treachery. It was also reconfirmation of the reality of the menace that the Persian Empire continued to pose for Athens and the Delian League.

This nonstop sequence of wars on different fronts was most likely taking place in the absence of Athens' most effectual general, Cimon, who was, it seems, still in exile as a result of his ostracism. He was, however, evidently eager to return home rather than seek the rewards of working for the Persians. To help keep his profile high with the Athenian public, Cimon had made a truly massive donation to the city-state from his war spoils to finance the foundations of a set of giant walls to link Athens with its main ports on the coast to the southwest, Piraeus and Phalerum. These so-called Long Walls, like those recently constructed at Megara, guaranteed that even in the face of a Spartan land attack Athens could import food to feed the population, export goods and silver to pay for imports, and send naval aid to its allies. Cimon's money also paid to construct and decorate a prominent civic building in the center of town known today as the "Painted Stoa" that was originally named for Cimon's brother-in-law. The stoa's walls were covered with paintings done by famous artists that depicted the aftermath of the Greeks' capturing Troy in the Trojan War; the victory of the hero Theseus and an Athenian army over the Amazons, who according to legend had attacked Athens; the victory over the Persians at Marathon attributed to the leadership of Miltiades; and the Athenians fighting the Spartans in a battle. Cimon probably also paid for a monument commemorating the Battle of Marathon to be erected in the sanctuary of Apollo at Delphi. All these works of art displayed in conspicuous locations explicitly emphasized Athenian military glory and implicitly expressed Cimon's continuing loyalty to his homeland.

In about 457 Cimon made an even more personal demonstration of his devotion to his homeland when the Athenians and their allies faced off against the Spartans and their allies in a land battle at Tanagra in Boeotia; the Spartans were fighting in that region on a mission of support for allies in central Greece. The Peloponnesians won this confrontation, but they suffered a large loss of manpower that was especially significant for Sparta, whose population, never large, was shrinking. For reasons hard to determine but perhaps related to official regulation of sexual relations, reproduction at Sparta was not succeeding in maintaining, let alone increasing, the number of citizens. Their failure to reproduce themselves made the Spartans a little weaker every year, and that realization made them more and more resolved to assert their power in relations with their flourishing enemies the Athenians.

Cimon showed up at Tanagra fully armed, ready to join his fellow citizens in the battle line. When the Athenian Council of 500 heard about his arrival, they ordered their generals to forbid Cimon's participation because the majority of the councilors feared that he was a double agent aiming to sow confusion in the Athenian battle ranks and then lead the Spartans against the city. This suspicion reflected the bitter split at Athens between the majority of citizens in the radical democracy and at least some very wealthy Athenians, and it was perhaps spurred by the memory of the conspiracy at the time of the Battle of Plataea that Aristides had quashed. The antidemocrats were rich landowners whose country estates were threatened by the strategic implications of the Long Walls: in a war with Sparta, the Athenian army would take refuge behind the impregnable walls to wait out the superior Spartan infantry, abandoning all the property outside the walls to be sacked and burned by the invaders. This strategy threatened to impose serious losses on the wealthy.

As it turned out, this suspicion of treachery was well founded: members of the elite now formed another conspiracy to overthrow Athens' democracy, this time with the immediate goal of preventing the walls from being completed. They then sent secret messengers to the Spartans asking for help. Fortunately for the majority of Athenians who favored direct democracy, that aid for their hometown enemies did not arrive. As a matter of fact, Cimon was not part of this traitorous plot, and he left the field at Tanagra in obedience to the Council of 500. As he departed, he urged his friends in the Athenian army to kill the rumors of pro-Spartan disloyalty against them by fighting bravely. They took his advice as an order: every single one died in the battle. Struck by this demonstration of courage, the Athenians subsequently regretted their hostility to Cimon and again wished to have his great generalship in their service. In a startling move, Pericles supported a decree to recall his exiled rival. As so often, the surviving sources leave us in the lurch concerning crucial details, in this case the date of Cimon's return. We simply cannot tell how soon it took place after the battle at Tanagra; it may not have been until the later 450s.

It is recorded that two months after the battle at Tanagra the Athenians and their allies defeated the Spartans and their allies in the Battle of Oenophyta in Boeotia. The victors then tore down the wall protecting Tanagra. In the aftermath of this major Athenian success against Spartan interests, the island of Aegina surrendered to Athens. The penalties imposed on the Aeginetans included destroying their fortification wall, turning over their fleet, and joining the Delian League. They were also forced to make the largest payment known to have been assessed on any member at that time. The Aeginetans were the first Greeks who had fought against the Persians in the Persian Wars – and they had fought well – but were nevertheless compelled to join the league. This act of compulsion points to a further shift away from the principles of a democratically structured league by the Athenians in their leadership of the alliance, but their justification was presumably that it was more pressing than ever to maintain a robust defense against the Persians, now that the Spartans were openly hostile, too. The latter point is clear from the report that the Athenian general Tolmides burnished his reputation mightily when he subsequently commanded a naval expedition that circumnavigated the Peloponnese to sack coastal locations and launch inland raids with its hoplites carried on the triremes' decks.

The military needs of the Delian League soon became agonizingly crucial. Persian reinforcements had arrived in Egypt to besiege the Greeks who were there to support Inarus' rebellion. In probably 454, after some six years fighting overseas, the league's troops were defeated, in fact crushed. Most of the men were killed. The league then sent a relief expedition with another 50 triremes, but they, too, were mostly destroyed. The loss of life and of warships was enormous. The crews of 250 triremes would amount to some 50,000 men and represent approximately half of the total manpower of the Delian League. Some scholars today assert that a substantial number of these ships and their men actually left Egypt before the great catastrophe. Otherwise, the argument goes, the league could never have recovered from this massive loss of men and ships. According to Thucydides (1.110), however, only "a few" of the original expedition and "the minority" of the relief force escaped. On his evidence, the conclusion of the Egyptian expedition in the 450s seems clear: the Delian League suffered a body blow, and the Persians reestablished their hold over the rich and strategically located territory of Egypt.

The serious nature of the situation emerges plainly from the league's decision in 454/3 to move its treasury from storage on the Aegean island of Delos to the Acropolis of Athens. In this new location in the heart of the city that headed the alliance, the money would be less exposed to a Persian naval attack, and it could still have the protection of a god's oversight, now Athena instead of Apollo. A set of mammoth inscribed stone pillars was erected in the Athenian sanctuary to record the sixtieth of the tribute that was given to Athena each year in return for her protection. These so-called Athenian Tribute Lists, when they are not too damaged to be read, allow us to see which city-states were in the Delian League from year to year from 454 on and to calculate how much each paid annually.

Shifting the treasury to Athens is often seen as the tipping point in the Athenians' transformation of the Delian League from a confederacy to an empire, a time when the annual payments made by the members began to seem like the mandatory *phoros* imposed by the Persian king on his subjects. Such a judgment, however, is not as easy to sustain as it might appear. We lack sufficient evidence to determine to what extent the decision-making process in the Delian League had changed over the previous twenty-five years. Some of the allies surely had supported the move because it would have been ill advised to ignore the prudence of removing their joint funds to a more easily protected strongpoint following the disaster in Egypt. Plutarch indeed reports (*Aristides* 25) that it was the Samians who proposed the move. They were located at the western edge of the Persian Empire and knew how real the danger was from that direction. But Plutarch also says that there was controversy over the decision, with other allies arguing it represented an unjust alteration of the original terms of the alliance. It seems therefore that the controversy over the terms of league membership that had erupted some time before had only become more heated.

It is highly relevant in this context that it is clear from Thucydides' general account of the fifty years between the Persian Wars and the (second) Peloponnesian War (1.89–118) that he believed the Athenians became more and more dominant and more and more autocratic, even tyrannical, in their leadership of the Delian League. Evidence to support his view may perhaps be found in a terribly damaged inscription from probably the 450s that admittedly has been restored in widely divergent ways (Fornara, *Translated Documents* no. 71). The text appears to set strict terms for the behavior of the people of Erythrae, a city in Ionia that perhaps had tried to leave the Delian League. As before, I think it is right to give Thucydides' account great weight and to recognize that the Athenians eventually did come to exercise, to use the Greek word, *archē* over their allies. As said at the start, this term is commonly translated as "rule," but in the spirit of trying to understand the situation in its own context, we should note that the translations "to be the head of" and "to have control over" are also possible, as opposed to the meaning of rule as the domination over subjects. This implication is clear in the language of Athenian democratic government, in which nine annually selected officials bore the title of *archōn*, which if *archē* means "rule" would mean that they were called "rulers." No official in Athenian democracy "ruled" over his fellow citizens as far as they were concerned. When the law required citizens to obey their instructions, then citizens were supposed to do so, but this was not domination of subjects based on illegitimate force. So, we would do well to be careful not to attribute modern connotations to Thucydides' language automatically.

At the same time, however, it must be said that there is no question that the historian means to say that Athenian control of the Delian League became severely strict and deeply unpopular with many members. Whether this development deserves to be termed imperialism depends on the implications that one sees in that highly emotive modern concept when applied to the Athenians' communal decisions in this particular ancient context. Regardless of what we might think today, most Athenians of Pericles' time, it seems clear, would not have agreed that their actions in foreign policy were wrong or that their *archē* was unnecessary for, as they phrased it, the "salvation" of their city-state. What we therefore need to do is to try to understand why they believed that, before we move on to judge the wisdom of what they did or did not do and to evaluate its moral significance.

Pericles' role in most of these very significant events is, as so often before, not directly recorded by our sources. It is evident, however, that he acted vigorously in support of Athenian (and therefore league) policy during this period of Greeks' continuing to wage war on Greeks. In about 454, he commanded a large naval expedition sent out to harass Athens' enemies. These warships, sailing from the westernmost port of Megara, raided and perhaps even captured a large region on the northern coast of the Peloponnese. They then sailed to northwest Greece, on the crucial sea route to Italy and Sicily. There, Pericles won over almost all the cities to Athens' side. Despite this distinguished military service, Pericles still had his detractors, to judge from two ostracism ballots carrying his name that archaeologists date to this general period.

The end of the decade of the 450s introduced significant changes for Athens and for Pericles. In 451, the Athenians made a five-year peace treaty with the Spartans. The sources give no background on how the two bitter enemies reached this agreement. Most likely, both sides felt exhausted and were unwilling to continue fighting each other in what amounted to a bloody stalemate in which neither one could overcome the other. Surprisingly, given the huge losses of personnel in the expedition to Egypt, a decline in the population of Athens appears not to have been a factor (as it may have been at Sparta) in deciding to take a break from having more men killed in war. This conclusion is based on the next (after "pay for jury service") major piece of legislation for which Pericles is given credit. His so-called Citizenship Law stated that only children born to two Athenian citizen parents could themselves be enrolled as Athenian citizens. Previously, all that was required for full citizenship was for a child to have an Athenian father. By reducing the number of possible citizens – all (future) children born to foreign mothers, including women who were officially resident aliens in Athens, were now blocked from any path to citizenship – the law effectively raised the value of Athenian citizenship. At the same time, the new regulation elevated the status of Athenian citizen women.

Since children such as Cimon's offspring who had been born to foreign women before the passage of the law did not lose their citizenship, the law was not an attempt by Pericles to ruin the family lines of the numerous upper-class Athenian men such as his main rival who had married non-Athenian wives. More likely, Pericles was trying to strengthen ordinary Athenians' attachment to their citizenship as a way to combat the danger from subversion of the kind mentioned earlier concerning the plot by certain wealthy landowners to betray the city-state to the Spartans when the Long Walls were being completed. If the mass of citizens could take greater pride in simply being citizens, women as well as men, then they would, Pericles could hope, become ever more vigilant in detecting subversive activity by those richer citizens with whom they had contact as laborers, small merchants, nursemaids, and coparticipants in religious ceremonies. These citizens could, like their ancestors who had spontaneously rallied to oppose the Spartans when they had threatened Athens' new Cleisthenic democracy in the late sixth century, feel new satisfaction in their status and therefore more strenuously defend the stability and independence of their city-state from all its enemies, internal and external. They could also confer their enhanced enthusiasm for Athens' radical democracy on their participation in the assembly and the juries that determined the course of public life in their city-state. On this interpretation, Pericles was working to keep the power of Athens strong in the only way that he saw as viable over the long term: promoting the morale and the material well-being of the mass of Athenians.

If this is what Pericles was thinking, he was proven correct that danger was still omnipresent for his city-state even after it made peace with Sparta in 451. In this very period, Argos broke its alliance with Athens and concluded a peace for thirty years with Sparta. The Argives also sent envoys to the current Great King of Persia to try to reconfirm their formerly positive relations with that empire, repeating what they had done back in the time of the Persian Wars, when they had agreed with King Xerxes not to oppose his actions against Greece. This shift of allegiance by Argos was a severe blow to any Athenian hope for containment of the Spartan threat. In this period, the Athenians hired the most famous Greek urban planner, Hippodamus, to upgrade the main harbor at Piraeus, a massive project indicating that the assembly was conscious of the need to keep the navy's facilities in optimal condition.

By this date, Cimon had returned from ostracism, and he apparently sensed that the public mood was perilously close to returning to a state of war with Sparta despite the recent peace treaty. To forestall the possibility of his aggressive fellow citizens' sending a naval expedition around the Peloponnese, Cimon instead convinced the assembly to send him out as the commander of a large naval force aiming to gain a foothold on the island of Cyprus, a gateway to the eastern Mediterranean and the heart of Persian naval strength. His goals were to keep the Athenians in a state of battle readiness through hard training and to win them spoils. From Cyprus, 60 of the 200 triremes were dispatched to support another rebellion in Egypt against the Persian king, demonstrating that the Delian League was still ready to oppose their archenemy and remained resolute even after the disaster in Egypt not so long before. This far-flung military activity yielded initial victories, but then Cimon fell deathly ill. As he lay on his deathbed, he told his companions to conceal his death so that the allies and the enemy would not hear about it until later. As a result, the expedition was able to regroup and return home safely. His remains were taken back to Athens, where monuments were erected to perpetuate his memory as the city-state's all-time most successful general against the Persian Empire.

There is no record of any further battles at sea between the Delian League navy and the Persian fleet. For this reason, some scholars place the Peace of Callias (or its renewal) at this point. A treaty (re)confining the Persians to the eastern Mediterranean would have also meant the end of legitimate raids by the league on Persian outposts to seize plunder. Finally, it would have lessened the perceived need for an active allied defense force against possible future Persian attacks, perhaps encouraging some of the allies to be less and less willing to make their annual payments. In the end, there is not enough evidence to decide whether a formal treaty was struck between the Delian League and Persia at this point, or whether both sides simply concluded that further military action against the other was fruitless for the foreseeable future. Whatever the case, whether the change happened de iure or de facto, the overwhelmingly important point is that there was no longer an active state of hostilities between the Athenian-led alliance and the empire of the Persians. Of course, at the time no one could have confidently predicted for how long this new state of affairs would hold good. It is only from hindsight that anyone could have known that the Persians would not directly affect the history of Athens until some forty years later, long after the death of Pericles, when the Great King at the time financed the naval buildup by the Spartans that would eventually help them defeat the Athenians in the Peloponnesian War.

There is, however, one piece of mysterious evidence suggesting Pericles judged that the chance that open warfare would resume between Greeks and Persians in the Mediterranean had now become substantially smaller. This is the so-called Congress Decree, which Plutarch, the only source to include it (*Pericles* 17), says Pericles persuaded the Athenian assembly to pass. The measure called for envoys to be sent to all Greek settlements in Europe and in Asia to invite the communities to send representatives to meet in Athens to discuss a triple-pronged agenda: determining what to do about the Greek sanctuaries of the gods that the Persians had burned down (and which had been left in ruins as memorials), fulfilling the sacrifices that had been vowed on behalf of Greece during the struggle with the barbarian invaders, and ensuring safe passage by sea for all and preserving the state of peace.

Teams of Athenian ambassadors, all fifty years old or older so as to be sufficiently distinguished for this crucial initiative in international diplomacy, were duly dispatched in every direction to urge Greeks to take part in a congress to establish peace and, as the proposal put it, "shared activity" for Greece. Pericles was therefore outlining a visionary plan to generate Greeks unprecedented power by forging a unity that they had never even attempted to achieve before. The Persian king Xerxes had long ago observed that Greeks ought to "negotiate with one another and unite" (Herodotus 7.9). He had been glad that they never did so because their disunity made them a much weaker target. Pericles had set out to fix that vulnerability with his inspired vision of Greeks working together to their mutual benefit.

He failed to achieve his goal, however, because the Spartans torpedoed the initiative with their vociferous opposition. It has been suggested that Pericles knew this would happen all along and simply wanted to expose the Spartans as selfish opportunists by proposing a plan to which he knew they would never agree. That deduction is not impossible because Greek history up to this point made it obvious that no one could ever be surprised by the Spartans' refusing to cooperate with any movement that did not give them a distinct chance to aggrandize their own strength at the expense of everyone else. Moreover, Pericles could well have calculated that a Spartan-caused debacle would win Athens greater support among other Greeks. It seems to me more likely, however, that Pericles had instead concluded, on the basis of a reasoned assessment of the new situation in the eastern Mediterranean region, that that precise moment presented the best opportunity ever to support the power, safety, and flourishing of all Greeks – or at least as many as possible – by creating an alliance aimed not just at establishing a permanent defense against a return of the Persians, but also at securing the universal goodwill of the divine. In other words, unity that included the Spartans would let Greeks seize the ultimate opportunity to be proactive in establishing a positive gain in their security and prosperity rather than only responding when yet another threat arose. This vision was not to be, thanks to the Spartans. The bitter failure of the Congress Decree only added to the pointed lessons that Pericles had been accumulating throughout his life about the intentions of Sparta, which were now again going to move to center stage in the determination of Athenian policy.

8

Pericles Becomes the First Man of Athens

In the 440s Pericles won his way to the top in the contest for leadership in democratic Athens. It was a time of almost nonstop conflict in foreign affairs and domestic politics. The Spartans followed up their rejection of Pericles' proposal for Greek unity by sending a military expedition to Delphi to secure their own primacy at Apollo's shrine. The Athenians countered this move after the Spartans returned home by sending Pericles to command an expedition to the god's sanctuary to reverse the arrangements that their enemies had made. He had the name of the Athenians inscribed on the statue of a bronze wolf in the sacred precinct to show that petitioners from Athens received the privilege of going to the head of the line of people waiting to consult the oracle, displacing the Spartans from that treasured advantage. The five-year peace that Athens and Sparta had agreed to in 451 was obviously fraying.

As usual, the chronology of events is confused in the ancient sources, but it is clear that Pericles was now playing a major role as a military commander in campaigns outside Athenian territory. Still, Athens had no second Cimon in the sense of a general whom the people regarded as far and away their best, and Tolmides' military reputation seems to have been as prominent as Pericles' in the early years of the decade. Pericles did, however, win great acclaim for the expedition he led in about 447 to the Thracian Chersonese. Ancestors of Cimon had long before settled Athenians on this peninsula, whose cities controlled the strait through which crucial imports of grain and timber were transported south from the shores of the Black Sea. The Thracians had never been happy about this encroachment, and they constantly raided the Greeks' settlements.

Pericles reestablished the Athenian presence in this strategically important region by recruiting and transporting a large group of new settlers to occupy the land and building a defense wall four miles long to reach from shore to shore across the neck of the peninsula. It seems possible that Pericles was aided in this innovative plan by recalling information about the region that he had long before learned from his father, who had been the Athenian commander in a victorious campaign in the Chersonese at the end of the Persian Wars. Moreover, similarly to the way in which Themistocles had prepared the Greek attack for the Battle of Salamis, Pericles analyzed the topography and calculated the technical limitations of the enemy to reason out a successful set of tactics. The victory that his forces won supported the economic well-being of Athens by securing an essential supply route and giving entrepreneurial citizens a chance to improve their own financial situation by risking a new start in a location rich with resources – and dangers.

Soon thereafter, the competition for reputation at Athens heated up when Pericles and Tolmides clashed in the assembly over a military campaign in Boeotia, the region just north of Athens, whose city-states frequently fought one another. Pericles commented on the instability of interstate politics there by saying that the Boeotians were like holm oaks, trees known to sway so much in the wind that they whacked into each other hard enough to knock themselves down. Tolmides, known for his reckless daring as a commander, persuaded a group of volunteers to go on the mission. Pericles concluded by saying, "If Tolmides won't listen to Pericles, he couldn't go wrong by waiting for the wisest advisor of all, time" (Plutarch *Pericles* 18). This aphorism was sadly proven accurate when Tolmides' men first succeeded in taking Chaeronea, garrisoning the urban center and selling its population into slavery, but then were decisively defeated at Coronea by a force that included Boeotians who had been exiled from cities there that had been under Athenian domination since the victory at Oenophyta a decade earlier. Tolmides and many of his troops died, and Athens lost its control over territory in Boeotia. The terrible defeat also had personal consequences for Pericles: among the dead was Cleinias, an Alcmeonid relative of his. After their father's death, Cleinias' sons lived as Pericles' wards in his household. One of the boys was the later notorious wild-child Alcibiades, whose brilliant but infamous career as a military commander and a political firebrand spanned the second half of the Peloponnesian War.

Tolmides' death elevated Pericles to the status of Athens' leading general. He was therefore next up on the rotation of command when in

446 the city-states on the nearby island of Euboea northeast of Athens rebelled against the Delian League. The Euboeans were perhaps induced to revolt by the expiration of Athens' five-year truce with Sparta and their hope that the Peloponnesians might march against the Athenians as a common enemy. Pericles knew from the history of the dangerous events involving Euboea long ago in the time of his relative Cleisthenes and then again during the Persians Wars that Athens' defense interests were on the line when there was trouble on this nearby island. The obvious military danger only escalated after Pericles led an expedition against the rebels because the Megarians to the immediate west of Athens seized the opportunity to break their alliance with the Athenians. They then obtained the support of Sparta's allies in the northeastern Peloponnese, killed the members of the Athenian garrison stationed in their territory, and reallied with Sparta. With a pro-Spartan foe located immediately on its border, Athens now lay open to direct attack from its bitter enemies in the Peloponnese.

The Spartans wasted no time in capitalizing on the situation by sending out an infantry expedition to help Megara. Their troops inflicted widespread property damage during their advance into the western sector of Athenian territory. The simultaneous threats to Athens from west and east seemed overwhelming, much as they had when the Spartans in the late sixth century had arranged a similar two-pronged attack to try to overwhelm the Athenians. Pericles quickly marched his troops back from Euboea, but after observing the Spartan army in the field he decided, unlike his ancestors some sixty years earlier, that it would be suicide to confront them in a pitched land battle even at this moment of extreme crisis. As he often said to his fellow citizens, it was his goal, so far as it was up to him, that they should be immortal for all time. It was part of Pericles' judgment based on knowledge never to waste human life, the scarcest resource in his world, in some ill-considered demonstration of bravado that he could predict would end in disaster.

As everyone looked on in bewilderment, however, the Spartan invaders abruptly and mysteriously returned home despite not being directly confronted by the Athenian army. What had happened?, onlookers wondered. The answer was that Pericles had not simply given up in the face of superior Spartan power in the field. Instead, he used his reason to devise a secret tactic, based on his knowledge of the tendencies of Spartan generals away from home. That is, he arranged to bribe the chief adviser of the Spartans' young general to convince his commander to abandon the expedition supporting the Megarians. The general was the twenty-five-year-old Spartan king Pleistoanax, son of the infamous Pausanias of the time of the

FIGURE 14. Athenian silver coin. © The Trustees of the British Museum/Art Resource, NY.

Persian Wars. In concocting his undercover plan, Pericles no doubt remembered not only Pausanias' corruption but also how in the 470s the Spartan king Leotychidas had been bribed by the enemy when he was commanding a military expedition to punish the Thessalians for having aided the Persians in the Persian Wars. To save Athens, Pericles exploited the demonstrated weaknesses of at least some Spartan leaders when tempted by riches to betray their homeland's requirement forbidding its citizens to make money a focus of their ambitions. That year, during the annual public examination of Pericles' conduct and financial probity during his service as a general (the yearly audit that every top Athenian official had to pass), he was asked what a certain large expenditure with no description attached to it had been for: "What was necessary" was his reply. This aphorism, too, became a famous saying (Plutarch *Pericles* 23; Aristophanes *Clouds* lines 858–859). What had been necessary, it seems clear, was using heaps of Athenian silver coins (Figure 14) to bribe Pleistoanax's trusted adviser to prevail on the inexperienced king to give up the mission that threatened to destroy Athens. It is dramatic evidence for Pericles' political predominance in this period that he could expend a large amount of public money on his own initiative without prior approval by the assembly – and then have his decision accepted after the fact by his notoriously cantankerous fellow citizens, who usually insisted on a full accounting of the expenditure of public funds, often inscribing the results on stone for all to see, and who were never reluctant to come down hard on leaders whose actions displeased them.

After having induced the Spartan army to evacuate Athenian territory with this covert bribery, Pericles led his troops back to Euboea, regaining control of that strategic location and expelling a number of wealthy citizens from the city-state of Chalcis there, presumably because he suspected they would undermine a democratic government sympathetic to Athens. Next, to punish residents of the city-state of Histiaea on Euboea for having murdered the captured crew of an Athenian warship, he compelled them to leave their home territory so that Athenian settlers could occupy it. Once again, his actions made perfectly clear that he supported Athens' strengthening itself by exploiting resources to which allies had, in his view, forfeited their right in just retribution for their disloyalty to the alliance to which they had sworn eternal loyalty.

To strengthen further their ability to command the Delian League effectively, the Athenians around this time began the construction of a third Long Wall inside the two widely spaced walls built a decade earlier. Erected parallel and closer to the northernmost wall, this new fortification enclosed a corridor directly connecting the city center and the main port of Piraeus. This additional wall completed a barrier that was sure to be impenetrable even to Sparta's top-notch infantry, ensuring that the Athenians could always send out warships to join their remaining allies in naval attacks on their enemies and could constantly import the foreign grain that they needed to feed themselves adequately and the timber they needed to build and repair triremes.

During this period the Athenians also made changes to try to buttress their military strength on land. Most significantly, they voted to spend public money to finance building up their cavalry contingent from 300 to 1,000 mounted warriors. This expensive commitment seemed necessary because their erstwhile allies the Thessalians had not sent their cavalry to help the Athenians against the Spartan invasion of 446. No other Greek city-state had a substantial cavalry at this time, so the Athenians were embarking on a military innovation based on thinking about the future, which Pericles could foresee would be an ongoing struggle with the Spartans. It would not always be possible to buy off their enemy's attacks, and so being able to harass Sparta's hoplites with Athens' own cavalry would be a useful tactic in what we could call a "rope-a-dope" approach when the army faced battle with a superior enemy (to recall the way in which the great twentieth-century world champion boxer Muhammad Ali characterized his winning defensive tactics when fighting a more muscular opponent).

Similarly, it was probably also Pericles' initiative to persuade the assembly to finance a corps of archers to serve in skirmishes on land

and on the decks of triremes in naval battles. These missile troops could be effective in repelling light-armed troops and disrupting the carefully ordered battle line of heavy infantry by showering them with a cascade of arrows. By the outbreak of the Peloponnesian War in 431, Athens had 1,600 of these light-armed artillery troops. Pericles' reasoned reluctance to send heavy infantry into set battles against the Spartans amounted to a radically new tactical attitude for Greeks who were imbued with the idea that men looking like noble heroes of old with their heavy armor, huge shields, and long thrusting spears were not just the safeguard of the community but also the bulwark of its honor. Pericles was able to persuade his fellow citizens to accept this departure from tradition, which some might denounce as cowardly, through his effective reliance on judgment backed by knowledge.

These military developments – a third Long Wall, more cavalry, and archers – were intended to support Athens' military self-sufficiency, as necessary responses to the seemingly perpetual state of high international tension in which the Athenians of Pericles' time lived. Equally, if not more, important in this context was maintaining the supremacy of the Delian League fleet. Pericles addressed this defense imperative by backing the assembly's vote to keep the triremes at sea eight months of the year, practically the entire span of time that the Mediterranean was reasonably calm. Wintertime high winds were hard for these specialized ships to handle because their narrow hulls built for speed did poorly in heavy weather. The trireme crews trained constantly so that their fitness and skills could be the best in the Greek world. All this cost a great deal of money. Existing ships had to be equipped and repaired, new ones had to be built, and the rowers had to be paid. The payments made annually by the members of the Delian League covered these expenses. Ever since the time of Cimon (who is said to have encouraged the trend), more and more allies had decided that it was less trouble for them just to pay cash into the league treasury than to provide ships and crews on their own. They therefore allowed the Athenians to build the triremes in the Piraeus shipyards and recruit the crews from Athens' citizens and whatever other populations were willing to do this exhausting job. By the mid-440s, only a few larger league members still sent ships from their home fleet to join the Athenian-dominated navy of the alliance.

Given that the large majority of the number of triremes was now under direct Athenian control, it was true that, if push ever came to shove in a dispute with the other allies, then the Athenian assembly could exercise effective control over the league's navy because most of the warships were commanded and rowed by Athenians and their supporters. It is, unfortunately, impossible to determine how league decisions were being reached at this point. Thucydides, as mentioned earlier, claims that the initial democracy of the league had fallen away under the pressure of Athenian ambition. If the inscriptions that deal with relations between Athens and Delian League members were better preserved and more securely dated, then we could have more confidence in evaluating the dynamics of these interactions between the most powerful state in the alliance and its weaker members, but as matters stand there is no evidence to refute Thucydides' judgment.

For example, one relevant epigraphical document is the so-called Chalcis Decree (Fornara, *Translated Documents* no. 103), whose date is proposed to be either in the mid-440s or the mid-420s. It says that the people of Chalcis (a city-state on Euboea) will swear to remain loyal to and "to obey the people of the Athenians." This phrasing certainly sounds oppressive to a modern ear, but it is only fair to remember that this text also lays out the reciprocal obligations of the Athenians to the Chalcidians, especially the guarantee against depriving them of their legal protections, property, or revenues without due judicial process. Nevertheless, if this decree actually belongs to the turbulent period of the rebellion on Euboea during which the Spartans invaded Athenian territory, then the argument is buttressed that these regulations imposed on Chalcis by Athens established a state of clear inequality between the two parties and therefore indicate an erosion of the original democracy of the league. That development would certainly amount to a trend toward increasing Athenian imperialism during the time of Pericles' political predominance.

On this topic, it has also been argued that a very damaged and again undated inscription (it is disputed whether it is to be placed in the 440s or decades later during the Peloponnesian War) shows the Athenians' ordering allied states to stop minting their own coinage and to use only Athenian currency (Fornara, *Translated Documents* no. 97). This suppression of independent city-states' mints in favor of an Athenian monetary monopoly is then interpreted as Athens' denial of full sovereignty to its allies. It is certainly true that the rich veins of silver ore in Athens' mines allowed its mint to produce vast quantities of coinage in the mid- and later fifth century. Instead of outright suppression by Athens of the currencies of other states, however, what actually seems to have happened is that the Athenians produced so much money in this form and in such dependable fashion (that is, with consistent purity of the silver in the coins and consistent weights of the denominations) that Athenian currency became the money of choice in the markets of the eastern Mediterranean region. The so-called Coinage Decree (which is also called the Standards Decree because it dealt with the standards set for units of weight and measure) probably mandated for coinage only that payments by members of the Delian League should be paid in Athenian currency, to make the counting and determination of the total value of such a tremendous number of coins more efficient and more accurate, and to preclude the trouble and expense of having to exchange many different foreign currencies in funding the league's treasury. On this interpretation, the Coinage Decree (if it in fact is from the 440s) would not be an index of growing imperialism at the time of Pericles in the same way as would be the Chalcis Decree (if it in fact belongs to the 440s).

Even if these epigraphical documents are from the time of the Peloponnesian War after Pericles' death and are therefore not relevant to an evaluation of his political leadership, it is clear that the issue of the league's money and how it should be spent does belong in this earlier period. In fact, the controversy became explosive in the 440s. It climaxed in a political showdown between Pericles and his political opponents. The dispute centered on the financing of the most enduringly famous – and expensive – architectural achievements of Golden Age Athens. The premier monument of this building program was the Parthenon ("Temple of the Virgin Goddess"), a huge new sanctuary on the Acropolis dedicated to Athena in her capacity as a warrior deity whose goodwill blessed the Athenians with victory (Figure 15). Its construction began in 447 and took fifteen years to complete. Pericles is not mentioned by name in the surviving inscriptions that document the financing of the Parthenon, but the ancient sources explicitly give him the credit for convincing the Athenian assembly to vote for this ambitious public works building program. He was also said to be a close friend of the architect and artist Phidias, who got the top job overseeing the design and construction of the works.

Following the standard form of a Greek temple, the Parthenon served as the god's private residence and was therefore, like all temples of the time, not a building that worshippers could ordinarily enter. Public worship ceremonies, especially sacrifices, took place outside in front of the building, where a massive altar stood. The ground plan of the temple was also standard, a rectangular stone box on a raised platform lined with columns. The Parthenon, however, was bigger than almost all other temples of the time, stretching 230 feet long and 100 feet wide. Twenty thousand tons of local marble was required to finish this giant monument. Its

FIGURE 15. View of the Acropolis and Parthenon. Album/Art Resource, NY.

surrounding porches had a larger number of columns than other sacred buildings. These soaring tubular supports for the roof were carved in the restrained style called Doric. Subtle curves and inclines were also built into the Parthenon's raised base, which was lined with steps, to produce an illusion of completely straight lines – absolutely rectilinear architecture appears curved to human perception – and to enhance the temple's impression of massive size. This design by Phidias and the subarchitects working with him demonstrated the capacity of human knowledge and reasoning to improve on nature, a hint at the tone of the message that this striking temple conveyed about the power of those who were paying to construct it for the world to admire.

A major component of that message was expressed by the many sculptures placed inside and outside the Parthenon. In the interior, a statue made of gold and ivory soared nearly forty feet high to depict Athena in armor with a great shield in front of her. In her outstretched arm she held a six-foot statue of Nike, the divine personification of victory. On the exterior, figures carved in relief decorated the upper parts of the Parthenon. The pediments (the triangular spaces atop the columns at the eastern and western ends of the temple) featured different scenes portraying Athena as the city-state's benefactor. The metopes (panels sculpted in relief above the outer columns around all four sides of the building) portrayed victories over hostile centaurs (creatures with the body of a horse but torso and head of a man) and other enemies of civilization. Most strikingly of all, a frieze (a continuous band of figures carved in relief) ran around the top of the four walls inside the porches. The sculptures were painted in bright colors and fitted with shiny metal highlights to make them more lifelike and visually striking (see Figure 19).

The Parthenon frieze was architecturally distinctive for a temple with Doric columns because usually only buildings in the more elaborate Ionic style had this kind of "film-strip" decoration. The frieze showed men, women, children, and horses parading before the gods. This complex procession implied motion, similar to the way in which the illustrations function in a graphic novel today. The identification of the figures in the frieze and the interpretation of its meaning remain much-discussed and controversial among modern scholars. The key point for a biography of Pericles is that the human beings in the frieze were almost certainly meant to be seen as Athenians, whether from the present of Pericles' time or perhaps from the distant past when Athens was being founded.

No citizens of any Greek city-state had ever before commissioned a temple decorated with sculptural representations of themselves (or their ancestors). The Parthenon therefore proclaimed a unique connection between the Athenians and the gods that outshone any other city-state's relationship with the divine. This competitive assertion of civic confidence reflected Athens' success in defeating the Persians at Marathon and Salamis, gaining the leadership of the Delian League, and increasing its wealth to the highest level through the spoils of war and the profits of international seaborne commerce. To express it bluntly, the Athenians were claiming for all to see that more than anyone else they enjoyed the protective goodwill of the gods in general and of Athena in particular. This new temple manifested their gratitude for this special divine favor, which allowed them to triumph over human foes and the cosmic forces of chaos.

It is also significant that the Parthenon housed a giant statue of Athena that prominently emphasized her function as a goddess of war. Some years before (the precise date is controversial), the Athenians had hired Phidias to erect an almost equally huge bronze statue of an armed Athena to stand outside on the Acropolis. Called the Athena Promachos ("In the Forefront of Battle"), it held a thrusting spear whose shiny point could be seen gleaming from as far away as the entrance to the port of Piraeus. The great amount of bronze required to finish it was gained from the spoils of the Battle of Marathon. The Athena Promachos and the Parthenon Athena both expressed the same message: the fierce and wise daughter of Zeus stood ready to rally the Athenians to defend themselves against their enemies.

This statement of confident power by the Athenians was echoed by the imposing size of another building erected on the Acropolis as part of this project promoted by Pericles. This structure was the massive marble gateway decorated with columns that framed the main entrance to the sacred space atop this promontory at the center of town. The exterior of this Propylaia ("Gatehouse") loomed above people as they approached it while walking up the eastern slope of the Acropolis. It then funneled them through a comparatively low ceiling and confined interior space before suddenly presenting them on its other side with a spectacular view of the even more imposing Parthenon, now in front of them at the highest point of the Acropolis' plateau. People who experienced this "over-the-top" entrance building regularly commented on how spectacular it was that the Athenians had spent so much on a gatehouse. They were right that the building program was expensive: the Parthenon and the Propylaia cost more than the equivalent of $1 billion today, a phenomenal sum for any ancient Greek city-state to expend on public works.

And these were not the only buildings constructed during the heyday of Pericles' leadership. Another large marble temple was begun on a rise just above the western edge of the agora, dedicated to Hephaestus, the god of technology. It, too, boasted extensive sculptural decoration, some of which portrayed the heroic exploits of the legendary founder of Athenian democracy, Theseus. On the southern side of the Acropolis, an innovative concert hall, the Odeon, was built for musical performances to be enjoyed by citizens. It purposely imitated the shape of the luxurious tent that the Great King of Persia used to host entertainments, as an architectural demonstration that Athens under Pericles' influence was providing its citizens with an amenity previously reserved for royalty. A little farther from the city center, the gymnasium called the Lyceum was also refurbished and improved on Pericles' initiative, to provide a site for the intense physical exercise and training that Athenian men were expected to undertake to make themselves both good-looking and fit enough to serve in the citizen militia. In far western Attica, extensive construction took place in the sanctuary of Demeter at Eleusis, where pilgrims traveled from around the Greek world to be initiated into the Mysteries, whose secret knowledge promised a better life on earth and a happier fate in the afterlife.

This large-scale building program backed by Pericles, begun in the 440s and lasting for years, was more than just a concrete expression of

Athenian confidence. It also yielded material benefits for many poorer citizens because it offered countless opportunities for employment for skilled and unskilled workers alike and supported contractors supplying raw materials. Plutarch offers a detailed and colorful list of the many different professionals and artisans involved in supplying and completing these public works, from artists and stonecutters to wagon drivers and road construction crews (*Pericles* 12). Though Plutarch from his anachronistic perspective as an upper-class Greek living in the Roman Empire was not in favor of populist policies, he nevertheless acknowledges that the money that all these workers and suppliers earned in Periclean Athens increased the general prosperity of the city-state because the funds reached people all up and down the socioeconomic pyramid. Earning more money, ordinary people could spend more money, and the overall economy benefited from this upsurge in exchange. The rich in Athenian society, however, for the most part seem to have severely disapproved of this policy. As Plutarch puts it, Pericles designed his policies to support the interests of the masses rather than of "better" (meaning "richer") citizens. In the eyes of these members of the socioeconomic elite at Athens, Pericles was a "traitor to his class," to recall the words of accusation hurled against the wealthy Franklin Delano Roosevelt, U.S. president from 1933 to 1945. Roosevelt's program, referred to as the New Deal, used public funds, among other purposes, to finance jobs in public works programs for the unemployed during a severe depression.

Opposition from the upper class was not the only problem for political stability caused by this populist spending program that Pericles promoted. Material support naturally meant a lot to poorer citizens, so much so that in 445 these benefits evidently were at the center of an extremely bitter dispute over who was truly a citizen and therefore eligible to receive this kind of support. The trouble began when an Egyptian king sent a huge shipment of grain as a gift of friendship to the Athenian people. The reason for this generous donation is not recorded. Perhaps there had been a food shortage at Athens caused by prolonged bad weather, or maybe the magnificent present represented the king's attempt to establish a new diplomatic connection with an increasingly powerful Greek state. In any case, arguments over who was entitled to receive a share of the grain became volcanic. Many people were accused of falsely claiming to be citizens. According to Plutarch, nearly 5,000 were convicted of maintaining fraudulent identities and punished by being sold into slavery (*Pericles* 37). That so many people were so harshly treated reveals how terribly sharp-edged political strife had become by this point in Pericles' career.

Of course, we have to remember that Pericles was not alone in supporting the policies for which Plutarch makes him responsible, especially for conceiving and promoting the far-reaching and expensive public works program of this period. Athenian government always made decisions through the deliberations of large committees such as the council, and mass meetings such as the assembly. Moreover, when Pericles was elected to the highest civic office of general, he was always a member of a board of ten. To have his policies put into practice, he had to persuade others. Neither he nor anyone else could simply dictate policies for Athens.

Nevertheless, there is clear evidence of how highly influential Pericles had become. One of the most remarkable projects from this period reveals his highly imaginative and even idiosyncratic ways of supporting the interests of less well-off citizens. This ambitious plan centered on the foundation of a new settlement in southern Italy. There, the people of Sybaris had appealed both to the Spartans and to the Athenians to send people to help them establish a new city-state after they had lost a war to their neighbors. The Spartans rejected the call, but the Athenians responded at the urging of Pericles.

Called Thurii, this new settlement was apparently open to Greeks from anywhere to join; the historian Herodotus reportedly moved there. With Athens having taken the lead in the project, however, it seems likely that poorer Athenians looking to improve their economic circumstances would have been first to sign up for the opportunity. Athenians were well aware of the reputation for prosperity and culture of the Greek settlements already existing in southern Italy and Sicily. Even if they did not personally relocate to Thurii, they could see it as an advantage for Athens to have a special connection with a flourishing community in that rich region. In short, by promoting the ambitious and complex project of founding Thurii, Pericles was supporting the interests of the Athenian people both as potential settlers and as recipients of benefits to flow from this new foundation. He was also demonstrating that Athens had the resources and the courage to embark on an ambitious project that, he could pointedly say, had intimidated the stodgy stay-at-home Spartans.

Pericles' decidedly distinctive approach to political matters shows up in his choices for directors of the project. The Athenians appointed a ten-man committee to organize the new settlement, among whom was Lampon, the religious expert who knew Pericles. This appointment shows that, on the one hand, Pericles recognized the importance of gaining legitimacy for such a risky plan by paying close and public attention to honoring the gods in the process. On the other hand, he also persuaded the citizens to accept one of the most controversial sophists of the era as the designer of a constitution for the new community. This astonishing choice was Protagoras.

Immigrating to Athens from Abdera in northern Greece around 450, Protagoras taught ideas about the subjectivism of truth and the relativism of morality that outraged many Athenians. On the former topic, he argued that no absolute standard of truth existed because every question had two contradictory answers based on the subjective nature of how human beings experience the world. For example, Protagoras maintained, if one person sensing a breeze thinks that its temperature is warm but a different person judges it to be a cool breeze, neither judgment can be correct in absolute terms. The wind is purely and simply warm to one person and cool to the other. The difference in their judgments is irreconcilable. Protagoras summarized this doctrine of subjectivism – the principle that there is no absolute reality behind and independent of appearances and human perceptions – with a conclusion expressed in his work *Truth* that became infamous because it seemed to imply that the gods were not the source of ultimate knowledge: "The human being is the measure of all things, of the things that are that they are, and of the things that are not, that they are not" (Plato *Theatetus* 152a).

Many ordinary Athenians also objected to the views of Protagoras on the grounds of the implications for public life of two of his main concepts, which other sophists also shared: (1) human institutions and values are not creations of *physis* ("nature") but rather only matters of convention, custom, or *nomos* ("law"), and (2) since truth is subjective, speakers can and should argue either side of a question with equal persuasiveness and rationality, not on absolute moral grounds. The first view implied that traditional human institutions were arbitrary and changing rather than natural and permanent, while the second seemed to many people to make questions of right and wrong irrelevant. Critics saw these ideas as proclaiming moral relativism and therefore as threats to the shared public values of the democratic city-state because they taught students to use persuasive techniques in court and in the assembly that would make the weaker argument seem the stronger argument. Protagoras (and others who taught such ideas), the accusation ran, would cause the moral ruin of Athens by eliminating considerations of justice from public policy and law.

Protagoras strongly disagreed with this criticism. He defended his teachings by explaining that they definitely were not hostile to democracy. To the contrary, he added, his ideas were essential for people in a democracy to understand because every individual had a natural capacity for excellence that needed to be developed by thought and practice, and because the preservation of human society depended on the rule of law rooted in a shared concept of justice. These truths required that members of a community, if they were to live together in harmony, be persuaded – not compelled – to obey the established laws. They were to be persuaded to this position not by the false claim that laws were based on absolute and unchanging truth: that ideal did not and could not exist in reality. Instead, people had to become law abiding because reasoning showed this behavior to be advantageous for everyone in the community. A thief, for example, might claim that stealing was a part of nature, but he would need to be persuaded by reason to stop this behavior harmful to others, convinced by intellectual judgment that a man-made law forbidding theft was to his personal advantage because it protected his own property as well as that of the community in which he, like all humans, had to live in order to survive.

The fears that citizens felt about the potentially corrosive effect of Protagoras' relativism on the moral basis of persuasion in legal and political oratory was exceeded only by the worries they had about his ideas concerning the gods. Protagoras deeply upset religiously minded people, a category that included the overwhelming majority, with his blatant agnosticism (the belief that supernatural phenomena are unknowable): "Whether the gods exist I cannot discover, nor what their form is like, for there are many impediments to knowledge, [such as] the obscurity of the subject and the short duration of human life" (Diogenes Laertius *Lives of Eminent Philosophers* 9.51). This conclusion angered all those who thought he was saying that conventional religion had no meaning. They further worried that his words would provoke divine anger against the community where he now lived because it had not expelled this religious offender, as they saw him.

Pericles became close to Protagoras, spending hours and hours discussing intellectual quandaries with the controversial sophist. One time, for example, an athlete accidently killed another man when the javelin he was throwing in a contest flew off line and fatally impaled his competitor. Pericles and Protagoras filled an entire day disputing whether the thrower, the organizers of the competition, or the javelin itself should be held responsible for homicide. Given the widespread suspicion of and even overt hostility to Protagoras in many sectors of Athenian society, it is highly significant that the notoriously cautious Pericles thought it worth the risk to his reputation to associate with him. Even more striking is that he proposed Protagoras as the architect of a social contract for Thurii – and that he succeeded in persuading the Athenian assembly to accept his choice of the sophist as a lawmaker for what was going to be a new democracy based on equality. It is unfortunate that we have no record of the arguments that Pericles used to persuade his fellow citizens to approve this revolutionary appointment. They must have been among his most spectacular oratorical achievements in reasoning from a judgment based on knowledge because they somehow convinced skeptics that he could foresee what was the best policy for the future, even when he was proposing as the implementer of that policy a sophist who seemed to be an extreme outlier in terms of traditional ways of thought and perhaps even an offender against the gods.

Similarly, Pericles' advocacy of public spending to support the nonelite section of the population carried political risk because it could remind people of the policies of Pisistratus, Athens' tyrant of a century before. Pericles' political prominence therefore was liable to arouse not just the jealousy of his social equals but also fears that he might become so prominent that he could dominate Athenian democracy in much the same way that Pisistratus had. As Plutarch puts it, Pericles' political opponents recognized that, with Cimon dead, Pericles had become "the greatest of the citizens" (*Pericles* 11). There was no one with a military reputation brilliant enough to dispute with Pericles over policies for the city-state, but those who wanted to bring him down found the next best candidate, a good speaker (and a relative of Cimon) named Thucydides son of Melesias (a different person from the historian, Thucydides son of Olorus). Pericles' rivals began referring to themselves as the "Fine and Good," and they started grouping together on the open-air floor of the assembly so that they could raise a concerted noise when they wanted to heckle Pericles' speeches. They furiously criticized him for, they claimed, having ruined the reputation of Athenians by (they asserted) stealing the funds of the Delian League in moving its treasury from Delos to the Acropolis, and then, worse, by spending this money that belonged to the allies on costly baubles, statues, and temples to adorn the city of Athens like a woman boasting of her beautiful appearance.

This sexist taunt in fact misrepresented the facts. As Pericles pointedly replied, the allies' payments were being expended only to finance the alliance's very expensive navy. (Modern research confirms this; see Giovannini 2008.) The money for the new buildings, the wages of the laborers on public works, the settlements of Athenians abroad, and benefits for poorer citizens were financed not through payments made by Delian League members but by the fortunately now abundant non-League resources of Athens itself drawn from taxes and the donations of wealthy private individuals. In addition, Pericles adamantly insisted that the Athenians did not owe an accounting to the allies so long as the Persians were kept at bay (by the league navy, now of course dominated by Athenians). He went on to say (admittedly in an overstatement) that the allies were contributing not a single horse, or trireme, or heavy armed infantryman, but only money. And the money, he argued, belonged to those who took it in, so long as they provided the service for which the funds were being paid.

This argument was sternly rigorous, but it was also hard to refute on the facts. As Thucydides son of Melesias had said, Pericles was such a skilled public speaker that just when he, Thucydides, thought that his arguments had pinned his rival on the ground in a (metaphorical) choke hold, Pericles, that supreme oratorical wrestler, would persuade the judges of the match that he had never been thrown down at all. Nevertheless, Pericles' reason-based refutations of the financial slanders against him did not stop his political enemies. They tried to turn public opinion against him with startling accusations of misconduct. They claimed he had conspired with Phidias to conduct adulterous affairs with freeborn women under the very eyes of Athena in the Parthenon. And not only that: they alleged that Pericles had authorized the blatant sacrilege of having his own portrait included among the figures of fighting heroes sculpted on the great shield of the goddess inside the temple (Figure 16). All these hostile rumors had an effect, with Thucydides son of Melesias and the other "Fine and Good" also keeping up their barrage of accusations that Pericles was mishandling the public finances of the city-state. In exasperation, Pericles finally stood up in the assembly to pose the question to its attendees whether it seemed to them that he had authorized excessive spending on Athens' splendid new constructions. They roared back that he had. "In that case," he exclaimed, "it won't be your expenditure, but mine, and I am going to inscribe my own name on these dedications to the gods!" (Plutarch *Pericles* 14).

His oratorical tactic worked an immediate transformation: the assembled thousands of male citizens now shouted at him to spend absolutely as much public money as he saw fit. This episode reveals Pericles' knowledge of crowd psychology. It was, frankly, unrealistic for him to promise to pay for major public works himself. In terms of wealth, he was nowhere near capable of operating at the same level of philanthropy as

FIGURE 16. Copy in stone of the shield of the statue of Athena in the Parthenon. © The Trustees of the British Museum/Art Resource, NY.

Cimon had with his huge benefactions to Athens, such as financing the foundations of some of the Long Walls. What Pericles must have calculated was that the citizens would be ashamed to think that their communal identity would not be formally linked with Athens' wonderful accomplishments and monuments for all to see in perpetuity. Sentiment now turned so strongly in favor of Pericles that it was also decided to hold an ostracism in about the year 443. The balloting sent his political rival Thucydides son of Melesias into exile.

Pericles was now indisputably the first man of Athens in terms of his political influence. He was elected to the board of generals for the next fifteen years in a row. In a radical democracy that stressed term limits and wide participation by as many male citizens as possible in public office, that run of electoral success testified to Pericles' now-unrivaled respect and status in domestic politics. The international situation had stabilized – or so it could be hoped – a few years before the ostracism. In 446/5, the Athenians and the Spartans agreed to another peace treaty, this one to last for thirty years. Both sides swore oaths before the gods as witnesses to their sincere pledges to abide by the terms of the agreement. The military stresses and expenses of the previous years had forced both sides to realize that they could not easily prevail over the other and therefore had to cut their losses to prevent further fruitless losses of men and resources. The Athenians consented to withdrawing their military from the island of Euboea, giving up the areas they controlled in the northern Peloponnese, and removing their garrison from Megara's western port. Otherwise, they retained their current possessions and control. The Spartans were therefore conceding official recognition of the legitimacy of Athenian dominance of its allies. Most important for the future, it would turn out, the treaty also formally specified that any disputes between the two signatory states must be submitted to arbitration, so that the issues could be settled without flaring into war.

This long-term treaty added fuel to the fire of dissatisfaction burning among some Delian League allies. If the Persians were restricted to the eastern Mediterranean and now the Spartans had sworn not to make war on the allies, then, they complained, there was no longer any decisive reason to keep making payments to maintain a hypervigilant defense. The Athenians, by contrast, agreed with the argument that Pericles had made about the finances of the league: the allies' annual payments were being expended on the intended purpose of protection against the Persian Empire, that purpose was being fulfilled for the League Members, and all the league members had a sworn, eternal duty to honor their promises to pay. In their exasperation at their allies' complaints, perhaps Pericles and his fellow citizens even recalled to themselves the fable of Aesop that Themistocles had once alluded to when complaining that the people were ungrateful for what he had done for them. Once upon time, the story went, two exhausted travelers walking along on a steaming hot day took their rest in the shade of a plane tree, but while lying there comfortably out of the sun they commented on how useless the plane tree was because it produced no fruits. The tree then said (Aesop's animals and plants often speak Greek), "You really are lacking in gratitude, denouncing me for not bearing fruit at the very time that you are enjoying my protection!" (Plutarch *Themistocles* 18 = Gibbs, *Fable* no. 82).

Pericles' unrivaled level of political dominance in Athenian democracy in this same period inspired the authors of comic plays to lampoon him in every possible way, but especially by accusing him of having become as dominant as a god, or a tyrant like Pisistratus. Cratinus called him "the greatest of all tyrants" and labeled him "Zeus the Onion Head" (referring to the shape of Pericles' apparently bulbous skull [see Figure 1], whose appearance comedians regularly mocked, according to Plutarch *Pericles* 3 and 13). Teleclides, who began competing in Athens' comic festivals in this period, blasted Pericles in a comedy now lost by saying that the Athenians had handed over to him the ability "to tie up or to release the payments (*phoros*) of the cities [of the Delian League] and even the cities themselves, to construct walls of stone or tear them down again, to [do the same] to treaties, power, strength, peace, wealth, and happiness" (Plutarch *Pericles* 16). If all that power did not amount to a level of control exercised by one man that was completely unfitting in a democracy, the play was suggesting, then what possibly could?

The unhappy members of the league of course strenuously rejected the argument that they had to observe the terms of the original agreement now that international conditions had changed, with Persia restricted to the eastern Mediterranean region. At the same time, it seems clear from the historical record that Pericles – and a majority of the Athenians – held to a very clear belief that the agreement was to be maintained. It therefore is not surprising that there is no indication in the surviving ancient sources that Pericles saw any reason, whether practical or ethical, to seek to change Athenian policy. And even if he had, he most likely would have agreed with Aristides, the famously just statesman of Pericles' youth, who reportedly believed that a leader had to remain personally incorruptible but sometimes had to put aside considerations of justice to support the public policy of his homeland, including leadership of the Delian League (Plutarch *Aristides* 25). That approach to statesmanship was soon going to be on full display in Athens' most controversial action against an ally during Pericles' entire career.

MAP 6. Athenian and Peloponnesian Leagues 431 B.C.

9

Pericles' Responsibility for the Samian Revolt and the Peloponnesian War

The fiercest challenge yet both to Pericles' leadership and to the unity of the Delian League arose in 441 from a dispute with the island city-state of Samos, one of the few alliance members still fielding a strong navy of its own. The Samians and their neighbors on the mainland in the city-state of Miletus, also a league member, had reached an impasse in a heated conflict to take over some nearby territory. The Athenians instructed their arguing allies to go to arbitration, but Samos refused. Pericles probably proposed the decision made by Athens as leader of the Delian League to respond very forcibly by installing a new, and democratic, government on Samos; in supporting this policy unfavorable to the elite of Samos, Pericles was perhaps recalling the treachery of those Samian commanders fifty years earlier who had made a deal with the Persian king Darius to save their city-state from what they feared would be devastation and therefore deserted the Ionian alliance in the heat of the Battle of Lade. A fine of 80 talents was imposed, and 100 citizens were taken away as diplomatic hostages to an Athenian stronghold on the island of Lemnos. In keeping with his conspicuous incorruptibility, Pericles refused a king's ransom in bribes offered him by a group of rich antidemocratic Samians and the Persian governor to ease the conditions.

The next year, the dispute blew up into a crisis that restored the Persians to the status of an active threat to the member states of the Delian League when the Samian rebels allied with the Persian governor in western Anatolia. Now flush with money supplied by the Persian king's governor, they hired mercenaries and violently overthrew the newly installed democracy allied with Athens. The anti-Athenian Samians also freed the hostages and captured some Athenian citizens. These fellow Greeks they turned over to their Persian backer. The city-state of Byzantium then joined the rebellious Samians in rebelling against the league.

To meet this serious crisis to the league's unity and to the safety of his fellow citizens who were being held as hostages, Pericles was tasked with commanding a force of warships from Athens supported by the fleets of Chios and Lesbos. These were island allies that, like Samos, still had navies, but that, unlike the Samian rebels, remained loyal to their oath of allegiance to the Delian League. Some of the ships were sent to head off the Persian triremes that were reported to be on the way to Samos from the eastern end of the Mediterranean Sea. Pericles' tactics succeeded in defeating the rebels at sea and then on land. When they retreated inside Samos' fortification wall, he had the city surrounded on land and its harbor blocked by ships on patrol. Pericles then ordered that the league infantry and engineers deploy a new technology to pressure the encircled Samians – siege machines that could batter walls and towers made of stone. Finally, he detached a large number of warships from the blockade fleet to confront the approaching Persians off Cyprus.

Pericles' judgment – that he could safely reduce the size of the Greek navy remaining in position at Samos – turned out to be mistaken, and the Samians defeated the remaining blockaders. Pericles therefore had to return to Samos with the other ships from the expedition that had been looking for the Persians and reinstate the full blockade confining the rebels. So as not to repeat his earlier miscalculation, Pericles maintained the passive tactics of the siege, rather than allow more of his citizens to die after they began clamoring to avenge their earlier defeat by trying to scale the city's walls in a headlong attack. The hostility in this war between former allies became so poisonous that both sides burned brands into the skin of the prisoners of war they captured. After months of increasing deprivation, the rebels finally had to surrender in 439. The terms of their punishment were crushing, even more so than in the past when members of the Delian League had broken their oath and unilaterally tried to exit the alliance: the Samians' fortifications were torn down, their fleet confiscated, their leaders punished with crucifixion, diplomatic hostages taken away, and large payments imposed to recover all the allies' expenses in fighting the war.

Was Pericles believed to have been personally responsible for the horror that was the course and the result of the Samian revolt? The majority reaction at Athens to this bloody episode and the ruthless and humiliating punishment of the rebel Samians is difficult to gauge accurately. One of Pericles' fellow generals elected to serve in the war had been Sophocles, the famous author of tragedies, who like most Athenian artists also served in public office. A few years earlier, the playwright had fulfilled a term on the board of high-ranking officials overseeing the collection of payments in the Delian League. Pericles while at Samos memorably chided Sophocles for showing more interest in a handsome adolescent male than in his military duties, but this anecdote is not evidence that Sophocles was anything other than a supporter of the Athenian side in the war. Even so, some modern scholars have suggested that Sophocles' famed play *Antigone*, which was probably produced in this period, indirectly criticized Pericles' leadership. The heroine, Antigone, confronts Creon, whom the play makes the "general" (*strategos*) of Thebes and therefore the fictional equivalent of the position that Pericles (and his fellow officials) filled at Athens. With furious anger she denounces him for what she heatedly condemns as his narrowly rigid decisions. She accuses Creon of privileging political reason in punishing disloyal citizens and ignoring eternal and unwritten rules descended from the gods when he denied burial to the dead rebels. Sophocles' horrifying story in this famous drama of rage, gender-based confrontation, and multiple family suicides exposes the right and wrong of both Antigone, who dies, and Creon, who lives on in disgraced despair. The play in fact offers no simple solution for resolving the competing and sometimes incompatible interests of divinely sanctioned moral tradition, family relationships, the differing authority of women and of men in Greek public life, and the state's necessary policies. As a result, a feeling of deep ambiguity, even acute anxiety, about the right and wrong of the situation seems to be a plausible reaction to posit for the Athenian people to the deeply troubling events of the Samian revolt. That they would have held Pericles responsible for their disturbing feelings would have been in character with the tendency of Athenian democracy to blame its leaders and advisers for any policy that was less than an overwhelming success.

Authors of comedies certainly took direct aim at Pericles over the outcome of the Samian revolt. (As so often, the original texts have not survived, and we have to speculate on the strength of later references.) They had the most fun in their comic plays with the accusation that Pericles had backed the war against Samos as a way to please Aspasia (Figure 17); her uncommon Greek name meant something like "Joy" in English. She was originally from Miletus, so in backing her hometown in its dispute with Samos, the accusation went, Pericles was favoring his lover over the best interests of Athens. Aspasia and Pericles had become a couple at some point in the 440s. That Apasia was extremely intelligent and

FIGURE 17. Stone bust of Aspasia. Album/Art Resource, NY.

shrewd was confirmed by later authors including Plato and Xenophon. They report that Aspasia was so astute in argument, rhetoric, and political reasoning that Socrates often visited her to hold conversations about politics and ethics and that she wrote Pericles' public speeches for him. The literal truth behind the stories about Aspasia as a teacher is naturally impossible to recover, but the unanimous impression given by the ancient sources is that Aspasia was the love of Pericles' life and that he loved her for her brains as much as for her physical charms.

Lines from comedies staged at Athens poked fun at what the plays portrayed as the openly affectionate, even erotic nature of the relationship between Aspasia and Pericles. The famously reserved and careful political leader, who always so strictly monitored his behavior, was ridiculed on stage for kissing his love when he left her in the morning and returned in the evening. Aspasia herself was mocked as the owner of a brothel that trained high-class prostitutes (an accusation that seems unlikely to be true for the woman with whom Pericles chose to live after his failed marriage). Comic authors could be scathing about Aspasia: in one of Eupolis' plays she was openly called a "whore," while Cratinus upped the intensity of this insult by labeling her a "whore with the face of a dog" (Plutarch *Pericles* 24). These insults were especially painful because Aspasia and Pericles had an illegitimate son whom they named after his father instead of his maternal grandfather. It was a much-commented-upon irony that Pericles the younger, born to a foreign mother by about 440, was not an Athenian citizen as a result of the Citizenship Law that his father had passed in 451.

Pericles' love for Aspasia did nothing to calm his rocky relationship with his two legitimate sons from his marriage. Pericles made his children furious by imposing a family budget based on preset spending limits that did not allow the buying of luxuries even when there was surplus income, and he designated a single slave, ironically named "Good News," to enforce the household's financial rules. The elder boy, Xanthippus, was nevertheless said to behave as a debauched spendthrift, as sometimes happens with the offspring of famous and wealthy families. His father's renowned ability to persuade the citizens to make reasoned decisions evidently had little effect on this son. Xanthippus in frustration at his lack of funds borrowed a large sum from a friend of his father by falsely claiming that the loan was for Pericles. When the friend asked Pericles for repayment, the father brought legal action against the son to make him repay the money. Xanthippus retaliated by making fun of his father for filling countless hours in absurdly abstract discussions with sophists. He even became so enraged that he made up the charge that Pericles had seduced his daughter-in-law. In other words, the happiness that Pericles experienced with Aspasia failed to carry over to his private life, just as it failed to stem the cruel gossip that his political rivals spread about the couple in public.

If we could be sure that it was true (the ancient evidence is contested), the most astonishing evidence for political conflict at Athens at the time of the Samian war would be the report from some sources that the ridiculing of Pericles (and other leaders) in comedies became so vituperatively personal and so politically combustible that the Athenian assembly may have voted a ban on "making fun of people by name on stage" (scholia on Aristophanes *Acharnians* line 67 = Fornara, *Translated Documents* no. 111, and *Birds* line 1297). It is uncontested that the Athenians prided themselves on their freedom of speech (*parrhesia*, "saying everything") in their civic life, and though they recognized slander and blasphemy as legal offenses, they nevertheless traditionally valued a level of free expression that rivals, or even exceeds, that of many modern cultures. Comedy in particular seems to have been granted exceptional leeway in insulting public figures on stage. If in fact the Athenians did approve this suppression of free expression (and if they did, it was temporary), it was surely because the political atmosphere at Athens had become as disturbing as had the hatred between the Athenians and the Samian rebels.

A hint of the bitterness that characterized the opposition to Pericles at this point is found in the story that Elpinice, who despite her advanced age was still the unquenchable firebrand of Cimon's family, publicly upbraided her dead brother's former rival when other women began crowning Pericles with garlands in response to the speech he had given commemorating the Athenian dead from the war with Samos. The citizens always commissioned the leading speaker of the time to deliver an official funeral oration for those lost in battle, and this one by Pericles had been a great success oratorically. In it, as alluded to earlier, he compared the city's eternal memory of the men who had been killed to the immortality of the gods. He also memorably compared the loss of so many young men in war to the disappearance of the spring from the year. Cimon's sister, however, expressed a bitterly sarcastic reaction: "This is amazing, Pericles, and deserving of garlands, that you destroyed so many of our good citizens, not by making war against Phoenicians or Persians, but by overturning a city-state that was our ally and our relative." He then retorted by quoting a line of poetry that implied Elpinice was meddling with topics that should be off limits: "You are gray to be smelling of such perfume!" (Plutarch *Pericles* 28).

If any censorship on comedy had truly been imposed, its restrictions were revoked in 437, perhaps as an attempt to calm the situation by restoring the traditional expectation of freedom of speech on the comic stage. In this same year, a young political ally of Pericles named Hagnon led a campaign to settle Athenians and other volunteers at Amphipolis near the Strymon River in northern Greece on the border with Thrace. This region was valued because of its timber and precious metals, but it was also exposed to deadly raids by Thracians of the kind that had wiped out the 10,000 Athenians who had earlier attempted to settle Amphipolis. Pericles' support for sending out this risky mission – and having it succeed this time – was a sign that, whatever blasts his opponents might direct at him, he remained totally dedicated to policies designed to protect Athens and support its international power.

Within another year or so, Pericles gave a further demonstration of this commitment by gaining the approval of the assembly to lead a large naval expedition to the Black Sea. Access to its shores was absolutely crucial to Athenian survival because large amounts of grain were imported from there. The great defeat in Egypt in the late 450s had made it more difficult to import food from that region, so the Black Sea area to the north had to be kept open to Athenian cargo ships. Pericles signaled his recognition of the overwhelming importance of this necessity for the population's survival by embarking on a diplomatic initiative to reinforce Athens' relations with both Greek settlements and indigenous communities in the region. He even detached part of his fleet to help the citizens of a Greek city-state on the Black Sea's southern shore to expel a tyrant. He then persuaded the Athenian assembly to authorize a troop of 600 volunteers to move to the location as support for the new, Athens-friendly government, a connection publicized by the name given to their settlement: Piraeus. This name made the point that, to survive, Athens needed a port whose security zone reached as far as the distant Black Sea.

Pericles recognized that it was more important than ever to do everything possible to keep Athens strong because relations with Sparta were deteriorating despite the peace made in 446/5. Sparta's allies and would-be allies were constantly complaining that Athens was trampling on their interests, and they were demanding a Spartan military response, meaning direct attacks on Athens and its allies. As Pericles remarked to his fellow citizens, he could distinctly see war bearing down on them from the Peloponnese. To give his fellow citizens more time to prepare militarily and psychologically, during the mid-430s Pericles had ten talents sent secretly to the leaders in Sparta every year to bribe them to delay what seemed to him an inevitable attack. He knew their susceptibility to money from the lessons of the past. At home, his political opponents stepped up their efforts to dislodge him from his status as the people's most trusted adviser. Their motives for trying to undermine him in this period of increasingly dangerous foreign affairs are not recorded. Were they simply jealous of his popularity? Did they believe that his policies gave too much support to poorer citizens at the expense of the rich? Were they in favor of accommodation with the Spartans?

There is no direct evidence, but it was presumably some mix of these sentiments that motivated the notorious (but very poorly documented) prosecutions of Pericles' friends in the fraught environment of Athenian politics in the mid- and late 430s. What seems to have happened is that grave legal charges were brought against Phidias, Aspasia, and Anaxagoras. (Scholars vigorously dispute the dates, the results, and, in some cases, the historical reality of these trials.) The accusations were meant to cast suspicion on Pericles by association. Since a defendant's character, previous acts, and personal life were relevant, even necessary, topics of discussion in cases before Athenian courts (as opposed to the allowed procedure in contemporary American law), the accusers could mention Pericles' name and his alleged conspiracy with the accused as much as they liked in their speeches for the prosecution.

In the case of Phidias, the prosecutors alleged that he had cheated the people by using less gold on the statue of Athena in the Parthenon than the city-state had paid for. They added a charge of sacrilege that Phidias had also covertly sculpted the face of one of the figures on the goddess' shield to look like himself – and they then implicated Pericles, as mentioned earlier, by saying that Phidias had included his friend's likeness with a similar trick (see Figure 16). Speaking in defense of his friend, Pericles instructed the court to have the gold parts of Athena's statue taken off and weighed; he had advised Phidias to make them removable just in case this kind of slander arose. When the weight of the precious metal was in this way verified to be correct, the accusation of theft collapsed. Whether Phidias was acquitted or perhaps convicted on other charges remains unclear. He may have fled Athens to escape any risk of punishment. In any case, modern archaeologists have discovered evidence to show that Phidias did not die in prison at Athens, as one ancient source reported. Instead, he went to Olympia on a contract to produce the giant sculpture of Zeus for the sanctuary's main temple, where a cup inscribed with his name has been excavated from his workshop. Whatever the outcome of Phidias' trial, it was the first time that Pericles was ever implicated, even if indirectly and without any valid grounds, in a charge of personal financial corruption.

Aspasia was reportedly also prosecuted for impiety, a potentially capital charge. Her accuser was said to have been Hermippus, an author of comedies full of verbal attacks on Pericles. The crime of which Pericles' lover was charged can be understood under Athenian law as an accusation of "not engaging in proper worship of the gods." The offenses that counted as impiety were not precisely defined under the law, but this type of wrongdoing was regarded as extremely serious because, as explained earlier, most people believed that the gods would punish the entire city-state if it allowed even a single impious resident to remain among its residents. The precise form of impiety alleged seems to have been that Aspasia, a foreign-born brothel madam, had arranged for Pericles to have sexual liaisons with freeborn women in religious sanctuaries. Pericles convinced the jury to acquit his lover with a speech that seems to have been unique in his history as an orator: he made an emotional appeal to the jurors, with tears streaming down his face. This sort of response was in fact the expected one: speakers for the defense in major court cases were supposed to express their deep feelings in an obvious fashion as a way to help convince the jurors that they were hearing the truth. So, it was appropriate by Athenian standards for Pericles to cry on this occasion, but he had never before let his emotions show in public. We can guess that he realized that there was no way to disprove the charge with objective evidence and that the life of his beloved Aspasia was hanging in the balance. For Pericles to have behaved in this (for him) extraordinary way reveals both how deeply he cared for Aspasia and how intensely he was feeling the stings from his enemies' attacks.

The pressure on Pericles escalated with the indictment of a third close friend, the thinker/philosopher Anaxagoras. An Athenian with the evocative name Diopeithes ("Obedient to God") had the assembly pass a decree outlawing anyone who taught about celestial phenomena and did not observe the city-state's traditions about the gods. As the controversial thinker who had explained the sun as a flaming rock and identified "Mind" as the moving force in the universe, Anaxagoras was an obvious target for this category of accusation. The surviving evidence for a trial of Anaxagoras is so confused that it is unknown what actually happened to him, but it seems that many people were persuaded that there was real danger to the city-state from its most prominent leader's being personally close to this seemingly impious foreign intellectual.

The campaign to weaken Pericles' political dominance became direct when the successful politician Dracontides (another remarkable name, perhaps meaning "Son of a Snake") had a decree passed to require Pericles to justify his financial accounts as the official who had been in charge of the expensive contract for the construction of the gold and ivory statue of Athena in the Parthenon. This trial was seen as so special that the jurors would use ballots rendered sacred by having been laid on the altar of Athena on the Acropolis. With its combination of religious and financial issues, this case represented a severe threat that deeply worried Pericles. His reputation for financial probity might not be enough to save him in the face of the current storm in the political climate at Athens, and the fear clearly showed in Pericles' bearing. In fact, at one point his distress was so obvious that his ward Alcibiades found him sitting at home in despair over how to present a sufficiently documented accounting of his expenditures. The irrepressible youngster told his foster father that he should instead be planning how not to explain himself. The situation finally eased a bit when Hagnon, a supporter of Pericles with a strong military reputation, was able to persuade the assembly to return the case to the normal judicial procedures for financial fraud, separate from any implications of religious criminality.

Once again, to repeat the mournful mantra of ancient Greek history, the sources do not clearly reveal the outcome of this dramatic episode. Almost certainly, Pericles escaped conviction, but not without damage to his reputation – and his sense of personal security. He knew at first hand the pain caused by his father's ostracism, to say nothing of the compulsory exiles of other prominent leaders throughout his lifetime. He realized that even a highly successful general could be deposed from his elected office and punished at any time, and that this hard truth applied especially to him in the blast-furnace conditions of the moment. We can surely imagine that he was angry about what had been happening in the fire of Athenian political rivalry and anxious about what might happen next.

This consciousness of the treacherous insecurity of prominence in Athenian democracy helps explain the focus of the ancient sources on the story that the tornado of troubles afflicting Pericles' public and private lives in the 430s led him to push Athens into the Peloponnesian War (431–404). The charge was that he urged war not because it was the best choice for Athens under the circumstances but only because he needed to divert the citizens' attention from the alleged crimes of his close friends and his own reputed misdeeds. Was Pericles responsible for bringing on the Peloponnesian War? The accusation that he started the war principally to protect himself presents the culminating issue in any evaluation of Pericles' public career because in the end Athens suffered a terrible defeat and then a bloody civil war as a result of the Peloponnesian War.

By far the most detailed surviving account of the opening events of that fateful conflict and of its course while Pericles was still alive is that of Thucydides in book 1 and book 2.1–65. In this section of his history Thucydides includes speeches put into the mouth of Pericles. Analysis of the notoriously difficult syntax of the original Greek texts indicates that these versions cannot be strictly verbatim transcripts of the words that Pericles spoke in oral presentations that had to be understood by crowds of thousands in outdoor venues. Nevertheless, in my judgment, we can rely on Thucydides' explanation (1.22) that, in composing these speeches for inclusion in his narrative, he stayed as close as possible to the speaker's judgment based on knowledge (that is, on the speaker's *gnomē*, the same word that Thucydides has Pericles emphasize in his speeches in the *History* in referring to his thoughts). Therefore, I believe that we get from Thucydides the most accurate surviving version of the essential elements of Pericles' advice to the Athenians during this immensely tense period.

Thucydides famously states (1.23) that he believes the ultimate cause of the Peloponnesian War was that "the Athenians having become great struck fear into the Spartans, which generated a necessity for war." In other words, the growth of Athenian power, the very thing that Pericles and, to be fair, the majority of his fellow citizens, saw as Athens' salvation, so frightened Sparta that the long-simmering hostility between the two city-states inevitably flamed up into an open warfare that could not be avoided. The word that the historian uses for "necessity," *anangkē*, expresses the idea of a cosmic-level force that generated the war, raising his judgment to the level of an abstract truth of human existence.

The immediate reasons that the conflict finally broke out, however, centered on disputes between Athens and allies of Sparta, especially the Corinthians and the Megarians. Corinth had become embroiled in a violent dispute with Corcyra, originally founded from Corinth on a large island off the northwest coast of Greece. These two former allies were now fighting each other over a city-state on the mainland opposite Corcyra. Both Corcyra and Corinth had substantial navies, and both appealed to Athens for help in their war. The Corcyreans said allying with them would gain the support of Greece's second largest fleet of warships in the war with Sparta that was sure to come. The Corinthians countered by demanding that the Athenians repay the aid they had received from Corinth in the wars with Aegina and Samos. The Athenian assembly decided that their interests were best served by supporting Corcyra, which was a key stopping point on the sea route to the rich lands of southern Italy and Sicily.

In 433 the Athenians sent triremes to Corcyra, where, contrary to the intentions of the assembly that had ordered them to sail there, the warships were sucked into a naval battle against the Corinthian fleet in which both sides claimed victory. Thucydides says nothing of any role for Pericles at this point, but Plutarch reports (*Pericles* 29) that he convinced the assembly to send out an initial fleet of only ten ships because the commander was going to be Cimon's son named "Spartan" and Pericles retained hostile feelings against this scion of his former rival, even some two decades after his father's death. Public criticism of the paltry size of this expedition then compelled Pericles to propose a supplementary force to be sent as well. This anecdote, which asserts a motive for Pericles that seems out of keeping with his other behavior as a leader, at least underlines the depth of the political disunity in Athens at this point.

International relations soon grew even more tense, if that was possible, when the Athenians ordered Potidaea, an ally of Athens in northeast Greece but a colony of Corinth, to sever all its continuing ties with its mother city in the Peloponnese. This command enraged the Corinthians. The situation in the critical northeast region deteriorated yet further when Athens allied with the rivals of the king of Macedonia, their former supporter. He responded by calling on the Spartans to attack Athens, as did the Potidaeans. They agreed to take that ultimate step in breaking the peace treaty from 446/5 if open war broke out in the north. That additional factor did come into play when the Athenians sent a naval group north to enforce their orders to their allies.

A meeting of Sparta's allies took place in 432 to address the looming crisis. Thucydides presents the Corinthians as giving a speech that vehemently pressures the Spartans to take action against Athens. They conclude with a thinly veiled threat to go over to the Athenian side if the Spartans continue to procrastinate (1.68–71); this possibility could only have panicked the Spartans because without the support of Corinth they had no chance of overcoming Athens. Some Athenian envoys who coincidentally happened to be in Sparta responded with a vigorous defense of their city-state's policies (1.73–78). They candidly explained that they, like all human beings, had been motivated by fear, honor, and profit to acquire power over their allies and in fact had shown more justice in their rule than a preeminent state usually did. Though it might sound boastful, this justification seems to be a fair presentation by Thucydides of what the majority of Athenians at the time actually believed. The Athenian representatives then added that they were unwilling to relinquish their position of dominance because they knew the Spartans, out of hatred, would take advantage of any weakness. The Athenians concluded by adhering to the terms of the treaty: they offered to go to arbitration to settle the disputes. One of the two Spartan kings, Archidamus, urged caution on his fellow citizens and supported relying on the arbitration process to stave off war. The Spartans as a whole, however, stirred up by a belligerent speech from Stenelaidas, one of their chief elected officials (called ephors, meaning "overseers"), voted to launch an attack on Athens, peace treaty or no peace treaty.

As usual, the Spartans did not go into action immediately. In 431, they convened another meeting of their allies, this time with no Athenians in town. The Corinthians told the Spartans they absolutely must go to war to save Greece from slavery at the hands of the Athenians, a mission of national salvation that would ensure divine support regardless of the terms of the earlier treaty (1.120–124). At this point, the Spartans finally resolved to ready their invasion of Athenian territory. To paint Athens as being on the wrong side of the gods, weaken Pericles' influence, and give themselves more time to organize their military campaign, the Spartans sent messengers to the Athenians instructing them to drive out the polluting curse still attached to the Alcmeonids from the murders of the conspirators with Cylon 200 years before. Recalling the life lessons taught him early on by his parents, Pericles needed no reminder of the effect that this ancient pollution could have on the popular imagination. To support Pericles, the Athenian assembly turned the tables on the Spartans by telling them to cleanse their land of the curses hanging over it from the sacrilegious executions of some helot suppliants and of the traitorous general Pausanias decades earlier. The Spartan attempt to undermine Pericles' influence only reinforced the many lessons he had learned from his childhood about the necessity of never making any concessions to such untrustworthy enemies. Pericles clearly held the same opinion of the Spartans as dramatically enunciated by Andromache, the heroine of a heartbreaking tragic play of Euripides staged probably not long after Pericles' death: "Oh you inhabitants of Sparta, the most hateful of mortals to all human beings, deceitful advisors, commanders of lies, contrivers of evils!" (*Andromache* lines 445–447).

Soon after sending their embassy concerning the Alcmeonid curse, the Spartans then sent yet more ambassadors to announce specific changes for the Athenians to implement in their foreign policy if they wanted to avoid a war: lift their siege of Potidaea, let Aegina be independent, and revoke their decree that banned the Megarians from conducting any business in the central market at Athens or in any of the harbors of the members of the Delian League. As Plutarch says (*Pericles* 31), it is not possible to recover the circumstances in which the so-called Megarian Decree was passed, but Pericles was said to be its principal backer. At one point, the story goes, Pericles told one of the Spartan representatives that a law prevented him from taking down the official plaque on which the Megarian Decree was inscribed. The Spartan then exploded, "If you can't take it down, then turn the plaque to the wall. There's surely no law preventing that!" (*Pericles* 30). Unwilling to budge an inch, Pericles persuaded the assembly to send a herald to the Megarians to announce to them that they had committed sacrilege by appropriating land from the sanctuary at Eleusis along the border with Athenian territory and by giving refuge to runaway slaves from Athens. He also convinced the assembly to dispatch a second herald to the Spartans to inform them of this situation. According to the Athenians, the Megarians then committed another religious crime by murdering the herald sent to them, though they denied it and blamed Pericles for persecuting them. In Aristophanes' later comedy *Acharnians* (lines 523–529), Pericles' motive for his policy at this point was to get personal revenge for a monetary dispute between Megarians and Aspasia over kidnapped prostitutes. This satirical fiction shows how insultingly personal the dialogue could be in Athenian comedies, but there is no other evidence that it contains even a scrap of truth.

Pericles never wavered in his determination to stonewall the Spartans. The tipping point occurred when the Spartans in 432/1 dispatched three high-ranking spokesmen to Athens to announce their simple-sounding but sweeping ultimatum: "The Spartans want there to be peace, and there would be, if you let the Greeks be independent" (Thucydides 1.139). The Athenians promptly held an assembly to decide what to do. There was strong disagreement among the speakers concerning whether to stay the course of no concessions or to revoke the Megarian Decree to avoid war. At this crucial moment, Thucydides presents the first of the three complex orations of Pericles that he gives in direct speech (1.140–144, 2.35–46, and 2.60–64; 2.13 includes an oration in indirect speech).

Thucydides prefaces his first of these public addresses by Pericles with a description of him as "at this time the first man of the Athenians, the most powerful in speech and in action" (1.139), a two-pronged characterization recalling Homer's famous description of Achilles as having been educated to be "of words an orator and an accomplisher of deeds" (*Iliad* 9.443). The very first thing Thucydides presents Pericles as saying is that he always has the same judgment based on knowledge, the same *gnomē*: not to yield to the Peloponnesians. Pericles acknowledges that events sometimes turn out contrary to what reason calculates should occur, but he urges his fellow citizens to stick to their assembly's decisions nevertheless. The Spartans have been plotting against Athens for a long time and are ignoring the treaty's specification of arbitration to settle disputes. Therefore, no Athenians should think that if they refuse to reverse the Megarian Decree they would be going to war "over some tiny thing." In fact, it is a test of their judgment that the ostensible cause of the war is small. We cannot, he insists, care whether the reason is tiny or big because if we concede even a minor, but unfair, ultimatum from an equal, then that would be sliding down a slippery slope, which, in turn, would lead our opponents simply to keep returning with greater and greater demands. It would, in short, amount to slavery (1.140.4–141.1).

Pericles then details the reasoning behind his calculation that Athens has superior resources in a conflict with the Spartans. The latter have a much weaker agricultural base, he explains, only limited expertise in naval warfare, a cumbersome decision-making structure in their alliance, a tendency to be slow to take action, and, above all, only a small amount of money available for the expenses of the war. He next sets out the strategy that will prove so controversial: We Athenians can prevail if we will think of ourselves as islanders guarding our urban center and maintaining supremacy at sea. This strategy will admittedly exact the high cost of sacrificing our land and houses in the countryside when the Spartans invade. Under no circumstances, however, can we risk regular land battles with the stronger infantry of the Peloponnesian alliance. All we can care about is preserving our soldiers, not our property. Pericles next adds a detail that underlines how tense the situation had become in the Delian League: We must conserve our human resources, he says, because our allies will no longer remain tractable if we do not have enough men to march against them.

Thucydides then has Pericles offer the advice that the historian will subsequently criticize the Athenians for failing to follow later in the war after the death of Pericles. While this war is being fought, Pericles insists to his audience that they must not try to conquer any new territory or become involved in any other dangerous foreign entanglements. For the immediate present, the assembly should tell Sparta's representatives that the Athenians will vote to allow the Megarians back into their market and the league's harbors if Sparta will stop its hostile actions against them and their allies; that the Athenians will let the Greek city-states be independent if they were independent when the treaty was made in 446/5 and if the Spartans let the city-states subjected to them be independent; that the Athenians are ready to follow the requirements of the treaty (meaning, submit to arbitration); and that the Athenians will not open hostilities themselves but will confront anyone who does begin a war. In short, Pericles says in a memorable concluding phrase evocative of the language of Aeschylus in the *Oresteia*, his fellow citizens must understand that "there is a necessity to go to war" (1.144.3). Like our ancestors who resisted the Persians with far fewer resources than our city-state can currently marshal, he urges his fellow citizens, we must rely on judgment more than luck, on daring, and on power. Standing up to Athens' enemies in every possible way, they have to fight to hand down to those who follow them resources no less great than Athens now enjoys.

Pericles' reasoning proved persuasive. The assembly decided to tell the Spartans that Athens would not respond to orders but was ready and willing to go to arbitration to settle all the disputes on an equal and fair basis. Sparta's representatives took this message home; no further embassies arrived at Athens. The war was not yet formally under way, but it was for all practical purposes now imminent. That is the outcome that Pericles had foreseen all along on the basis of everything he had learned from the history of Sparta's relations with Athens, going back to the time of his relative Cleisthenes, and from the many relevant experiences of his own life during the Persian Wars and afterward for nearly 50 years.

The actions of the two major states' allies finally ignited open warfare between the rival city-states. The Thebans, allies of Sparta and the largest city-state in Boeotia, launched a surprise invasion of their minuscule neighbor Plataea, an ally of Athens, but when the sneak attack went wrong, the Plataeans massacred the captured Thebans before a message from Athens could arrive advising their allies not to harm the prisoners of war. Both the Athenians and the Spartans recognized this bloody incident as shattering their peace treaty, and they began final preparations for war. Both sides decided to send representatives to ask for support from non-Greek powers – especially the Great King of Persia. His governor in western Anatolia had provided a lot of money to the Samian rebels against the Athenians a decade earlier, and there was every reason to believe that this new Greek-on-Greek war was going to draw the autocrat of the world's superpower back into the affairs of mainland Greece in pursuit of his own interests. Both sides knew the Persian monarch could spend his limitless resources to strengthen the military campaigns of the side he supported – or worse, from the perspective of loyal Greeks, to bribe the leaders of the side that he opposed to betray their homelands. Pericles once again had had a lifetime of lessons about the reality of this latter danger, remembering the many instances of influential Greeks – Athenians as well as Spartans – who had sold their loyalty to their countrymen, corrupted by the lure of power and riches that a Persian connection could provide: Hippias, Miltiades, Themistocles, the Athenian conspirators at the Battle of Plataea, Pausanias, to name the most famous of these sellouts. The danger to Athens in this ultimate crisis over its security, Pericles knew, arose from supposed friends as well as from proclaimed enemies.

In addition to seeking foreign support, Athens and Sparta tried to convince neutral Greek city-states to join their respective alliances. The majority of Greeks favored Sparta because they feared that if Athens won, it would succeed in expanding control over all of them; they knew that the limitations imposed on the Spartans by their ever-dangerous reliance on the helots made that kind of international expansion highly improbable. In the summer of 431, the Spartans decided to capitalize on the support for them from other Greeks who feared Athens' power by assembling their allies for a march on Athenian territory. In command was Archidamus, who dutifully but reluctantly led the Peloponnesian army onward toward Athens. Before arriving, the Spartan king sent a herald to ask the Athenians whether they wanted to surrender now that they saw the Peloponnesian infantry on the way. The messenger never made it into the city because Pericles had already persuaded the assembly to pass a decree stating that no representative of the Spartans would be allowed to enter once the Peloponnesian army had taken the field. He clearly wanted to keep his fellow citizens as far as possible from the temptation to yield once the ferocity of the threat to them was clearly in their vision.

As the enemy approached, Pericles took the dramatic step of announcing publicly that if the Spartans during their invasion spared his own country properties as a provocation to stir up hostility against him among his fellow citizens, he would donate his landed wealth to the people. It was known that he had a guest-friend relationship with Archidamus, and he promised to make the donation even if the Spartan king passed by his properties out of loyalty to that special bond. How Pericles came to be a guest-friend with a prominent Spartan is unknown, but presumably the connection with the cautious Archidamus reflected a shared belief that they were compatible in wanting to keep Sparta and Athens at peace with each other.

Now that this hope of preventing open warfare had vanished, Pericles had to do everything he could to prevent the citizens from deviating from the harsh necessity of his "Athens as an island" strategy. He therefore advised the citizens to transport their movable property – and themselves – from the countryside to safety behind the fortification walls of the city. Victory in war, he said, depended on two things: judgment based on knowledge and money. He then displayed his ability to weave information and reasoning into a persuasive speech by giving them specifics first on the amount of coinage and precious metal objects that had been stored up to pay war expenses, and then on the numbers of different kinds of soldiers that were available and the number of triremes ready for action. These material resources, he said, would be used for Athens' "salvation" (*soteria*). As other Greek texts show, this term specifically indicates the ultimate level of a community's political and physical existence. Pericles' message, therefore, was that in this war of attrition, money and manpower would determine the outcome – as is in fact what happened in the long run, when after years and years of war that weakened both sides the Persian king provided huge sums to the Spartans so that they could finance the triremes and the crews needed to defeat the Athenians, whom the king regarded as the bigger threat to his empire.

The Athenians recognized the wisdom of Pericles' advice and adopted his policy of behaving as if Athens were an island, but they complied only with great difficulty and deep discontent because so many were accustomed to making their homes outside the city, some of which had only recently been fully restored from the enormous devastation inflicted by the Persians long before. There simply was not enough space inside the city's walls to house all the refugees from the countryside without overcrowding, and the majority had to camp out in any open space, even moving into sanctuaries of the gods. Urban Athens became a massive shantytown with terrible problems of sanitation and supply.

Archidamus advanced slowly, giving the Athenian country dwellers time to escape, hoping that their panic would induce a general surrender. When that plan failed, he ordered his army to ravage Acharnae, a community located several miles north of the city center but visible from the top of its wall. The largest village in the Athenian countryside, Acharnae provided 3,000 hoplites to the citizen militia. When the Acharnian infantrymen standing atop the city fortifications saw the flames and smoke flaring up from their burning homes, in fury they demanded a mobilization of infantry to stream out of Athens' gates to take the fight to the Spartans. Others opposed their abandoning Pericles' plan never to meet the Peloponnesians in a land battle. But many, many people began fiercely blaming Pericles for the loss of their country property and the humiliation they felt at remaining inside the walls. Some even lashed out at him as a coward for having refused to allow the Athenian army to confront the Spartan invasion. In Greece's male-dominated society that idealized the macho warriors of Homer's epics, no insult could be more inflammatory. The comic author Hermippus, who had prosecuted Aspasia, made this charge as public as could be by including it in his (now-lost) play *The Fates*: "You king of the satyrs, why aren't you willing to carry an infantry spear, but instead you produce clever speeches about the war, inhabited by the soul of Teles [apparently the name of an Athenian infamous for cowardice]?" (Plutarch *Pericles* 33). Cratinus returned to his theme of equating Pericles with Zeus by putting on a comedy entitled *Plutuses* whose plot envisioned the return of an ancient Golden Age by overthrowing the tyrannical ruler of the gods – and thereby suggesting that Athens would regain its prosperity if it got rid of Pericles (fragments in Rusten, *The Birth of Comedy*, pp. 199–202).

Despite the buffeting from this furious hurricane of criticism and insults, Pericles maintained his characteristic public imperturbability, his *praotēs*. He also somehow – scholars debate the possible procedural options he might have employed – prevented the assembly from holding a special meeting to authorize an infantry battle with the Spartans. His success in restraining his fellow citizens from forcing a confrontation with the superior infantry of the enemy while they were roiled by emotional fury is the most striking example of Pericles' ability as a leader to oppose the citizens' wishes in crucial moments and prevent them from abandoning his policies based on reason and calculation for ensuring Athens' power and security against its enemies. This success was proof to his critics, we can imagine, that he had become a virtual tyrant controlling Athenian democracy.

To try to lift the mood of helplessness among the citizens, Pericles convinced the assembly to authorize a series of different military expeditions that would support his overall strategy. Cavalry squads were sent outside the walls to disrupt marauding bands of the enemy. A giant naval expedition was organized of 100 Athenian triremes and 50 more from Corcyra, to conduct raids all around the coast of the Peloponnese using 1,000 hoplites and 400 archers on board for lightning attacks on land targets. A smaller naval task force was sent to guard Euboea. Next, the Athenians' communal anger was redirected at the people of Aegina, who were vilified as having been the most responsible for the war. The entire population of the island city-state was uprooted and their land given to Athenian colonists (Figure 18). The Spartans gave many of the Aeginetan refugees a place to live in the western Peloponnese. The rest had to scatter throughout Greece looking for asylum.

Finally, after the Spartans had left Athenian territory (they could stay away from home no longer than several weeks at a time because they always feared another helot rebellion), Pericles himself led an attack on Megara. He assembled the largest land army that Athens had ever fielded, numbering well more than 10,000 heavy infantry supplemented

FIGURE 18. Temple on the island of Aegina. HIP/Art Resource, NY.

by a mass of light-armed troops. They ravaged Megarian territory before returning to Athens as the military campaigning season of the year was coming to a close as a result of the approach of winter.

In this first year of the Peloponnesian War, Pericles had been able to use his influence to persuade his fellow citizens to stick to his "Athens as an island strategy" despite their anger at the destruction of so much property outside the city walls and the intense discomfort experienced by so many while they were crammed so uncomfortably for several weeks inside Athens' fortifications. Moreover, the offensive operations against the Peloponnesians had gone well, and it seemed likely that Pericles' strategy was eventually going to succeed by exhausting the Spartans' lesser resources and therefore compelling them to drop out of the war. There would be no clear-cut conquest of Sparta, but the attacks on Athens would end, and that would be victory enough. It would be the salvation of Athens' power and therefore of its safety in a world filled with enemies.

Pericles well knew, however, and indeed had said as much in his first speech urging no concessions to Sparta, that the changing and often unpredictable fortunes of war always exacted a heavy toll on human resolution and confidence. How much longer the conflict would go on until Sparta lost its resolution to continue he could not predict exactly, but he did know that the Athenians would need stirring encouragement and stern admonition to keep their spirits healthy enough to withstand the pain and losses of war. He would shortly have a chance to administer that prescription on an occasion that became by far the most famous public appearance of his long and distinguished history of leadership in Athenian democracy, a career that fate was not to extend much longer.

10

Pericles' Fate, Then and Later

Pericles' attack on Megara in 431 was the last of Athens' major battles in the first summer of the Peloponnesian War; with winter approaching, bad weather made it difficult to engage in effective military operations. As in all of their wars, at this point in the annual calendar the Athenians held a large public funeral ceremony to honor those who had been killed by the enemy in the previous campaigning season. This multiday occasion culminated with an oration by a speaker chosen for the intelligence of his judgment and the eminence of his reputation. This time, that man was Pericles, who was still Athens' most respected adviser, despite the criticism from more than a few citizens of his martial policy. His speech as reported in Thucydides (2.34–46), today called the "Periclean Funeral Oration," has become the most famous passage in ancient Greek prose. It is also as important – and challenging – a piece of evidence as we have for Pericles' developed views on Athens.

For these reasons, it seems fitting to describe the Funeral Oration in some detail here, even though no summary can convey the full complexity – and deeply provocative character – of the speech's arguments. Worded by Thucydides in the dense style characteristic of direct speeches in his *History*, this passage portrays Pericles as taking a self-consciously contrarian approach to a traditional assignment. Rather than rely on the usual format of Athenian funeral orations, which focused heavily on the exploits of the recent war dead, he presents judgments based on knowledge to express his view of the exceptional nature of the Athenians' way of life, the power that its special characteristics produced for their community as a whole, and the depth of commitment that they all must maintain to preserve the level of superior power that was Athens' only source of ultimate salvation from the constant threats to its existence presented by its fearsome enemies.

Pericles begins his remarks in a startlingly untraditional way by announcing that he does not believe that a speech of this kind should be given on such a solemn occasion because the natural human jealousy characterizing everyone who is still living makes persuasive praise of the war dead nearly impossible. Nevertheless, he does proceed to fulfill his public duty by giving a full speech, an implicit demonstration that at Athens the needs of the group take precedence over the desires of the individual, no matter how distinguished.

He then moves on to the main body of his oration by praising the several generations of Athenians, including the current one, that established and then increased the rule (*archē*) over the Delian League that their city-state now enjoys. He next describes the preparations, form of government, and ways of life that have gained "great things" for the Athenians. In presenting this strongly self-confident argument, Pericles unflinchingly and explicitly asserts that the Athenians' government does not reflect the traditions and laws of their neighbors but is instead a paradigm for others, a model of how conditions should be in a Greek city-state. Their city-state is a democracy, he asserts, because it supports the interests of the many rather than of the few, rewarding capability rather than social class or wealth.

The freedom underlying Athens' governing institutions and principles also characterizes its private life, Pericles goes on to say. Citizens behave justly through fear of the written laws, while a sense of shame prevents them from breaking the unwritten laws of society, especially those that help any citizens who have been wronged. For some modern observers, fear and shame may seem to be inappropriate mechanisms for promoting law-abiding behavior as opposed to a desire for justice and a respect for decency. If we are honest with ourselves, however, we must admit that human nature means these motivations continue to occupy prominent places in the conduct of people to this very day. Pericles is speaking here as a frank realist whose insights express truth as he sees it based on his knowledge and experience, and he sugarcoats nothing.

Pericles continues on a strongly affirmative note by reminding his fellow citizens that their city-state provides many opportunities for recreation and imported luxuries while also maintaining an open-door policy to visitors. We, he says in a direct slap at the Spartans, live with relaxed ease instead of being subjected to painful discipline, yet we still field an equally, or even more, valiant military force.

Pericles elevates the level of praise for Athens even further by saying that for other qualities, too, it should evoke a sense of wonder. "Wonder" is a strikingly resonant term in ancient Greek; it is what Herodotus explains at the start of his *Histories* that he is investigating with his narrative of the deeds of Greeks and non-Greeks. The wonders that Pericles credits to his fellow citizens include their loving beauty and wisdom without weaknesses, valuing wealth not for its own sake but for what they can do with it, and not denigrating poverty but still believing that the poor should work to overcome their condition. And, he adds, again unlike in other city-states, we Athenians regard the citizen who does not participate in public life as "of no value." Here, then, Pericles is directly expressing the primacy of the public over the private, at the same time describing what he sees as the Athenians' admirably free private and personal life. There is an inherent contradiction in these two points, to be sure, but Pericles is asserting that at Athens they can coexist in a way that is not prevalent in other Greek city-states.

Pericles next introduces a topic that sheds light on his singular approach to oratory: he praises his fellow citizens for understanding that reasoning and argumentation must precede action. We are, he says, better than other people because we are both full of daring and especially ready to calculate the best course to take instead of just reacting out of ignorance, and because we still act with courage even after we have made a knowledge-based judgment in calculating the pain that we are likely to experience when we implement our decision. This point presumably reflects why Pericles believed – correctly, more often than not – that he could be most effective in guiding the Athenians by presenting speeches that emphasized his special brand of knowledge and reasoning. He also makes another flattering argument based on what he says is an uncommon reality: Athenians are different because they secure friends and allies by doing rather than receiving favors, motivated by their trust in their freedom.

All that Pericles has said so far he sums up in a stunningly assertive phrase: Our entire city-state is an education for Greece. This is the truth, not an empty boast, he explains, because Athenians are so self-sufficient and because Athens has such great power as a result of the special Athenian way of life. He is of course praising his fellow citizens for their self-determined independence of mind and life, but he is also alluding to a truth that everyone there knew only too well: it was more than anything else Athens' military and economic strengths that made it possible for its people to take care of themselves, down to the literal subsistence level of securing their nutrition by importing food from abroad under the protection of the most potent navy in the world. There was no other way for them to survive. Power is their salvation, Pericles is reminding them.

It should not be surprising, then, that Pericles proceeds to make exceptional claims about the nature of Athens' power: It is even greater than what others say about it; it is indeed so overwhelming that enemies overcome by it are not upset by their defeat at the hands of such a superior; and those subjected to it do not complain that they are not ruled by people worthy to dominate them. The nature of Athens' power, he tells his audience, will fill others with wonder (using that remarkable term again) at our accomplishments, not just now in our own day but indeed also in times to come. We Athenians have achieved so much that we have no need of a Homer to immortalize our deeds. Finally, Pericles offers a neck-snapping conclusion to his analysis of the extent and significance of Athenian power: We have required every sea and every land to give access to our daring, and everywhere at all times we have established undying memorials of good and bad. This is the city-state for which the war dead nobly gave their lives, and for which its living citizens, too, should be willing to sacrifice. It is hard to imagine a more tough-minded appraisal than this of the history of Athens in its Golden Age.

After this provocatively proud exposition of his city-state's power, Pericles at last turns to the topic that usually occupied the majority of a public funeral oration, namely, praise of the military service and courage of those whose funeral was being conducted. He characteristically performs this ceremonial duty in his own innovative way, omitting specific reference to any of the battles in which the soldiers lost their lives. Instead, he argues that, whatever the dead men's personal shortcomings might have been in their private lives, their valor in war redeemed their reputations and won them glory in the hearts of the citizens who survive.

Pericles' gnomic praise of the dead culminates with two unforgettable axioms directed at those who are still alive. First, you must pay attention to the power of Athens every day – and become lovers of it. This was a very strong, in fact blunt statement about the relationship the male citizens should develop with their city-state's power. The word "lovers" expressed an erotic passion whose effect on human beings, by the tenets of Greek thought, exceeded every other force in the cosmos. Therefore, Pericles is instructing the Athenians to put their commitment to their community's salvation at the same emotional level as their feelings for the people to whom they are the most closely bonded by ties of love. Second, Pericles coins a ringing phrase to sum up the message that those still alive must take from the sacrifice of those fallen in battle for Athens so that they, the living, can achieve the required depth of commitment: "Emulate them by deciding that happiness is freedom, and freedom is courage."

The sentiments that Pericles next prescribes have led some modern scholars to condemn him as cold-blooded and unfeeling. To the grieving parents of the dead soldiers, he says that he recognizes their deep emotional pain but believes that those couples still young enough to have more children should do just that, because only citizens with children whose lives will be at risk in war are truly able to participate on equal and just terms in making plans for the city-state. Those too old to bear more children should rejoice in the fortunate part of their lives that is now past and especially in their sons' honor, while recognizing that only a short time remains to them to live. No matter how flinty some of us today might find this judgment, the emphasis on the honor that the family had gained was recognized at the time as a genuine consolation in the midst of suffering. What Pericles is saying here reflects both judgments based on reason that fit with intellectual ideas of the sophists and assumptions about life and death that were accepted by many in his time. What Athenians in that era thought were appropriate points of consolation might sound disconcerting today, but that seems an insufficient reason to evaluate Pericles as emotionally tone deaf or cruel.

Pericles' strictly reason-based counsel continues when he next tells the sons and brothers of the dead that the inevitable impact of jealousy (a theme raised at the start of his speech) means they face a daunting obstacle in trying to gain the same level of recognition and reputation that their dead siblings have won. Again, this was true, if not comforting in any immediate way. He then concludes with an admonition to the war widows listening to his words. His comments to these women certainly sound condescending today (at least in some societies of our world), but in their ancient context these statements were on a par with the logic-driven themes of consolation that he had just made to parents and siblings reminding them of the steepness of the road to respect in Athenian society. This path was so difficult, he did not have to explain further to his audience because they already knew it, for the reason that it reflected the high level of personal reward and satisfaction conferred by winning a respected status. Therefore, however we may judge his remarks, he is not saying anything inappropriate by the social standards of his time and place when he tells the grieving wives that they can indeed have great respect and reputation, if they do not become worse than their existing nature and if they give men the least possible reasons for talking about them, whether for blame or fame. As shocking as this might seem to modern ideas of gender equality, this admonition was meant as an encouragement to the widows to focus on a central purpose for their lives (whose limits were of course defined for them by men) while they were experiencing intense personal pain and doubt.

Pericles then ends his speech with a reminder of the Athenians' concern for one another by announcing that the city-state will reward the bravery of the war dead by paying to support their children until they grow to maturity. He concludes with a gender-specific reference alluding to the service of males in the citizen militia and in democratic government at Athens: "Where there are the greatest prizes for excellence, there the best men are citizens."

At this point, Thucydides immediately returns to his narrative, making no comment about the audience's reception of Pericles' Funeral Oration or the historian's own opinion of it. He leaves his readers to reflect for themselves on the speech's content and implications, in particular on Pericles' boldly frank assertion of Athenian exceptionalism. Thucydides' account briskly returns to the military operations of the Peloponnesian War, which had recommenced in the spring of 430 not very long after the delivery of Pericles' Funeral Oration. At the start of this new campaigning season, Archidamus again led a Spartan invasion of Athenian territory, driving the citizens living in the countryside back inside the city walls.

Not long after the Peloponnesians arrived, the kind of unpredictable disaster that Pericles most feared actually occurred. An epidemic disease, today commonly referred to as "the Plague," began devastating the Athenian population now confined in close quarters in the jam-packed urban area. Thucydides, who says he had the illness but recovered, provides an exhaustive description of its symptoms (2.48–50). Modern medical experts can deduce from the details of his harrowing report that the sickness was not in fact bubonic plague. No current disease produces exactly the same set of symptoms, though typhoid seems close, so the health disaster at Athens perhaps resulted from some virulent and highly contagious infection that has since mutated into a related but not identical form.

Nothing in the medical practice of the time had any healing effect, and multitudes at Athens died in agony. Those who tried to help infected relatives or friends often became sick themselves and perished. The physical devastation of the population and the failure of prayers to the gods to alleviate the suffering led many people in their desperation to behave as if all the traditional assumptions of society had disappeared, almost as if the end of the world was at hand and all that was left was to keep partying without stopping. The community-minded adherence to norms and laws that Pericles so highly praised in the Funeral Oration degenerated into social chaos, Thucydides reports (2.51–53). Some Athenians began openly to blame Pericles for the catastrophe, especially for having filled the city with so many suddenly homeless people forced to exist in such crowded and unsanitary conditions.

Neither the epidemic nor the fault finding led Pericles to back down from his wartime strategy to preserve Athens. As before, he stuck to his advice to his exasperated fellow citizens not to act on their emotions and rush out of the city to battle the Peloponnesians' fearsome infantry. To show that his strategy was not entirely passive, however, he organized a massive naval expedition that he personally commanded for another operation to attack coastal sites around the Peloponnese. Not only did he man it with 4,000 hoplites, he also had innovative ship transports constructed that carried 300 cavalry horses. Although these raiders failed in their major thrust against Epidaurus in the northeastern Peloponnese, they did conduct several other successful attacks. When, however, the epidemic decimated its troops, the expedition had to return home without achieving any decisive victories. Pericles' younger colleague Hagnon and another general then took this same naval force to the north. They intended to help the league troops already there capture Potidaea, but the epidemic raged so fiercely among the army that the generals had to return their men to Athens after a fourth of the contingent died of disease in only forty days.

This cascade of setbacks drove many citizens to a frenzy of recriminations against Pericles. The majority even voted to send representatives to Sparta to try to arrange a peace. When the enemy rejected that overture, the Athenians' desperation peaked. Pericles then appeared before the assembly to deliver what Thucydides makes his last speech (2.60–64). In it, Pericles pulls no punches in expressing his deep unhappiness with the attitude of those citizens who are now raging at him. He begins by saying that he had expected everyone to become angry with him and now wants to remind them of the principles guiding his strategy. The foundation of his policy, he explains, is that individuals benefit when the community as a whole does well, but that they can never maintain their private good fortunes if the city-state falls to its enemies. The harsh truth is that in this contest for ultimate stakes, their individual interests must be traded for their "common salvation." Citizens therefore cannot allow private hardships to imperil the existence of their community. He then flatly declares that he knows as well as anyone else what needs to be done and has not been influenced in his conclusions by money. As a loyal patriot whose arguments persuaded them to decide to go to war, he insists, he does not merit their accusations of wrongdoing.

If we wanted to remain free, he continues, we had no choice except war. Your sufferings have changed your minds, but not mine. It is natural for people to be shocked and depressed by the unexpected and the unpredictable, by that which could not be calculated. That certainly describes the epidemic, he says, but as citizens of a great city-state raised in the ways of greatness (referring implicitly to what in the Funeral Oration he had said were their exceptional qualities), you have to bear up under your calamities, preserve your reputation, and attend to the salvation of us all.

That can happen, he explains, if you comprehend the special nature of the greatness of our rule: no state on earth, not even Persia, can match us at sea. So, let the property in the countryside go. If we maintain our naval strength, we can always reacquire those land-based possessions. Our courage needs to be grounded in reasoning based on knowledge because that is the best way to predict the future. And that future concerns not merely freedom or slavery as determined by our enemies. No, losing our rule (over our allies in the Delian League) would not just deprive us of resources but also expose us to grave danger from the hatred of those whom we currently dominate. After this exceedingly tough advice – "Give up caring about your homes and land that lie outside our walls!" – Pericles then pulls no punches in describing Athens' situation: Our rule is like a tyranny, he baldly states, which it can seem unjust to take but is dangerous to let go. There is no safety in slavery, so do not listen to anyone advocating anything other than action. Pericles here rips off any remaining polite front masking the harsh reality of the power that he insists is necessary to ensure the salvation of his homeland. There could be no starker assessment from the Athenian side of the "necessity for war" that Thucydides had identified (1.23) as the most fundamental cause of the conflict.

Pericles then returns to his argument that he should not be blamed for the single unexpected event that has taken place – the epidemic – because human beings simply have to endure "what comes from a divine source." He again reinforces the major principle behind his strategy: Athens today enjoys the greatest power and reputation that any Greek city-state has ever won, and even if someday it, like all things, must decay, still there will remain the memory that of all Greeks its citizens ruled the most Greeks, that they persevered in the greatest of wars, and that their city-state was the richest in every way and the greatest. This breathtakingly proud – and valid – claim leads Pericles to his conclusion: It is inevitable that we will be hated for our dominance, but this is the source of our honor. Those who maintain their judgment based on knowledge in the face of sorrows and who fight back the hardest in their actions, whether city-state or individuals, are the strongest.

Pericles' ruggedly candid arguments based on the overwhelmingly important concepts of power and honor convinced the Athenians to abandon their attempt to come to terms with the Spartans and to continue their stand against their enemies by sticking to Pericles' strategy of "Athens as an island." Nevertheless, many Athenians retained their resentment against him personally. His policy might be correct, they felt, but nevertheless someone had to pay for their losses and their pain, and that someone at Athens was always the most prominent leader. So, in a badly documented episode – it seems either to have been a prosecution for failed or deceptive performance in public office or a trial for financial fraud – Pericles was condemned to pay a huge fine and deposed from his elected position as a member of the board of ten generals.

This was without any doubt the lowest point in Pericles' public life, when the sterling reputation that he had worked so hard to establish by his cautious and reasoned behavior seemed to have been destroyed. Exactly how long his official deposition and disgrace lasted is not precisely known, but it seems to have been a relatively short period. Thucydides only says that the majority of Athenians changed their minds yet again and reelected Pericles to a generalship "not long after" (2.65.4). Now paying less attention to their own troubles, the historian reports from his eyewitness perspective, the citizens recognized that Pericles was the most worthy adviser the city-state had. He had kept Athens safe before the Peloponnesian War and taken it to the height of greatness, and at the start of the war he had foreseen how to preserve and exploit Athens' power. And now the wartime situation threatened to become even more dangerous: not only were the Spartans launching aggressive attacks on Athenian allies, they along with some of their Peloponnesian allies had dispatched an embassy to travel to the Persian king to request financial support and implore him to join their side in the war. The Athenians knew about this diplomatic mission because they had intercepted the enemy's representatives before they could reach the shores of Asia. The citizens displayed their anger and their fear at this development by summarily executing the ambassadors without trial on the very day they were taken to Athens and hurling the dead bodies into a ravine without proper burial rites.

Despite the near-panic among his fellow citizens at the current state of the war, Pericles was evidently reluctant to resume his public duties, a hesitation that suggests just how angry he had become at the opposition to his advice about the war and, I would add, how devastated and depressed he had been by his conviction by his fellow citizens. After a lifetime of basing his self-esteem on his service to Athens and his absolute incorruptibility, he clearly felt repudiated and humiliated. As Plutarch testifies (*Pericles* 15), even when wealthy foreign kings had appointed Pericles to be the guardian of their sons in attempts to buy his favor as a backdoor entry into influencing Athenian policies, he had never enriched himself by accepting their gifts. His refusal to yield to such temptations must have seemed pointless to him now.

Eventually Alcibiades, his ward, persuaded Pericles to rouse himself from his depression and resume active political participation. How Pericles himself felt at this moment is unfortunately completely unrecorded, but it is difficult to imagine that he felt anything other than a deep, almost debilitating melancholy. He had always known that a life spent in politics in Athens' democracy incurred the risk of rejection in election campaigns and even punishment for perceived failure, but the bitter brand of repudiation that he had suffered from the citizens whose best interests he had worked so long and so diligently to protect can only have seemed crushingly unfair and ungrateful.

Ironically and tragically, it was probably Pericles' family that, unintentionally, prevented him from resuming an active public role and perhaps regaining his enthusiasm for political leadership among his fellow citizens. The epidemic struck both his sons from his marriage, his sister, and other relatives. They all eventually died, though not at the same time; the sons lingered the longest, it seems. When Pericles got the news about the first death in his immediate family, he kept his composure, emulating the philosophical resignation of his teacher Anaxagoras when his son had died. In public, Pericles maintained his outwardly calm demeanor so as to give heart to others who were suffering, too. When he lost his second and remaining son from his marriage, however, he broke down weeping at the graveside, revealing how deeply moved he, too, was by the horror of the times. Like his crying while speaking at the trial of Aspasia, this behavior was not inappropriate for Athenian men, but it was extraordinarily uncharacteristic of Pericles and therefore indicative of how affected he had been by the troubles that were besetting him.

Losing both his legitimate sons left Pericles with no heir. He therefore took the unusual step of petitioning the assembly to grant citizenship to the younger Pericles, his illegitimate son by Aspasia. This request of course called for an exception to the rule defining citizenship – both an Athenian mother and an Athenian father were required – that he himself had successfully proposed twenty years earlier. Special grants of citizenship by the Athenian assembly were rare, usually being reserved as honors bestowed on foreign potentates who had provided large material benefits to Athens and had no intention of residing there. We can guess that it at least partially restored Pericles' spirits to learn that his request had been approved and that his bastard son would be elevated to the status of an Athenian citizen.

There is no record, however, of Pericles' taking any active part in the military operations that occupied the following warfare season of 429. The reason is probably that he had already contracted the deadly infection himself while visiting his family members during their illnesses. He was evidently ill for some time, and Plutarch paints a dramatic picture of Pericles during his dying days in the autumn of that year (*Pericles* 38). One time when a friend visited him as he was lying on his sickbed, he held up an amulet for his visitor to see; the women in his household had draped the charm around his neck to try to heal him. There was, he was implying, no other hope. As he lapsed in and out of consciousness, his associates gathered around his deathbed, discussing among themselves his excellence, his political dominance, and his nine great military victories as a general. Suddenly he startled them by opening his eyes and saying that they were crediting him with successes that chance could bestow on any commander. He then instructed them on what he regarded as the finest and greatest praise he could receive: "No one of the Athenians now in existence has put on the black clothing [of mourning for the dead] because of me." It was his personal fate to die in the autumn of 429.

Even though by the time of his death Pericles had regained public respect by being reelected to the office of one of Athens' ten annually elected generals, it seems impossible to think that he died a happy man. He would surely have been even sadder to know that it would be the fate of his family to be erased from history by the Peloponnesian War that he had so strongly advocated. Near the end of that long conflict, the younger Pericles, who had himself risen to the office of general, was executed in 406 on a vote of the assembly. He was among the naval commanders condemned in a group trial for allegedly having neglected to rescue Athenian rowers after their ships had been wrecked in a defeat by the new Persian-financed Peloponnesian fleet near the Arginusae islands in the northeastern Aegean Sea. In fact, a huge storm had prevented rescue operations, and in any case it was a violation of Athenian legal procedure to try defendants in a group on a capital charge. The citizens, however, had reacted with anger when the objection had been made that they were acting illegally in the prosecution. Their response was that they should be able to do whatever they wanted regardless. Sadly, this was just the sort of emotion-fueled and irretrievable blunder by the majority that the elder Pericles had been able to prevent through his persuasive speeches crafted to persuade through judgment based on knowledge. It seems horribly ironic that his son died because there was no leader at Athens persuasive enough to prevent this injustice.

The Peloponnesian War eventually ended in 404 when Athens surrendered to the Spartans, who approved the abolition of the democracy by a group of Athenian oligarchs. The collaborators' regime soon descended into a reign of terror whose violent injustice provoked a civil war. Supporters of democracy won back the city in 403. Restored to political power, the citizens in the assembly over the first decades of the fourth century reconfirmed their faith in the wisdom of Pericles' "Athens as an island" policy by authorizing the rebuilding of the Long Walls to reconnect the urban center with the city's main port and by assembling a new naval alliance (this time with a written constitution to protect the members from domination by Athens). But the Athenians would never recover the unprecedented levels of domestic prosperity and international power that as a community they had achieved in the time of Pericles.

The fate of Pericles' reputation after his death was just as contested as his political career had been during his life. Thucydides with his characteristic abhorrence of anecdotes says nothing about Pericles' final days or his apparent sadness at the way events had turned out in his public and family life. Instead, after the end of Pericles' final speech the historian immediately presents an evaluation of his career as a leader. This famous passage (2.65) presents Thucydides' analysis that Pericles' wartime strategy had been correct and that Athens lost the war because its citizens, motivated by ambition and private advantage, failed to follow his instructions as the war dragged on. In other words, Pericles might have been responsible for not trying to head off the Peloponnesian War, but his policies were not the reason why Athens finally lost the war.

Thucydides asserts that under Pericles' leadership, Athens had become the "greatest" it had ever been. Pericles' effectiveness as a leader, the historian states, emerged from the power of his reputation, his judgment based on knowledge, and his being transparently impervious to bribery and graft. He imposed restraint on the masses with an independent spirit, never stooping to flattery and willing to rouse the public's anger by opposing their will when that was necessary. With his speeches he could both combat the people's arrogance and buck up their confidence as the circumstances demanded. In short, Athens at the time of Pericles "was becoming a democracy in name but in fact rule (*archē*) by the first man" (2.65.9). With this statement, Thucydides equates Pericles' dominance of Athens with Athens' dominance of the members of the Delian League.

The historian continues his evaluation by saying that Pericles' successors, lacking his status and ability, were demagogues who pandered to the majority. Under their defective leadership, the Athenians committed horrible mistakes in the later years of the Peloponnesian War, especially the giant and catastrophic naval expedition to Sicily (in 415–413), which opposed Pericles' warning not to try to expand Athens' power internationally during wartime. The city-state's final defeat then resulted from the intervention of the Persian king in building a fleet for the Spartans (in the last decade of the fifth century) and the fatal rivalries among the leaders at Athens at that time. Pericles, Thucydides concludes, had foreseen how Athens' greater resources could surely have allowed it to prevail against the Peloponnesians.

Five hundred years later, Plutarch, in his final evaluation of Pericles (*Pericles* 39 and *Comparison of Pericles and Fabius*), recalls the "wondrousness" of Pericles' imperturbability (*praotēs*) and agrees with Thucydides' judgment that Pericles' influence had been the secret to preserving Athens' power during his career. He also agrees that Pericles accurately anticipated that Athens could have survived the long conflict with Sparta in the Peloponnesian War and that the city-state's downfall should be laid at the feet of Pericles' demagogic successors as political leaders. Plutarch adds that the Athenians came to appreciate how much they had lost when Pericles died. They therefore allowed his son by Aspasia to erect a bronze statue on the Acropolis to honor his dead father.

Not all later Athenians, however, recalled Pericles' policies as positive and constructive, even as they recognized his great influence as a leader. In the famous philosopher Plato's dialogues exploring ethical and political issues written in the fourth century B.C., Socrates describes Pericles as being the most accomplished expert ever at persuasive rhetoric. Pericles held that status because he learned high-level thinking about intelligence and understanding from Anaxagoras (*Phaedrus* 269–270), even if, Socrates alleges, Pericles did ask Aspasia to write his Funeral Oration (*Menexenus*).

Xenophon, too, has Socrates say Pericles was held to be "the mightiest advisor for his homeland" (*Symposium* 8.39). But, as mentioned earlier, Plato also has Socrates blame Pericles for corrupting the Athenians with pay for jury service, making them lazy, talky, and greedy; like Themistocles and Cimon, Pericles made them worse, not better, citizens. Therefore, says Plato's Socrates, Pericles had been a bad statesman (*Gorgias* 515, 519).

Plato's (non-Athenian) student Aristotle, who was not as dogmatically hostile to democracy as his teacher, takes a more nuanced view, judging that Athens' government was better while Pericles "was in charge of the people" but deteriorated after he died because it became too unrestrainedly democratic and demagogic (*Constitution of the Athenians* 28). In his discussion of personal ethics, Aristotle maintains that Pericles and other leaders of similar capability possessed practical wisdom (*phronēsis*) because through the use of reasoning they were able to determine what was good for them and for people in general. Therefore, they were good at managing both households and city-states (*Nichomachean Ethics* 6.5.1140b).

By the historian Diodorus' time in the first century B.C., Rome had been in control of Greece for a century. Given the overwhelming superiority of Roman strength in the Mediterranean world at this point and the evolution of Athenian government into a system requiring the ownership of property for full participation, there was little reason anymore to ponder the nature or significance of the former political nature of Athens as a direct democracy of all adult citizens. Oratory was still important in Diodorus' time, however, so he finds it worthwhile to remember Pericles' fame as a public speaker and his status "far exceeding the other citizens in his distinguished ancestry, his reputation, and his awesome power of reasoning and speech" (12.38.2). In this same era, Marcus Tullius Cicero, the greatest orator of the Roman republic, depicts the famous Roman commander Scipio describing Pericles at the beginning of the Peloponnesian War as "the first man of his city-state in influence, eloquence, and judgment" (*On the Commonwealth* 1.25).

In the centuries following the time of Cicero, there was comparatively little reason to ponder the lessons of Athenian democracy and its leaders throughout this long period when empires and kingdoms were the norm. Fifteen hundred or so years later, however, when Renaissance Europe was experiencing epochal changes in state formation and in political theory, the attention of statesmen and thinkers returned, at least in some quarters, to the history of democracy in ancient Athens and the role of Pericles. This interest has continued to the present day. Readers interested in investigating the rich materials relevant to these topics from the premodern and modern eras can find detailed and stimulating treatments in English in Jennifer Tolbert Roberts, *Athens on Trial* (1994) and in chapters 11–12 of Vincent Azoulay, *Pericles* (trans. Janet Lloyd, 2014). Here, for reasons of space I can only present a handful of citations to give some sense of the major shifts in the fate of Pericles' overall reputation since antiquity.

Azoulay offers a helpful summary of the premodern history of that trajectory:

> From the Renaissance right down to the beginning of the nineteenth century, Pericles was seldom raised to the rank of a model. For most of the time, he was arrogantly ignored and remained in the shadow of the great men of Sparta and Rome. When his memory was recalled, it was mainly to his disadvantage; depicted, as he was, now as a corrupting demagogue, now as a corrupt warmonger, for the elite groups of the modern era his role was that of a scarecrow. (p. 192)

The founders of the American republic were overwhelmingly not admirers of democratic Athens, regarding it as having been ruled by the "mob," with Pericles as the facilitator. Alexander Hamilton, for example, in words of blazing vitriol reflecting accusations from Athens' comic playwrights and the benefit of hindsight, blames Pericles for the outcomes of the Samian revolt and the Peloponnesian War: "The celebrated Pericles, in compliance with the resentments of a prostitute, at the expense of much of the blood and treasure of his countrymen, attacked, vanquished and destroyed the city of the Samians. The same man ... was the primitive author of that famous and fatal war which, after various vicissitudes, intermissions and renewals, terminated in the ruin of the Athenian commonwealth" (*Federalist Papers* No. 6, November 14, 1787).

In the mid-nineteenth century this negative evaluation of Pericles received an eloquent rebuttal by the liberal British politician and historian George Grote, whose twelve-volume *History of Greece* (1846–1856) reflects Grote's support for parliamentary democracy as well as the growing nationalism of this period in European history. Grote deserves mention here because his *History* was the most influential work in the English-speaking world in promoting a highly positive evaluation of Pericles resonating with triumphalist praise. Grote sums up his detailed analysis of Pericles' career in a rousing conclusion:

> Taking [Pericles] altogether, with his powers of thought, speech, and action – his competence, civil and military, in the council as well as in the field – his vigorous and cultivated intellect, and his comprehensive ideas of a community in pacific and many-sided development – his incorruptible public morality, caution, and

FIGURE 19. Alma-Tadema painting of Pericles and Aspasia viewing the Parthenon frieze. © DeA Picture Library/Art Resource, NY.

firmness, in a country where all those qualities were rare, and the union of them in the same individual of course much rarer, we shall find him without a parallel throughout the whole course of Grecian history. (vol. VI, ch. XLIX)

Grote's influential history exercised a strong effect on the thinking of many: "Within a few decades [after the publication of Grote's work], Pericles became the very embodiment of the Greek miracle, to the point of being celebrated as the genius who had bequeathed to posterity two imperishable monuments: the marble creation of the Parthenon [Figure 19] and the verbal creation of the funeral oration" (Azoulay 2014, p. 193).

Grote as an experienced politician and academic was far from naive about human behavior, and his extended treatment of Pericles and fifth-century Athens deserves respect for its subtle insights into the workings of power. Still, its optimism about the possibility for human flourishing under democratic principles depends on a belief in conventional ideas of moral behavior. Not so long after Grote's history, praise for Pericles was channeled in a startling new direction by the controversial German philosopher Friedrich Nietzsche in his *On the Genealogy of Morality* (1887), a work composed to rebut common notions of moral values. Nietzsche's view is worth referencing because it elevated Pericles not on account of any widely accepted ideas of virtuous behavior but because of his success in supporting the Athenian drive for power, a central theme in Pericles' thinking, as the earlier narrative in this book has stressed. The first of the *Genealogy*'s three sections, which is entitled "'Good and Evil,' 'Good and Bad,'" discusses how the powerful ("masters") and the oppressed ("slaves") see these moral categories differently. The Athenians of Pericles' time Nietzsche puts into the former category, for whom power defines what is good:

> It was the noble races which left the concept of "barbarian" in their traces wherever they went; even their highest culture betrays the fact that they were conscious of this and indeed proud of it (for example, when Pericles, in that famous funeral oration, tells his Athenians: "Our daring has forced a path to every land and sea, erecting timeless memorials to itself everywhere for good *and ill*)." This "daring" of the noble races, mad, absurd and sudden in the way it manifests itself, the unpredictability and even the improbability of their undertakings – Pericles singles out the *rhathumia* [relaxed ease of life] of the Athenians for praise – their unconcern and scorn for safety, body, life, comfort, their shocking cheerfulness and depth of delight in all destruction, in all the debauches of victory and cruelty – all this, for those who suffered under it, was summed up in the image of the "barbarian", the "evil enemy." (*Essay* 1.11, trans. Carol Diethe)

For Nietzsche, then, Pericles' focus on power reflected how conditions should be in this world, regardless of what lesser mortals might think and heedless of any ordinary ideas about how conventional morality should constrain the behavior of the powerful.

The nonacademic world of the twentieth and twenty-first centuries has, it seems fair to say, paid relatively less attention to Pericles than the centuries immediately preceding. One notable exception, however, is the novelist Daniel Silva, who in his 1996 novel *The Unlikely Spy* (New York: Villard Books) about espionage in World War II portrays the British academic-turned-spy-catcher Alfred Vicary as wondering about the motivations of his archrival in the German counterintelligence service, Kurt Vogel. Silva's description of Vicary's silent musings at a moment of great crisis stands in fact as a perceptive summary of major questions raised in this biography of Pericles:

> By instinct [Vicary] attacked [the puzzle of understanding what the enemy was planning] like a problem of history. His area of expertise was nineteenth-century Europe ... but Vicary had a secret passion for the history and myth of ancient Greece. He was intrigued by the fact that much scholarship on the age had to be based on guesswork and conjecture; the immense passage of time and lack of a clear historical record made that necessary. Why, for example, did Pericles launch the Peloponnesian War with Sparta that eventually led to the destruction of Athens? Why not accept the demands of his more powerful rival and revoke

the Megarian decree? Was he driven by fear of the superior armies of Sparta? Did he believe the war was inevitable? Did he embark on a disastrous foreign adventure to relieve pressure at home? Now Vicary asked similar questions about his rival in Berlin, Kurt Vogel. (p. 138)

Among recent professional scholars of the ancient world, a few have offered positive evaluations of Pericles' leadership. One notable proponent of this view is Geoffrey De Ste. Croix, whose study *The Origins of the Peloponnesian War* (1972) places the responsibility for the war squarely on the Spartans, not Pericles and the Athenians. Donald Kagan has been much more expansive in expressing a strongly favorable judgment of Pericles, emphasizing what he sees as Pericles' vision and his ideal for society, as, for example, in this statement from his book-length study of 1991 (*Pericles of Athens and the Birth of Democracy*):

Pericles' greatness ... goes beyond his heroic character. He was right to claim immortality for Athens, although what made it so was not its power, as he thought; that power was soon surpassed and overcome. Rather, the real source of his city's undying fame was Pericles' unique and original vision of the good society and the good citizen. It was a vision of a free people who would achieve their highest goals and capabilities as members of a free community in which the people took turns governing and being governed and made the most important decisions in common. The Periclean vision valued intelligence and talent and was not embarrassed to reward both with public honor.... This is a vision of timeless value; and as long as there are human societies struggling with the problems posed by political freedom, that vision will continue to inspire and instruct. (p. 258)

In a subsequent article, Kagan again returns to his interpretation of what he calls the Periclean ideal: "The goal was understood to be the forging of a single people in pursuit of an excellence which all respected and to which all could aspire. It aimed to raise its citizens to a higher level by providing splendid models and the opportunity for all to seek to emulate them" ("Joe DiMaggio, Baseball's Aristocrat," *Weekly Standard*, March 22, 1999, Vol. 4, no. 26).

Other scholars, however, have not shared this unequivocally positive view of Pericles. Among this group, Russell Meiggs in his detailed work *The Athenian Empire* (1979) stands out with his measured judgment on the question of the moral evaluation of Athenian power during the mid-fifth century: "The Aegean world gained considerably from the use made by Athens of the wealth that she drew from the cities and, as the Athenians claimed at Sparta in 432, they made considerably less use of force than imperial powers are expected to use; but they could have made more concessions to the general Greek passion for autonomy without undermining their position" (p. 412).

More recently, leading scholars have tended to express decidedly negative evaluations of Pericles. Only a tiny sample of this important and provocative work can be offered here (and only of scholarship in English, to serve the intended readers of this biography). On the basis of a wide-ranging discussion of the history of Pericles and Athens in his lifetime (*The Cambridge Companion to the Age of Pericles* [2007]), Loren J. Samons II reaches a stark judgment from a contemporary perspective about the ethical implications of Pericles' speeches as presented by Thucydides: "Modern sensibilities recoil – or should recoil – from the naked nationalism of Pericles' orations, a nationalism that one cannot dismiss as merely empty rhetoric" (p. 284). Samons also points out that "it was Athens' power, and her cultural or political superiority, on which Pericles relied for Athens' future reputation" (p. 293). His concluding evaluation is complex and thought-provoking but certainly far from encomiastic: "As the leader of Athens' most progressive and militaristic faction, panegyrist of Athenian natural superiority and collectivism, proponent of Athens' greatest public construction project, and associate or friend of some of the city's (and era's) greatest minds, Pericles defined his age even as he radically altered it" (p. 301).

Martha C. Taylor, in focusing on the interpretation of Thucydides' history, argues that the historian's narrative implicitly but forcefully opposes Pericles' speeches' "radical" vision of Athens as an idea rather than a city grounded in its territory. Thucydides' work otherwise, she says, "emphasizes reconciliation, not partisanship, and favors political compromise, not ideological purity.... Thucydides implies that the loss of empire would be worth it – indeed, even compulsory – if it was necessary to preserve the Athens in Attica from the Spartans" (*Thucydides, Pericles, and the Idea of Athens in the Peloponnesian War* [2010], p. 4). Taylor is explicitly not trying to unearth the complete history of Pericles' life but rather the deep message of Thucydides' combination of orations and narrative. Nevertheless, her sharp-edged analysis leaves little room to judge Pericles positively on the basis of her view of the evidence of Thucydides.

Edith Foster in her work directly addressing the topic of Athenian imperialism under Pericles' leadership (*Thucydides, Pericles, and Periclean Imperialism* [2010]) also concentrates on interpreting Thucydides' text rather than on extrapolating from it to a direct exposition of what the historical Pericles actually said and did. She astutely analyzes how the speeches in Thucydides reveal that, for Pericles, the reason for the existence of Athens and the goal of its survival was the power that the city-state could project in war, a point that seems entirely convincing. Pericles as depicted by Thucydides, she argues, saw this power as driving an unlimited future for the city-state. Foster also argues, however, that the historian's narrative presents a damning critique of Pericles' position: as a leader Pericles is shown to be incorruptible but also "cruel to Athenian citizens and entirely materialistic in his attitude toward the value of nearly everything in human life" (p. 220). Thucydides, she believes, recognizes Pericles' intelligence and leadership ability, but, she also concludes, the historian shows that Pericles' qualities "did not secure him against delusions of power" (p. 188). To conclude that Pericles was in any sense delusional is surely to offer about as negative an evaluation of him as possible.

These scholars, to repeat an important point, appropriately pay close attention to Thucydides' history in their process of evaluating Pericles. The Athenian historian/commander is after all the most important witness that we have to the "real" Pericles, both because, to repeat what was said in the introductory discussion of ancient sources in this book, Thucydides was a (younger) contemporary of Pericles and because he had personal experience of a public and military career in a top office (member of the annual board of generals) in Athenian democracy. At the same time, Thucydides, as has any author and especially any author whose work is as complex and subtle as his, has messages to convey that sometimes float on the surface of things and sometimes dive back below it, requiring the audience to engage in the intellectual work (and, for some, the delight) of interpreting the evidence that is at hand.

As mentioned, Thucydides expresses the view that the Athenians exercised their power over recalcitrant allies in a harsh, even tyrannical fashion in the later decades of Pericles' career. It is worth saying in this context that we need to be careful of our terms when characterizing Athenian policy under Pericles' leadership by making direct comparisons with modern empires. The Athenians, as portrayed in particular in the Periclean Funeral Oration, certainly embraced the idea that their way of life in their city-state was exceptional and better than that of others, but at the same time their claims to rule did not rest on the kind of ideological and racist assertions of ethnic superiority that modern imperialist oppressors have often expressed as their justification for domination. Pericles in the Funeral Oration as represented in Thucydides makes a claim for Athenian exceptionalism compared to the rest of their fellow Greeks who share the same overall cultural roots; in his view, the Athenians did more with what they had than did their neighbors.

The wording of the Greek text of the Funeral Oration certainly underlines the overwhelming importance of power (*dunamis*) for Pericles as the key to protecting the independence, flourishing, and literal salvation of Athens. Athenians created the wonders of their special national identity through their (in Pericles' view) unique combination of democracy, freedom, relaxed ease of life, personal self-sufficiency, and political participation. As briefly documented previously, leading modern scholars, both pro- and anti-Pericles, have expressed negative judgments about this emphasis on Athens' power in the Periclean Funeral Oration in Thucydides. In my view, however, this critical position runs the risk of underestimating the harsh reality of Athenian history in Pericles' lifetime, of the extreme degree of fear that Athenians experienced like a persistent low-grade fever inflamed by the knowledge that enemies near and far constantly threatened the city-state in war and that starvation loomed for them all if any of those hostile states managed to put a chokehold on the sea-lanes that served as the arteries and veins of Athens.

It is a matter of fact that by the time of the Peloponnesian War the Athenians were confronted on land by enemies directly located on their northern and western borders and allied with their treacherous archenemy Sparta. And to make matters worse, the Spartans (like the Athenians) were actively trying to win the support of the Great King of Persia for their war effort. It would have been risky in the extreme to expect that the Spartans would ever stand down from their hostility to Athens, and therefore it was eminently reasonable for Pericles to believe with total sincerity that power offered the only available hope for the Athenians' salvation. Therefore, it seems unrealistic to assert that by giving up its empire – and therefore its power – Athens could have saved itself from the Spartans and its other enemies. The lessons of history, then and now, point in a totally different direction, a fact that can be lamented but cannot be buried.

It is, however, also true that Pericles' sincere belief in Athenian exceptionalism and the necessity for power might have itself ironically become an impediment to exercising the type of clear, reason-based policy making that he privileged in his political leadership. Recent research in cognitive neuroscience suggests that when people become tightly identified and affiliated with their own group, they lose their ability to enter into the thoughts and emotions of other communities, especially those perceived as being actively opposed or hostile to their own. This so-called empathy gap makes it very difficult for members of a particular group to become willing to compromise with, or even negotiate with, people who are outside their own community. If this is indeed a shared characteristic of human beings across time and space, then it is possible to imagine that Pericles' extremely close attachment to his own city-state, as evidenced most dramatically by the words of the Funeral Oration but also witnessed by all the other ancient sources about his career, created an insurmountable psychological barrier to his accepting the idea of trying to reach a compromise with the Spartans over the disputes of the late 430s. This is admittedly a very speculative suggestion, but perhaps it can give some texture to the assessment of Pericles as having been hardheaded or inflexible in his anti-Spartan policy.

Of course, even if this suggestion is valid in any significant way, it does not relieve Pericles from the responsibility of having persuaded the majority of Athenian citizens to rule out any attempts at negotiations with the Spartans and to agree to enter a war that not even Pericles thought would be easy to escape without horrible losses. On the other hand, however, to repeat the crucial point, this is not to say that he was wrong to hold the view that he did about the Spartans – to the contrary, the historical evidence was clearly on his side. It means only that our hindsight concerning the ultimate outcome of the Peloponnesian War makes it tempting to ask whether there could possibly have been any other viable course to take under the circumstances. I personally do not see that there was at the time when Pericles had to decide what the best course was to try to save Athens.

Moreover, the majority of Athenians agreed with Pericles about going to war with Sparta in 431 because they believed that they deserved their rule, their *archē*, on the grounds that they were better at acting on core principles of Greek culture than were their fellow Greeks. They were putting into practice what Plato has the youth Meno say to Socrates when the philosopher asks him to define excellence: "It's not hard, Socrates, to say what that is. If you mean the excellence of a man, it's easy [to see that] a man's excellence consists of accomplishing the affairs of the city-state, and in doing that to do well by his friends and to do harm to his enemies, while taking care not to experience any harm himself" (*Meno* 71e). Whatever many people today might publicly claim they think about the morality of a policy of helping friends and harming enemies, this credo was accepted in ancient Greece (and is not rare in our times, in my experience). It was in accord with this way of thinking that the Athenians in their rule over other Greeks decided to fund a large navy for defense and profit, to establish settlements numbering from hundreds to several thousand of their citizens in locations outside Athens' borders, to support seaborne trade for their food supply and other imported goods, and to favor democratic governments in allied city-states when possible.

As I have tried to indicate at various points in the narrative, beginning with the implications of Miltiades' promise to the Athenians that a victory at Marathon would make them the first city-state of Greece, Athens' rise to power in Greece followed from a fear of dangerous enemies and a desire for security and national flourishing. If those aims required ruling over other Greeks, then so be it, decided the voting citizens of Athens; their successes had earned them their predominance. A funeral oration attributed to the orator Lysias and purporting to have been prepared in the 390s, decades after the death of Pericles, shows that this extraordinarily self-confident view persisted:

> Through a huge number of painful exertions and conspicuous contests and the most noble dangers, [our predecessors as Athenians] made Greece free and made their homeland the greatest. Ruling the sea for seventy years and keeping their allies free from internal factional conflict, deeming it not right for the many to be enslaved to the few but compelling all to exist in equality, they did not make their allies weak but rather established them as strong, and they demonstrated that their own power was so great that the Great King no longer longed for the things belonging to others but instead gave up some of his own, in fear for what was left. At that time no triremes sailed from Asia, no tyrant was established among Greeks, no city was forced into servitude by the barbarians. [All this came about because] the excellence of [our immediate predecessors] provided such great self-restraint and fear to all people. It was for these reasons that they alone became the leaders and protectors of the Greeks and the commanders of the city-states. (*Epitaphios* 55–57)

The undeniable accumulation of greater and greater international power by the Athenians in the mid-fifth century and the evidently willing acceptance of this situation by the majority of Athenians do not of course make this development more acceptable in some ultimate moral sense than similar actions by modern imperial nations, or indeed make it just in any supranational way. At the same time, we moderns should perhaps be careful in assessing to what degree ideas of morality and justice have ever had significant actual influence in international relations, including in our own times. Constantly aware that our perspective is affected by hindsight, it seems only fair to strive to reconstruct and understand what the people of the past whom we are studying were thinking about their own actions and to ask to what extent they were correct in assessing their needs and necessities. Only then, I think, are we entitled to risk generalized judgments of right and wrong. And when we take that step, we would do well to avoid hubris in automatically asserting our moral superiority to that of other bygone eras. Can we honestly say that we would act with equal justice toward others if we sincerely believed that external threats seemed great enough to destroy our flourishing, indeed our very survival?

Reflecting on these (to me) extremely difficult and disturbing questions, my overall interpretation of Pericles is that the lessons from his family's history and his own experiences beginning early in his life taught him to believe that Athens' salvation depended first and always on maintaining its power to defend itself against foreign and Greek enemies, and that he was absolutely convinced that he understood the best policies that a leader should follow to support the development of that power in a society organized politically as a direct democracy with no property qualification for voters and dependent on a citizen militia for its army and navy. Athens' system of radical democracy had been given its original boost by his ancestor Cleisthenes, and Pericles spent his life doing his best to defend and to guide that family inheritance. Moreover, he realized that Athens could only remain strong enough to protect itself if the majority of citizens, many of them poor, were benefited by policies supporting employment and sharing of public resources. This realization made him, as mentioned, a "traitor to his class" in the eyes of the rich.

Pericles lived his life, in private and in public, with a fierce dedication to his vision of what it meant for his city-state to thrive and what it took to reach that challenging goal. I do not believe that he was seduced by the lure of power for its own sake or because he concluded that it was somehow intrinsically morally good, but rather because he had learned by hard experience that Athens lived in a world populated with fierce and unrelenting enemies, from aggressive Persian kings to untrustworthy Spartans. He feared down to the core of his being the real danger they posed to his beloved homeland. This judgment was no delusion. Negotiation had a role in ancient international affairs, but only those with power could have any confidence in their chances to defend themselves against the enemies who were always ready to take advantage of weaknesses, or break their word as allies. It is additionally no exaggeration to say, once again, that the physical survival of the Athenians depended on their maintaining the power to protect the sea-lanes and to keep their port open for the importation of food from abroad and the exportation of the silver and goods needed to pay for the essential supply of the calories that prevented them from starving. Athens was not self-sufficient in a literal sense – it could not feed itself from its own local resources. In that circumstance, its power could certainly be a source of pride, but the necessity for maintaining this power resided at the most fundamental level of existence and self-preservation.

Pericles knew that trust mattered in human affairs, and he scrupulously kept himself uncorrupted by money or social ties so that he would be trusted as an adviser to the Athenian public. States that showed themselves trustworthy, like Plataea, deserved to be treated as valued allies, but they were hard to find. Sparta was as far from that category as could be, Pericles knew from the lessons he had absorbed from an early age. Spirit and courage also mattered, he knew. After all, he had been alive and aware when Athens refused the seductive deal to become the ruler of Greece that the Persian king offered during the Persian Wars. But the power to defend against enemies mattered most of all, he had come to know. The sufferings of Athens and of his own family had taught him the sobering truth that Plato has a character in one of his dialogues express as an absolute necessity for statesmen to grasp: "What most people call 'peace,' that is only a name. In reality, there is by the nature of things always an undeclared war of all city-states against all city-states" (*Laws* 1.626A). This analysis might be a surpassingly sad truth about human existence, and it might not be a truth that works to build universal justice, but it seems impossible to dismiss as mistaken, then or now.

Plato's description of "the undeclared war of all ... against all" certainly applies to the landscape of reality that Pericles experienced throughout his life from his earliest years onward. In response, Pericles worked in innovative ways to develop his knowledge and to use it in reasoning about the best course to pursue so that Athens could have a successful future. Remarkably, he was able to employ that education and training to turn himself into the most persuasive leader his world had ever seen. To his own regret, however, not even the hyperrational Pericles could overcome the unpredictability present in this world, especially not in the confusion and conflict of war and especially not when it led to his own death and the loss of his leadership at the very time that his community needed it the most. In the end, not even his outstanding intellect could defeat the tragic truth of the enduring insecurity of human life, no matter how well fortified by judgment and knowledge and reason. Pericles conducted his political career and his personal life at an astonishing level of purpose and individual choice, but nevertheless they both came to what I can only call a tragic end, for him, for his family, and, unlike his companion in Plutarch's biographies Fabius Maximus, for his homeland in the long run.

This conclusion is not the same as saying that those outcomes were directly Pericles' fault, or that there were any obviously better options available for Athens or for him. It is simply not clear to me what decisions Pericles could have made that would have prevented the tragedy. Should he have been less of a "tyrant" in his leadership and advocated allowing the Delian League – the Athenian Empire – to dissolve? How then would Athens have had any reasonable chance of defending itself against attacks from the unreliable Spartans and the inevitable reassertion of Persian interference in Greek affairs, or of ensuring the importation by sea of necessary foodstuffs and wood for building warships? Should he have been more flexible and agreed to tell the Athenian assembly to rescind the Megarian Decree and to let the Spartans once more renege on their sworn word and avoid arbitration over the disputes that precipitated the Peloponnesian War? What then would have happened as Sparta supported its allies in weakening Athenian international power, especially in the north, where there were choke points controlling the route for the importation of Athens' essential supplies? Are these the kinds of choices that we today would expect our national leaders to risk if our flourishing, if indeed our very survival, seemed to be at stake?

If Pericles had made such concessions, would we be comparing him to, for example, the British prime minister Neville Chamberlain (1869–1940)? Chamberlain was sharply criticized by many, including his successor Winston Churchill, for having yielded to the aggressive plans of Adolf Hitler, chancellor and führer of Germany, at the infamous Munich Conference in 1938 and for having neglected to prepare his countrymen for the war that seemed sure to occur – and did occur, with disastrous consequences. What might historians be saying about Pericles today if he had compromised with the Spartans but nevertheless, like Chamberlain, ended up as a leader who was unable to keep his homeland out of a terribly destructive war that the enemy commenced despite the concessions granted them?

As reported earlier, in his dying declaration Pericles said that he took solace in his never having directly caused the death of any fellow citizens. Modern scholars sometimes regard this statement as a hallucinatory claim by a leader who had so adamantly argued against making concessions to the Spartans when the Peloponnesian War was at issue. It seems to me, however, that Pericles was simply remaining relentlessly committed to reason and knowledge, even to his last breath. On his military campaigns, he had always operated with the utmost caution to preserve his soldiers' lives, as when, to cite one example, he prevented them from storming the walls of Samos during the siege of that rebellious ally. More importantly on this point, as legalistic as it might sound to say it, as a matter of strict fact Pericles had not advocated initiating a war against Sparta. His position had been to adhere to the terms of the treaty of 446/5 that required disputes to be settled by arbitration and not to give way to the demands of an enemy whose history showed they would seize on any concession as a weakness they could exploit with their continually expanding complaints.

All this is of course not to say that Pericles was at all reluctant to see Athens go to war. Indeed, Thucydides says "he spurred on the Athenians to war" (1.127.3). The fundamental motivations for Pericles' policy recommendations derived from the lessons of the history of his family and of his own career, lessons that had convinced him that there was no chance that negotiations with the Spartans could be trusted to maintain peace over the long term. Nevertheless, although in the end it was the Spartans, not the Athenians, who formally started the war and the killing that it caused, it still seems necessary to acknowledge that Pericles' last words sound defensive and self-justifying in a way that clashes with what he said in his speeches at the start of the Peloponnesian War. Perhaps his dying remarks reflect the reality that not even someone as self-possessed as Pericles could escape the corrosive damage to his spirits caused by his having been deposed from his office as general and having been unable fully to implement his wartime strategy because of the unforeseen consequences of the epidemic.

In the end, it seems to me unfair to make Pericles "responsible for the Peloponnesian War" if that conclusion means holding him responsible for Athens' defeat in 404 and then the horrible aftermath of the war, decades after his death. Ancient Greek literature poignantly and repeatedly expresses the idea that the totality of human existence amounts in the end to a tragedy that no one can escape. It also suggests that this mournful but inevitable outcome for all things in mortal life has more to do with the nature of the cosmos, with Luck, with Fate (for which the Greeks had multiple terms, so complex was this idea for them), than with a person's individual choices or personality. Perhaps, then, one thing that a biography of an ancient Greek such as this one can hope to offer is an incentive to think about how its subject dealt with what for Greeks of Pericles' time was this cosmic truth. In my judgment, it takes a dedicated spirit to be able to keep on striving for achievement while living with the realization of such a debilitating reality. The ultimately tragic story of the life of Pericles seems to me to reveal a man who did just that, achieving the goal that his mother and father established for him when they gave him a name expressing the purpose in life that had meant the most to the heroes of Homer: to become "far famed." As he himself had said in the Funeral Oration concerning Athens' reputation, that fame encompassed both good and bad.

Suggested Readings

ANCIENT AUTHORS IN ENGLISH TRANSLATION

Aesop. 2002. *Aesop's Fables*. Translated by Laura Gibbs (Oxford: Oxford University Press).

Anaxagoras. 2007. *Anaxagoras of Clazomenae. Fragments and Testimonia: A Text and Translation with Notes and Essays*. Translated by Patricia Curd (Toronto: University of Toronto Press).

Aristotle. 2010. *Aristotle and Xenophon on Democracy and Oligarchy*. Translated by J. M. Moore (Berkeley: University of California Press).

Athenaeus. 2006–2012. *The Learned Banqueters*. Translated by S. Douglas Olson. 8 vols (Cambridge, MA: Harvard University Press).

Dillon, John, and Tania Gergel, trans. 2003. *The Greek Sophists* (London: Penguin).

Diodorus Siculus. 2010. *The Persian Wars to the Fall of Athens. Books 11–14.34 (480–401 BCE)*. Translated by Peter Green (Austin: University of Texas Press).

Herodotus. 1996. *The Histories*. Translated by Aubrey de Sélincourt. Revised by John Marincola (London: Penguin).

Homer. 2011. *The Iliad*. Translated by Richmond Lattimore. Introduction by Richard Martin (Chicago: University of Chicago Press).

Justin. 1994. *Epitome of the Philippic History of Pompeius Trogus*. Translated by J. C. Yardley. Introduction and notes by R. Develin (Atlanta: Scholars Press).

Plutarch. 1916. *Plutarch's Lives*. Vol. 3: *Pericles and Fabius Maximus, Nicias and Crassus*. Translated by Bernadotte Perrin (Cambridge, MA: Harvard University Press).

Plutarch 1960. *The Rise and Fall of Athens: Nine Greek Lives*. Translated by Ian Scott-Kilvert (London: Penguin).

Thucydides. 2013. *The War of the Peloponnesians and the Athenians*. Translated by Jeremy Mynott (Cambridge: Cambridge University Press).

Waterfield, Robin, trans. 2000. *The First Philosophers: The Presocratics and the Sophists* (Oxford: Oxford University Press).

COLLECTIONS OF ANCIENT TEXTS AND INSCRIPTIONS IN ENGLISH TRANSLATION

Crawford, Michael, and David Whitehead, eds. 1983. *Archaic and Classical Greece: A Selection of Ancient Sources in Translation* (Cambridge: Cambridge University Press).

Fornara, Charles W., ed. 1983. *Translated Documents of Greece and Rome. Vol. 1: Archaic Times to the End of the Peloponnesian War*. 2nd ed (Cambridge: Cambridge University Press).

Harding, Phillip, ed. 2008. *The Story of Athens: The Fragments of the Local Chronicles of Attika* (London: Routledge).

Osborne, Robin. 2000. *The Athenian Empire*, 4th ed. (London: London Association of Classical Teachers).

Rusten, Jeffrey, ed. and trans. 2011. *The Birth of Comedy: Texts, Documents, and Art from Athenian Comic Competitions, 486–280* (Baltimore: Johns Hopkins University Press).

Samons II, Loren J., ed. 1998. *Athenian Democracy and Imperialism* (Boston: Houghton Mifflin).

Samons II, Loren J. 2000. *Empire of the Owl: Athenian Imperial Finance* (Stuttgart: Steiner; *Historia Einzelschriften* 142).

Storey, Ian C., trans. 2011. *Fragments of Old Comedy*. 3 vols. (Cambridge, MA: Harvard University Press).

Tracy, Stephen, V., ed. 2009. *Pericles: A Sourcebook and Reader* (Berkeley: University of California Press).

MODERN STUDIES

Allen, Danielle S. 2000. *The World of Prometheus: The Politics of Punishing in Democratic Athens* (Princeton, NJ: Princeton University Press).

Anderson, Greg. 2003. *The Athenian Experiment: Building an Imagined Political Community in Ancient Attica, 508–490 B.C.* (Ann Arbor: University of Michigan Press).

Avramidou, Amalia. 2011. *The Codrus Painter: Iconography and Reception of Greek Vases in the Age of Pericles* (Madison: University of Wisconsin Press).

Azoulay, Vincent. 2014. *Pericles*. [2010. *Périclès: la démocratie athénienne a l'épreuve du grand homme* (Paris: Colin)] Translated by Janet Lloyd (Princeton, NJ: Princeton University Press).

Bakola, Emmanuela. 2010. *Cratinus and the Art of Comedy* (Oxford: Oxford University Press).

Balot, Ryan K. 2001. *Greed and Injustice in Classical Athens* (Princeton, NJ: Princeton University Press).

2014. *Courage in the Democratic Polis: Ideology and Critique in Classical Athens* (Oxford: Oxford University Press).

Banfi, Antonio. 2003. *Il governo della città: Pericle nel pensiero antico* (Bologna: Il Mulino).

Barringer, Judith M., and Jeffrey M. Hurwit, eds. 2005. *Periklean Athens and Its Legacy: Problems and Perspectives* (Austin: University of Texas Press).

Beaumont, Lesley A. 2012. *Childhood in Ancient Athens: Iconography and Social History* (London: Routledge).

Blamire, Alec. 2001. "Athenian Finance, 454–404 B.C." *Hesperia* 70, pp. 99–126.

Blok, Josine H. 2009. "Perikles' Citizenship Law: A New Perspective." *Historia* 58, pp. 141–170.

Boedeker, Deborah, and Kurt A. Raaflaub, eds. 1998. *Democracy, Empire, and the Arts in Fifth-century Athens* (Cambridge, MA: Harvard University Press).

Boersma, Johannes S. 1970. *Athenian Building Policy from 561/0 to 405/4 B.C* (Groningen: Wolters-Noordhoff).

Boukouvala-Anagnostou, Ioanna. 2002. *Aspasia: Apo pallikia, vasilissa. Historiko mythistorema* (Athens: Ankyra).

Bowden, Hugh. 2005. *Classical Athens and the Delphic Oracle: Divinization and Democracy* (Cambridge: Cambridge University Press).

Brulé, Pierre. 1994. *Périclès: l'apogée d'Athènes* (Paris: Galimard).

Cartledge, Paul. 2003. *The Spartans: The World of the Warrior-Heroes of Ancient Greece, from Utopia to Crisis and Collapse* (Woodstock, NY: Overlook Press).

Castriota, David. 1992. *Myth, Ethos, and Actuality: Official Art in Fifth-Century B.C. Athens* (Madison: University of Wisconsin Press).

Christodoulou, Panos. 2013. "Thucydides' Pericles. Between Historical Reality and Literary Representation." In Antonis Tsakmakis and Melina Tamiolaki, eds. *Thucydides between History and Literature* (Berlin: De Gruyter), pp. 225–254.

Cohen, Beth. 1991. "Perikles' Portrait and the Riace Bronzes: New Evidence for 'Schinocephaly.' " *Hesperia* 60, pp. 465–502.

Connelly, Joan Breton. 2014. *The Parthenon Enigma: A New Understanding of the World's Most Iconic Building and the People Who Made It* (New York: Knopf).

Cotterell, Arthur, Roger Lowe, and Ian Shaw. 2006. "Integrity: The Political Supremacy of Pericles." In *Leadership Lessons from the Ancient World: How Learning from the Past Can Win You the Future* (Chichester: John Wiley), pp. 89–102.

Davies, J. K. 1971. *Athenian Propertied Families 600–300 B.C* (Oxford: Clarendon Press).

Demetriou, Kyriakos N., ed. 2014. *Brill's Companion to George Grote and the Classical Tradition* (Leiden: Brill).

De Sanctis, Gaetano. 1944. *Pericle* (Milan: G. Principato).

De Ste. Croix, G. E. M. 1972. *The Origins of the Peloponnesian War* (London: Duckworth).

Dewald, Carolyn, and John Marincola, eds. 2006. *The Cambridge Companion to Herodotus* (Cambridge: Cambridge University Press).

Dressler, Jan. 2014. *Wortverdreher, Sonderlinge, Gottlose: Kritik an Philosophie und Rhetorik im klassischen Athens* (Berlin: De Gruyter; *Beiträge zur Altertumskunde* 331).

Duff, Tim. 1999. *Plutarch's Lives: Exploring Virtue and Vice* (Oxford: Oxford University Press).
Easterling, P. E., and J. V. Muir, eds. 1985. *Greek Religion and Society* (Cambridge: Cambridge University Press).
Eide, Tormod. 1981. "Thucydides' LOGOS PARAMYTHIKOS." *Symbolae Osloenses* 41, pp. 33–45.
Elizalde, Laura. 2010. *Pericles de Atenas* (Buenos Aires: Biblos).
Euben, J. Peter, ed. 1986. *Greek Tragedy and Political Theory* (Berkeley: University of California Press).
Evans, Nancy. 2010. *Civic Rights: Democracy and Religion in Ancient Athens* (Berkeley: University of California Press).
Fantasia, Ugo. 2003. *Tucidide: La guerra del Peloponneso. Libro II, testo, traduzione e commento con saggio introduzione* (Pisa: Edizioni ETS).
Ferrario, Sarah. 2012. "Political Tragedy: Sophocles and Athenian History." In Andreas Markantonatos, ed. *Brill's Companion to Sophocles* (Leiden: Brill), pp. 447–470.
Fornara, Charles W., and Loren J. Samons II. 1990. *Athens from Cleisthenes to Pericles* (Berkeley: University of California Press).
Forsdyke, Sara. 2005. *Exile, Ostracism, and Democracy: The Politics of Expulsion in Ancient Greece* (Princeton, NJ: Princeton University Press).
Foster, Edith. 2010. *Thucydides, Pericles, and Periclean Imperialism* (Cambridge: Cambridge University Press).
Frost, Frank J. 1964. "Pericles, Thucydides, Son of Melesias, and Athenian Politics before the War." *Historia* 13, pp. 385–399.
Gabrielsen, Vincent. 1994. *Financing the Athenian Fleet: Public Taxation and Social Relations* (Baltimore: Johns Hopkins University Press).
Garland, Robert. 1998. *Daily Life of the Ancient Greeks* (Westport, CT: Greenwood).
Garnsey, Peter. 1989. "Food Supply and Food Crisis in Athens c. 600–322 BC." *Famine and Food Supply in the Graeco-Roman World: Responses to Risk and Crisis*. Part III (Cambridge: Cambridge University Press), pp. 89–166.
Georges, Pericles. 1994. *Barbarian Asia and the Greek Experience: From the Archaic Period to the Age of Xenophon* (Baltimore: Johns Hopkins University Press).
Giovannini, Adalberto. 2008. "The Parthenon, the Treasury of Athena, and the Resources of the Athenian Empire." In Low, ed. *The Athenian Empire* (Edinburgh: University of Edinburgh Press), pp. 164–184.
Golden, Mark. 2015. *Children and Childhood in Classical Athens*, 2nd. ed. (Baltimore: Johns Hopkins University Press).
Gomme, A. W. 1945–1981. *A Historical Commentary on Thucydides*. 5 Vols. (Vols. 4 and 5 completed by K. J. Dover and A. Andrewes) (Oxford: Clarendon Press).
González Suárez, Amalia. 1997. *Aspasia (ca. 470–410 a. C.)* (Madrid: Ediciones del Orto).
Gottesman, Alex. 2014. *Politics and the Street in Democratic Athens* (Cambridge: Cambridge University Press).
Günther, Linda-Marie. 2010. *Perikles* (Tübingen: A. Francke).

Guthrie, W. K. C. 1971. *The Sophists* (Cambridge: Cambridge University Press).
Hale, John R. 2009. *Lords of the Sea: The Epic Story of the Athenian Navy and the Birth of Democracy* (New York: Viking).
Hall, Jonathan M. 2013. "Eleusis, the Oath of Plataia, and the Peace of Kallias." In *Artifact and Artifice: Classical Archaeology and the Ancient Historian* (Chicago: University of Chicago Press), pp. 55–76.
Hamel, Debra. 1998. *Athenian Generals: Military Authority in the Classical Period* (Leiden: Brill).
Hanson, Victor Davis. 2010. *Makers of Ancient Strategy: From the Persian Wars to the Fall of Rome* (Princeton, NJ: Princeton University Press).
Harrison, Evelyn B. 1966. "The Composition of the Amazonomachy on the Shield of Athena Parthenos." *Hesperia* 35, pp. 107–133.
Harrison, Thomas. 2006. "The Greek World, 478–432." In Konrad H. Kinzl, ed. *A Companion to the Classical Greek World* (Malden, MA: Blackwell).
Henderson, Jeffrey. 2012. "Old Comedy and Popular History." In John Marincola, Lloyd Llewellyn-Jones, and Calum Maciver, eds. *Greek Notions of the Past in the Archaic and Classical Eras: History without Historians* (Edinburgh: Edinburgh University Press), pp. 144–159.
Henry, Madeleine M. 1995. *Prisoner of History: Aspasia of Miletus and Her Biographical Tradition* (Oxford: Oxford University Press).
Hesk, Jon. 2000. *Deception and Democracy in Classical Athens* (Cambridge: Cambridge University Press).
Hornblower, Simon. 1991–2008. *A Commentary on Thucydides*. 3 Vols. (Oxford: Clarendon Press).
Hurwit, Jeffrey. 2004. *The Acropolis in the Age of Pericles* (Cambridge: Cambridge University Press).
Interlandi, Jennifer. 2015. "The Brain's Empathy Gap." *New York Times Magazine* March 22, pp. 50–55, 63.
Jennings, Victoria, and Andrea Katsaros, eds. 2007. *The World of Ion of Chios* (Leiden: Brill).
Jouanna, Danielle. 2005. *Aspasie de Milet: égérie de Périclès. Histoire d'une femme, histoire d'un mythe* (Paris: Fayard).
Kagan, Donald. 1991. *Pericles of Athens and the Birth of Democracy* (New York: Free Press).
1999. "Joe DiMaggio, Baseball's Aristocrat." *Weekly Standard*, March 22, Vol. 4, no. 26.
2010. "Pericles, Thucydides, and the Defense of Empire." In Hanson, ed. *Makers of Ancient Strategy: From the Persian Wars to the Fall of Rome* (Princeton, NJ: Princeton University Press), pp. 31–57.
Kallet-Marx, Lisa. 1993. *Money, Expense, and Naval Power in Thucydides' History 1–5.24* (Berkeley: University of California Press).
Karavites, Peter. 1977. "Abhandlungen [Realities and Appearances, 490–480 B.C.]." *Historia* 26, pp. 129–147.
Kimball, Roger. 2006. "Does Pericles Point the Way?" In David Fromkin, director. *Changing and Unchanging Values in the World of the Future: Inaugural Conference. November 8, 9, and 10, 2001* (Boston: Frederick Pardee Center for the Study of the Longer-Range Future, Boston University), pp. 12–16.

Krentz, Peter. 2010. *The Battle of Marathon* (New Haven, CT: Yale University Press).
Lape, Susan. 2010. *Race and Citizen Identity in the Classical Athenian Democracy* (Cambridge: Cambridge University Press).
Lehmann, Gustav Adolf. 2008. *Perikles: Staatsmann und Stratege im klassischen Athen. Eine Biographie* (Munich: Beck).
Levi, Mario Attilio. 1996. *Pericle e la democrazia ateniese* (Milan: Rusconi).
Loraux, Nicole. 2006. *The Invention of Athens: The Funeral Oration in the Classical City*. New ed. Translated by Alan Sheridan (New York: Zone).
Low, Polly. 2007. *Interstate Relations in Classical Greece: Morality and Power* (Cambridge: Cambridge University Press).
Low, Polly, ed. 2008. *The Athenian Empire* (Edinburgh: University of Edinburgh Press).
Ma, John, Nikolaos Papazarkadas, and Robert Parker, eds. 2009. *Interpreting the Athenian Empire* (London: Duckworth).
Maffre, Jean-Jacques. 1994. *Le Siècle de Périclès*. 2nd ed. (Paris: Presses universitaires de France).
Major, Wilfred E. 2013. "Old Comedy and Proto-Rhetoric in Athens before 425 B.C.E.: The Age of Pericles." In *The Court of Comedy: Aristophanes, Rhetoric, and Democracy in Fifth-Century Athens* (Columbus: Ohio State University Press).
Malye, Jean. 2008. *La véritable histoire de Périclès: Textes réunis et commentés* (Paris: Belles Letters).
Marginesu, Giovanni. 2010. *Gli epistati dell'Acropoli: edilizia sacra nella città di Pericle, 447/6–433/2 a.C* (Salerno: Pandemos).
Martin, Thomas R. 2013. *Ancient Greece: From Prehistoric to Hellenistic Times* (New Haven, CT: Yale University Press).
Mattingly, Harold. B. 2008. "Periclean Imperialism." In Low, ed. *The Athenian Empire* (Edinburgh: University of Edinburgh Press), pp. 81–110.
Mazzon, Daniela. 2011. *Aspasia: Maestra e amante di Pericle* (Treviso: Anordest).
McGlew, James. 2006. "The Comic Pericles." In Sian Lewis, ed. *Ancient Tyranny* (Edinburgh: University of Edinburgh Press), pp. 164–177.
Medem, Julio. 2012. *Aspasia, amante de Atenas* (Barcelona: Espasa).
Meiggs, Russell. 1979. *The Athenian Empire* (Oxford: Clarendon Press).
2008. "The Growth of Athenian Imperialism." In Low, ed. *The Athenian Empire* (Edinburgh: University of Edinburgh Press), pp. 58–80.
Meinhardt, Ekkehard. 1957. *Perikles bei Plutarch* (Frankfurt: Inaug. Diss.).
Monoson, S. Sara, and Michael Loriaux. 1998. "The Illusion of Power and the Disruption of Moral Norms: Thucydides' Critique of Periclean Policy." *American Political Science Review* 92, pp. 285–297.
Moreno, Alfonso. 2007. *Feeding the Democracy: The Athenian Grain Supply in the Fifth and Fourth Centuries BC* (Oxford: Oxford University Press).
Morrison, J. S. 2000. *The Athenian Trireme: The History and Reconstruction of an Ancient Greek Warship* (Cambridge: Cambridge University Press).
Mossé, Claude. 2004. *Périclès, L'inventeur de la démocratie* (Paris: Payot).
Munn, Mark. 2000. *The School of History: Athens in the Age of Socrates* (Berkeley: University of California Press).
Musti, Domenico. 1995. *Demokratia: origini di un'idea* (Rome: Laterza).

Neils, Jennifer, ed. 2005. *The Parthenon from Antiquity to the Present* (Cambridge: Cambridge University Press).
Nietzsche, Friedrich. 2006. *On the Genealogy of Morality and Other Writings.* Revised Student Edition. Edited by Keith Ansell-Pearson. Translated by Carol Diethe (Cambridge: Cambridge University Press).
Ober, Josiah. 2008. *Democracy and Knowledge: Innovation and Learning in Classical Athens* (Princeton, NJ: Princeton University Press).
Osborne, Robin. 2010. *Athens and Athenian Democracy* (Cambridge: Cambridge University Press).
O'Sullivan, Neil. 1995. "Pericles and Protagoras." *Greece & Rome* 42, pp. 15–23.
Parker, Robert. 1996. *Athenian Religion: A History* (Oxford: Clarendon Press).
Paspaliares, Panagiotes. 2009. *Perikles* (Athens: Skai Vivlio).
Patterson, Cynthia. 1981. *Pericles' Citizenship Law of 451–50 B.C* (New York: Arno).
Pelling, Christopher. 2000. "Thucydides' Speeches." In *Literary Texts and the Greek Historian* (London: Routledge).
Podlecki, Anthony J. 1987. *Plutarch: Life of Pericles. A Commentary to the Penguin Translation from The Rise and Fall of Athens.* Translated by Ian Scott-Kilvert (Bristol, CT: Bristol Classical Press).
1998. *Perikles and His Circle* (London: Routledge).
Powell, Anton. 2001. *Athens and Sparta: Constructing Greek Political and Social History from 478 BC.* 2nd ed. (London: Routledge).
Pritchard, David M., ed. 2010. *War, Democracy, and Culture in Classical Athens* (Cambridge: Cambridge University Press).
Ray, Fred Eugene. 2011. *Land Battles in 5th Century B.C. Greece: A History and Analysis of 173 Engagements* (Jefferson, NC: McFarland).
Rhodes, P. J. 1993. *A Commentary on the Aristotelian Athenaion Politeia* (Oxford: Clarendon Press).
2004. *Athenian Democracy* (Oxford: Oxford University Press).
2008. "After the Three-Bar *Sigma* Controversy: Athenian Imperialism Reassessed." *Classical Quarterly* 58, pp. 501–506.
Richard, Carl J. 2003. *Twelve Greeks and Romans Who Changed the World* (Lanham, MD: Rowman & Littlefield).
Roberts, Jennifer, and Tolbert Roberts. 1994. *Athens on Trial: The Antidemocratic Tradition in Western Thought* (Princeton, NJ: Princeton University Press).
Romilly, Jacqueline de. 1992. *The Great Sophists in Periclean Athens.* Translated by Janet Lloyd (Oxford: Clarendon Press).
1998. *La grandeur de l'homme au siècle de Périclès* (Paris: Fallois).
Rosenbloom, David. 2006. *Aeschylus: Persians* (London: Duckworth).
Russell, D. A. 1973. *Plutarch* (London: Duckworth).
Rusten, Jeffrey S., ed. 1989. *Thucydides: The Peloponnesian War: Book II* (Cambridge: Cambridge University Press).
2009. *Thucydides* (Oxford: Oxford University Press).
Salkever, Stephen. 2009. *The Cambridge Companion to Ancient Greek Political Thought* (Cambridge: Cambridge University Press).
Samons II, Loren J. 1998. "Kimon, Kallias, and Peace with Persia." *Historia* 47, pp. 129–140.
2000. *Empire of the Owl: Athenian Imperial Finance* (Stuttgart: Franz Steiner).

2010. "Athens: A Democratic Empire." In Kimberly Kagan, ed. *The Imperial Moment* (Cambridge, MA: Harvard University Press), pp. 12–31, 200–208.

Samons II, Loren J., ed. 2007. *The Cambridge Companion to the Age of Pericles* (Cambridge: Cambridge University Press).

Schubert, Charlotte. 2012. *Perikles: Tyrann oder Demokrat?* (Stuttgart: Philip Reclam jun.).

Schwarze, Joachim. 1971. *Die Beurteilung des Perikles durch die attische Komödie and ihre historische und historiographische Bedeutung* (Munich: Beck).

Scodel, Ruth. 2010. *An Introduction to Greek Tragedy* (Cambridge: Cambridge University Press).

Sidwell, Keith. 2009. *Aristophanes the Democrat: The Politics of Satirical Comedy during the Peloponnesian War* (Cambridge: Cambridge University Press).

Sommerstein, Alan H., and Andrew J. Bayliss, eds. 2013. *Oath and State in Ancient Greece.* (Berlin: De Gruyter; *Beiträge zur Altertumskunde* 306), pp. 154–156, 205–211 (Delian League oaths).

Stadter, Philip A. 1989. *A Commentary on Plutarch's Pericles* (Chapel Hill: University of North Carolina Press).

1991. "Pericles among the Intellectuals." *Illinois Classical Studies* 16, pp. 111–124.

Storey, Ian C. 2003. *Eupolis: Poet of Old Comedy* (Oxford: Oxford University Press).

Stow, Simon. 2007. "Pericles at Gettysburg and Ground Zero: Tragedy, Patriotism, and Public Mourning." *American Political Science Review* 101, pp. 195–208.

Strauss, Barry S. 2004. *The Battle of Salamis: The Naval Encounter That Saved Greece – and Western Civilization* (New York: Simon & Schuster).

Stuttard, David. 2013. *Parthenon: Power and Politics on the Acropolis* (London: British Museum).

Sweet, Andrew W. 2014. "Pericles and Solon on Happiness: Agonistic Echoes in Thucydides 2.44." *New England Classical Journal* 41, pp. 74–87.

Taylor, Martha C. 2010. *Thucydides, Pericles, and the Idea of Athens in the Peloponnesian War* (Cambridge: Cambridge University Press).

Thomas, Rosalind. 1992. *Oral Tradition and Written Record in Classical Athens* (Cambridge: Cambridge University Press).

Travlos, John. 1971. *Pictorial Dictionary of Ancient Athens* (London: Praeger).

Tritle, Lawrence A. 2010. *A New History of the Peloponnesian War* (Malden, MA: Wiley-Blackwell).

2010. "Pericles." In Michael Gagarin and Elaine Fantham, eds. *The Oxford Encyclopedia of Greece and Rome* (Oxford: Oxford University Press), pp. 209–211.

Tzanetou, Angeliki. 2012. *City of Suppliants: Tragedy and the Athenian Empire* (Austin: University of Texas Press).

Vanoyeke, Violaine. 1997. *Périklès* (Paris: Tallandier).

Vickers, Michael J. 1997. *Pericles on Stage: Political Comedy in Aristophanes' Early Plays* (Austin: University of Texas Press).

Vogt, Joseph. 2009. "The Portrait of Pericles in Thucydides." In Jeffrey S. Rusten, ed. *Thucydides* (Oxford: Oxford University Press), pp. 220–240.

Wade-Gery, H. T. 1932. "Thucydides the Son of Melesias: A Study of Periklean Policy." *Journal of Hellenic Studies* 52, pp. 205–227.
Wartenberg, Ute. 1995. *After Marathon: War, Society, and Money in Fifth-Century Greece* (London: British Museum).
Waters, Matthew W. 2014. *Ancient Persia: A Concise History of the Achaemenid Empire, 550–330 BCE* (Cambridge: Cambridge University Press).
Will, Wolfgang. 1995. *Perikles* (Reinbeck bei Hamburg: Rowohlt).
2003. *Thukydides und Perikles: der Historiker und sein Held* (Bonn: Habelt).

Index

Unless otherwise noted, everyone identified parenthetically is Greek.

Titles of written works are in *italics* and are followed by the author's name.